D0824902

SNORKELING
Rivers
and Streams

SNORKELING
Rivers
and Streams

An Aquatic Guide to
UNDERWATER DISCOVERY and ADVENTURE

KEITH WILLIAMS

STACKPOLE
BOOKS

Guilford, Connecticut

Published by Stackpole Books
An imprint of The Rowman & Littlefield Publishing Group, Inc.
4501 Forbes Blvd., Ste. 200
Lanham, MD 20706
www.rowman.com

Distributed by NATIONAL BOOK NETWORK

Copyright © 2020 by The Rowman & Littlefield Publishing Group, Inc.

Photographs by Keith Williams

All rights reserved. No part of this book may be reproduced in any form or by any electronic or mechanical means, including information storage and retrieval systems, without written permission from the publisher, except by a reviewer who may quote passages in a review.

British Library Cataloguing in Publication Information available

Library of Congress Cataloging-in-Publication Data available

ISBN 978-0-8117-3845-3 (paperback)
ISBN 978-0-8117-6847-4 (e-book)

∞™ The paper used in this publication meets the minimum requirements of American National Standard for Information Sciences—Permanence of Paper for Printed Library Materials, ANSI/NISO Z39.48-1992.

Contents

Introduction

WHY

I was leading a May trip on the White River in the Green Mountain National Forest, Vermont, with a group of students from Boston. We clung to a large boulder in the crystal-clear water a few feet downstream of a foot-high shelf and waited for fish to show up. A small brown trout emerged from somewhere and plied the current masterfully while we clumsily hung on. Carefully, the fish looked us over while our bodies played out downstream like streamers in a stiff breeze. The little fish observed the current as we watched it pluck morsels, invisible to us, with surgically precise movements. After a few minutes, a girl in the group picked her head from the water, dropped the snorkel from her mouth, and said, "I love him! He's beautiful!" She then put the snorkel back in her mouth and went back to watching the fish. A few minutes later, she picked her head from the water again and said, "How can we conserve something if we don't know it's there?"

At first, this seems like an absurd statement. We know that fish is there. We probably put it there, as I suspect this was a stocked brown trout. However, she raises a valid point: We really don't know what freshwater aquatic life is like on its terms, in the water where it lives. We don't know what brown trout are like in the stream. We know what they are like on a stringer, in a frying pan, and on a plate, but how many of us have watched these fish hunt and eat and explore and masterfully navigate complex currents? This young student got it. She understood that to really protect something, we need to know and appreciate and love it, and we can't fully know, appreciate, and love our freshwater life without watching and experiencing it on its own terms, in our rivers and streams.

Freshwater life is overlooked and forgotten. Rivers and streams are common in our landscape, and we don't give more than a passing thought to the life they contain. There can't possibly be anything of worth or beauty in the streams that wind their ways through our towns. However, there is incredible beauty, complexity, and intricacy hidden from view in all rivers and streams, even the most heavily impacted ones.

We are in the midst of a global extinction crisis, and freshwater ecosystems are at the epicenter. We are losing biodiversity from freshwater ecosystems faster than we are losing biodiversity from any other ecosystem on the planet. While local biological and socioeconomic factors drive that loss, a common underlying cause is a lack of knowledge about what we are losing. River snorkeling reveals the hidden treasures in our everyday streams and makes people aware of the astonishing freshwater life we share this planet with.

Students watch a brown trout in the White River.

There is stunning life to see, waiting to be discovered, which is another "why" behind freshwater snorkeling. Freshwater snorkeling is discovery and adventure accessible to all. It just takes a mask, a snorkel, and a curious spirit. The beauty experienced in our rivers joins us to aquatic life in deep and profound ways. Snorkeling is the most connecting experience we can have with a river.

HOW
Gear
Gear can be as simple or as complex as you like. At a minimum, you need a mask. Just about any mask will do, so if you are just starting out and aren't sure if you are really going to take to river snorkeling, go on the cheaper side. Once you are sure this is your thing, you can upgrade to a more expensive model. At a minimum, the mask should have a soft skirt of pliable silicone, and it should fit well. To test the fit, hold the mask to your face without putting the strap behind your head. Inhale through your nose. Does the mask suck to your face? Does it feel comfortable? If not, find another model. Masks really come down to

personal preference and comfortable fit. Hopefully, you will be wearing this for hours, so make sure it feels good.

The snorkel is the tube that connects you to the surface so that you can breathe while watching incredible underwater life unfold before you. The basic snorkel tube works well. It doesn't need a purge valve that helps water drain out after submerging. It doesn't need a float to plug the end of the tube when you submerge to keep water from getting in. However, those things make clearing water from a flooded snorkel easier. Things to consider are a flexible tube attached to the mouthpiece versus a rigid one. The flexible tubes are often more comfortable since they conform to the angle between where the snorkel tube connects to the mask strap and your mouth. On the downside, they can trap water so that your tube always gurgles, and they can crack over time. While purge valves are great for making clearing water from a flooded snorkel easy, they also leak. My personal preference is a flexible tube snorkel with a purge valve, and yes, mine leaks, so I almost always have a gurgle on inhalation and exhalation, which makes sneaking up on skittish fish difficult. I should upgrade.

Fins are entirely optional. It depends on the kind of river snorkeling you plan on doing. If you intend to get in at one spot and stay more or less in that same area of river, fins are not recommended as they tend to get in the way and kick up bottom. If, on the other hand, you plan on doing a downstream run or snorkeling some kind of distance, then fins come in handy to speed you through the slower parts. If you decide to go with them, get something that you can get on and off easily, as you will be doing that often.

The hike in was tough but worth it. This stream was about as pristine as they come, and the clear water had just a hint of aquamarine in its deepest parts. I

WEST BRANCH WHITE RIVER

Description: The West Branch of the White River is a 10-mile-long tributary to the White River, which flows 60 miles before joining the Connecticut River. The West Branch flows clear and cold, because it originates in the forests of the Green Mountain National Forest. The CCC camp is the site of a successful restoration project undertaken by the US Forest Service. Road crews scraped gravel out of the riverbed of the West Branch to restore roads that were washed out by Hurricane Irene. This destroyed habitat and did significant damage to the river. The Forest Service implemented a comprehensive restoration project that restored rock shelves, sills, and large woody material, and the river now supports a robust cold-water fishery.

Access: GPS Address: 3789 Brandon Mountain Road, Rochester, Vermont. The CCC camp is located off Route 73, Brandon Mountain Road, in Rochester, Vermont. Look for signs for the CCC camp and a small wooden building just off the road. It will be on your right if you are traveling west from the town of Rochester. A trail leads from the parking area to the river.

Above: West Branch of the White River, Green Mountain National Forest, Vermont.

pulled my mask out of my pack, pressed it to my face, slid the strap around the back of my head, and *snap*. . . . It broke. Now what? I was two hours in with no mask. Lesson learned. Always pack a spare: spare mask strap, spare snorkel keeper, the little plastic or rubber doohickey that attaches the snorkel to the mask, and a spare fin strap. When I travel long distances or fly to a destination, I pack a whole extra mask, just in case.

Wetsuits offer protection from cold water and abrasion. They trap a thin layer of water between your body and the neoprene, and your body warms it up. They also provide buoyancy, which can be a blessing or a curse depending on your reasons for snorkeling. I always like to be positively buoyant (i.e., float) when I river snorkel. I can usually see everything I want from the surface, so there is no need to submerge. Wetsuits provide the thermal and abrasion protection I need, plus they make me float like a cork. Wetsuit thickness depends on water temperatures: 3/2 mm provides comfort in water 60 degrees and up, 4/3 mm for 52 degrees and up, and 5 mm for 45 degrees and up.

There are times when I want to be on the bottom, and the buoyancy of a wetsuit is counter to getting there, so the addition of a weight belt is necessary to become neutrally buoyant. The amount of weight needed is based on individual body composition, so the only way to arrive at the right added weight is through experimentation in a pool.

When the water is just too cold for a wetsuit, the next level of protection is a drysuit. Where a wetsuit allows a thin layer of water between you and the suit, a drysuit, theoretically, doesn't allow any water to touch your skin. Drysuits by themselves offer no thermal protection, so an insulating underlayer is needed. I snorkel year-round. Polypropylene thermal underwear under a fleece jumpsuit, all protected by the drysuit, is usually sufficient to keep my core warm. Neoprene gloves and hood keep my hands and head warm for a while, though my hands are usually the limiting factor. In the mid-Atlantic, I switch from wet- to drysuit right around Halloween and back again right around Memorial Day. If I'm snorkeling Cascade Mountain rivers in the Pacific Northwest, I wear a drysuit year-round, and I wear my drysuit when I plan on being in the river all day regardless of geography. Drysuits can be expensive. A heavy-duty drysuit can run upward of one to two thousand dollars. I have been using a lightweight, low-end drysuit for four years without any problems. The lightweight suit before that lasted 4 years before the neck seal blew, a common problem regardless of price and thickness. However, lightweight suits don't have the same abrasion resistance that heavier suits do.

If you plan to make longer trips, a pack to hold drinking water, food, emergency gear, and warm, dry clothes is important. The pack obviously needs to be waterproof, though I know of some snorkelers who use army-surplus canvas gas mask bags and pack their contents in strong ziplock bags. My preference is a good, waterproof dry bag with shoulder straps so I can wear it like a backpack.

A waist belt is important to keep the pack secure to your body, and easy on/off is critical if you have to push through blowdowns or other obstructions, though a ton of caution needs to be exercised in these situations (see the safety section later in this introduction).

What you carry in the pack is up to you; however, I recommend, at a minimum, a basic first aid kit that includes a pocket mask for rescue breathing and basic wound care: BZK or other disinfectant pads, 4x4 gauze, and Band-Aids. A drysuit patch kit (duct tape) should also be included if you are wearing one. Think about what you would need for an extended time in nature. I carry dry fleece layers and high-energy food: granola and chocolate and, of course, drinking water. On longer trips, I carry a small-pack stove and fuel, along with something hot to make: hot chocolate and, even better, blackberry Jell-O. Just drink it warm as a liquid rather than eating it cold and sort of solid. A bivy sack provides protection from wind and rain if you find yourself stranded in the backcountry.

Snorkeling as an activity is very simple. However, since it is done in water and our lungs tend to stop functioning when too much water gets into them, serious caution is needed at a minimum, and formal instruction is recommended. But if you want to get started on your own, here are some instructions, and again, formal instruction is recommended.

Press the mask to your face. If you wear glasses, you need to take them off. Prescription mask lenses are available. You can leave contacts in. Once the mask is comfortably on your face, pull the strap over your head. Adjust the mask tightness with the ends of the straps on both sides of the mask. It should seal to your face without much headband pressure. There should be no need to cut the blood flow to your cheeks and nose to get a good seal. Masks tend to fog. The best deterrent is proper new mask treatment and spit. When you first get your mask, smear a dab of nonabrasive toothpaste on each lens. Really scrub the lens. Work the toothpaste in with your fingers, and then wash it all out. Spit on each lens and smear it around with your finger before each use. Rinse the spit out, and put the mask on. This should reduce fogging significantly. If your mask fogs while snorkeling, take the mask off and repeat, or just rinse it in the stream.

The operation of the snorkel is pretty straightforward. Put the mouthpiece in your mouth and breathe normally. The important part is to remember where the tube ends and to keep that above water. If you want to explore something in deeper water, hold your breath, surface dive to the bottom, and exhale hard through your mouth when you surface to clear the water out of the tube. Again, formal instruction here is really helpful.

Wetsuits can feel like neoprene vise grips when taking them off, but especially when putting them on. A nylon rash guard helps the neoprene slide over your skin, and socks help your feet slide through. However, the real key is folding the suit down as far as you can get it and stepping into it like pair of pants. Work each leg until your feet are through, grab folds of the neoprene, and work your way up until the knee areas of the wetsuit line up with your knees, the crotch lines up, more or less, with your crotch, and so on until your shoulders fit in and you can zip it up. Wet boots, gloves, and hood are needed in cooler water, and I usually wear them in water colder than 60 degrees.

Taking care of snorkeling gear is about as easy as its use. Rinse everything in fresh water after each trip. Dry wetsuits thoroughly but not in direct sun. Keep masks in a protective case.

Safety

River snorkeling is very safe. However, water is involved, and rivers are dynamic environments, which means they change. The current is always moving, and features in the river shift. Water is a dangerous element, so extreme caution needs to be used when river snorkeling. I always approach rivers with the utmost respect. Rivers that I have been in literally thousands of times will be the ones that kill me if I don't approach each trip with the same sense of vigilance and safety.

The current is your friend or enemy. It will help you get where you are going, and, when you learn how to use it, it will help you scoot across the river expertly. It will also push you into hazards that will kill you. Strainers are obstructions in rivers that let the water pass through but trap larger particles such as yourself. Strong currents in streams and rivers pin things against strainers and hold them underwater. Water is deceptively strong, and escape from strainers is nearly impossible. They are very dangerous features to anyone in moving water. Look for them downriver, and stay away.

Rocks are also problems. Hitting one is painful, and if you strike the wrong part of your body, such as your head or chest, it could lead to serious injury. Rapids are nothing more than a collection of rocks, so the chance of striking something vital increases. Snorkeling rapids gives a whole new perspective on rivers, but keep these adventures for after you have some river experience, and know you are flirting with a significant injury.

Finally, know how to call for help. Cell phone coverage is often spotty in river valleys. Know where you are and what your egress plan is so you can communicate that to 911 or the dispatch center. Not all parts of the country are covered by 911, so know the number for emergency services where you are snorkeling. Consider purchasing a personal locator beacon if you plan on snorkeling remote areas.

Know your limits, and don't exceed them despite the lure. I have placed myself in sketchy situations because of not paying attention to this tenet and was just lucky enough to not wind up in need of rescue or recovery. Finally, get training. Learn how to snorkel from a pro. Get CPR and first aid certified, and if you are going to make bigger trips in more remote areas, attend a wilderness first responder class. One of the best courses I ever took was swift water rescue, and I recommend that one if you plan on doing larger water.

Leave No Trace Underwater

I really hope this book inspires people to snorkel rivers. However, not too much. Our rivers are fragile, and some of the locations featured in this book can be overused. It's a weird tension. I want people to explore the amazing life in our streams, but by sharing these sacred places, I put them at risk.

That snail you just knocked off the rock is an individual of an endangered species. The rock you accidentally flipped over in the current housed a hellbender, the largest salamander in North America, whose numbers are declining. You just stomped on juvenile candy darters, an endangered species in the Southeast, as you walked into deeper water. Don't be that obnoxious river jerk. Recognize you are in someone else's home and act like it. Approach each river with reverence. Watch where you step, and minimize those steps. Get into the water and float. Don't disturb mating fish. Watch for redds, which are fish nests and look similar to bowls of fresh-churned bottom. Go as an observer, not an interrupter. If a spot looks overused, go somewhere else. Pick up after yourself, and pick up for other people who didn't pick up after themselves.

WHERE

One of the beauties of river snorkeling is we can do it anywhere there is a creek. The water doesn't need to be deep or big. Some of the most amazing experiences I have had exploring fresh water were small streams where half my body hung out of the water. Safety is the primary factor when selecting a snorkeling site. Look for hazards previously discussed, and make sure water quality won't make you sick. It is a sad statement that in 2020 we need to worry about getting sick after swimming in a river anywhere in the world, let alone the United States, but that is our reality. Make sure the water is clean enough for swimming. Typically, streams in forested areas are safe. Streams in rural areas may be contaminated by animal wastes, so a look at the watershed will tell you a lot. If cows are wading upstream of where you want to snorkel, there is probably fecal coliform in it. They aren't human coliforms but still fecal coliforms. Suburban streams may be contaminated with runoff from parking lots and overflowing sanitary sewer systems, and I usually stay away from most urban streams, but not all. The James River flows right through downtown Richmond, Virginia, and snorkeling there is fabulous! I have provided a few sites in this book to get you started, but there are so many more than I will ever have the opportunity to experience in my lifetime. That, to me, makes life exciting. There is always something new to discover, learn, and protect.

CAVEATS

This book is a really high-level overview of river snorkeling opportunities in the United States. It is 15 years of snorkeling across the country distilled into 60,000 words. The species accounts are abbreviated and touch on the high points. There are a lot of gaps, which I know. There are entire groups of organisms missing due to space and time constraints. Catfish, suckers, sturgeon, and gar are all incredible animals that aren't included here. It's not because they aren't worthy. It's simply because I ran out of space. There is a lot more to explore and discuss than what is here, which is the intent of this book: to provide a glimpse beneath the surface of our rivers and streams in the hopes people will want to snorkel them so that they experience the extraordinary life there and realize exactly what we stand to lose if we don't protect our rivers and the life they contain. There are so many more stories to tell.

HOW TO HELP

The hope is that as people snorkel rivers and experience streams on their own terms, they will be inspired to act to protect them. There are some really simple ways we can help all the amazing life we stand to lose in our generation. Don't overuse streams. Collect trash that isn't yours. Watch your runoff, and control it with rain gardens. Don't spray ditches with weed killer. Join water advocacy groups such as your local watershed association and regional river advocacy groups such as the Sea-Run Brook Trout Coalition, Downeast Salmon Federation, the Native Fish Society, your local land trust and Riverkeeper organization, and groups like American Rivers. The North American Native Fish Association is committed to native fish conservation, and international organizations such as Shoal and Alliance for Freshwater Life are committed to freshwater biodiversity conservation. However, conservation starts at home, and freshwater biodiversity conservation starts with snorkeling.

Sitting behind a tiny cabin in Maine, I notice that fall has arrived this last week of October. The ocean is in the distance behind a balsam forest, with a red blueberry field in front. I came here to document Atlantic salmon, a species impacted by climate change, among other things.

Six hours ago I squeezed into my drysuit in a freezing cold downpour, so it was almost a stupid proposition. I didn't even glove or hood up. I just jumped into the East Machias to photo and video the release of one of the last chances for a species: Atlantic salmon produced in the Downeast Salmon Federation Peter Gray Hatchery. The water was painfully freezing, and spears of cold stabbed my hands and face. I should have taken the extra minute to fully gear up. However, I needed to see this release, a release which might be the last hope for Atlantic salmon. And now I'm paying the price by sitting in the sun thawing out. It could be a lot worse.

As I reflect on the past week spent exploring cold dark water and watch the scene before me change with the setting sun, I wonder what will be left. The bold coast of Maine is also called the cold coast due to chilly ocean temperatures here. It is one of the fastest-warming parts of the sea, and the life I watched over the past week in bold coast rivers is directly affected by that warming. We are on the precipice of forever losing freshwater life that escapes description. It needs to be experienced to be understood.

I tried to give a broad overview of the life to be seen in our rivers and streams and the threats that life faces. During my 15-year freshwater snorkeling journey, I have been a firsthand witness to loss. Loss at an alarming rate. My hope is this snorkeling-induced change in perspective will at least slow this loss, if not arrest it.

This is the why.

I am grateful for the experiences, adventure, new friends, and inspired hope I encountered along the way.

Trout

I've always admired trout. They are usually keenly aware and wary, which makes them elusive, and when I spent more time fishing for them than snorkeling with them, tricking one into biting my hook was one of the ultimate challenges. Trout have an intelligence that makes it difficult to capture them. And now that I try to observe them, I find that they are just as challenging to watch.

I slid into the cold, clear water of Fishing Creek, a tributary to the lower Susquehanna, in June to scope it out for a trip I would be running later in the summer. The architecture of the place instantly impressed. Water cascaded over shelves of sparkling slate-blue schist bedrock into pools lined with smoothed and angulated slabs. Quicksilver air bubbles danced back to the surface through the crystal water.

I saw a group of minnows and crept in to try to get a good photo and positive identification. I noticed the speckled snout of a trout sticking out from under a rock. I watched the fish look intently at me trying to figure out what I was and plan its next move. I pointed the camera at the trout, and the fish allowed me to snap a few shots before it sped away into the main flow below a short waterfall, leaving the minnows in a cloud of silt.

I followed, and my little trout shot off and joined another larger fish feeding in a deeper, swift current. I hid behind a rock and watched the two trout hunt. They plucked insect morsels from the water with precise movements while maintaining their position in the river. Watching them was experiencing the most incredible ballet. They exemplified grace, power, agility, and keen knowledge of their surroundings. I wasn't fooling them by hiding behind the rock. They knew I was there and allowed me to watch them feed. Finally, they perceived me as a big enough threat to warrant the expenditure of energy to escape my presence, and they were gone. I swam through the pool, but the only thing I found was a puff of sediment in a bedrock crevice where one of the trout had hidden and burst out of when I passed overhead. I caught peripheral glimpses of the fish through the rest of the trip but wasn't able to spend any time watching them again. I enjoyed the beauty of Fishing Creek, looked for the trout, and admired their ability to dominate a pool one minute and completely vanish the next.

These were rainbow trout, likely a few holdouts from the April stocking. While stocked fish might be less able to navigate wild streams as their wild-born

1

cousins, these two certainly looked like they belonged here, though they didn't. It seemed these two had learned the way of the river with all its nooks and crannies and changes in flow compared to the smooth-walled, concrete-lined hatchery chutes where they were born and raised. It seemed they learned how to find their own food versus inhaling pellets tossed into the water by the scoopfull. These seemed to be as wary as their wild counterparts. Most rainbows don't survive the first few weeks of the season.

We raise rainbow trout in hatcheries and release them for fishermen to fish out. The put-and-take ritual is repeated every spring. The native trout populations in many streams have been replaced by nonnative rainbow trout. Rainbows are native to the Pacific Coast and are the most widely introduced trout globally. Antarctica is the only continent where rainbows aren't stocked. Putting them in a river changes the energy flow dynamics of the stream to the same degree as removing all of the trees surrounding it.

Streams get half their food from the algae that grow on the rocks and wood on the bottom. Aquatic insects feed on the algae and are in turn eaten by fish. The other half of a creek's nutrition comes from outside of the stream either as insects that fall directly into the water where they are gobbled by fish or as leaves and other vegetative matter that falls into the water, which is eaten by aquatic insects that are then consumed by fish. When the trees surrounding a stream are removed, a cascade of negative effects occurs. First, sunlight warms the water in the stream, possibly making it too hot to support cold-water fish such as trout. Second, 50 percent of the streams food source is removed, and the aquatic feeding structure is completely reorganized. Placing rainbow trout in streams has the same effect. They remove 50 percent of the stream's nutrition, and the energy flow of the stream is totally rearranged as a result. I understand the damage these fish do to our stream's. I also know the number of people drawn to rivers because of them. Moreover, I know their beauty and elegance underwater, so I enjoy swimming with them.

I got into the Gunpowder River in north-central Maryland in August, more to cool off than to see anything. I actually didn't expect much at this intensely used section of the river. There's a hole carved 10 feet into the bottom where the river bends left and splits around a large, submerged boulder. I jumped in and enjoyed the chilly water and weightlessness. I peered through my mask at the bottom, expecting a few minnows, maybe. Instead, I saw a foot-and-a-half rainbow holding steady in the gentle current at the base of the boulder. At first, I didn't believe my identification. It was too late in the season for a rainbow to have lasted in this heavily fished stream. Moreover, my noisy entry should have sent any trout in the vicinity flying for cover. It was probably just a big sucker that I mistook for a trout. I looked again and confirmed it was a rainbow. However, why was this fish here? I dove to the bottom on the side of the boulder opposite the trout and crept around the back of the rock until the fish came into view. The rainbow trout didn't move, which was very odd even for a hatchery fish. It was definitely a rainbow. Its silver body was dotted with clean-edged black dots and a blush of reddish-purple ran down its length. It held on the bottom, wagging its tail just enough to stay put in the current. I ran out of breath and came to the surface. Something wasn't quite right with this fish, as beautiful as it was. I dove for a closer look, and as I approached from the opposite side, I saw that its left eye was gone. It was blind on one side. I couldn't tell if this injury happened at the hatchery or since its release, but either way, I was amazed this fish was able to survive. I figured it wouldn't live for much longer and would soon fall victim to starvation, predation, or a hook.

The Loyalsock is a stream located in north-central Pennsylvania that runs wonderfully clear most of the time. It isn't without problems, though, and is afflicted by acid mine drainage. It was named the 2018 Pennsylvania River of the Year, and I embarked on a project to document the underwater changes of this river over 12 months. "A year in the life of the River of the Year," as I like to think of it. I started in February and hadn't seen a fish in the first two months of the project. I geared up for my April visit. The creek was clear and cold as usual, and it felt like a biological desert. I didn't see any life, as usual, except for an abundance of caddis and mayfly larvae. Yet, there was not one fish. I was starting to wonder if I had made the right choice to invest this much time and effort. Air and water temperatures were starting to rise, so I should start to see more fish. I should have already seen typical wintertime fish like sculpin. Maybe this creek was just too sick with acid mine drainage.

Stocked school of trout.

The river flowed hard, and getting swept downstream was a real possibility. I wasn't prepared to get bounced through a Class II rapid, so I fought to make my way across the channel. I caught my breath in the lee of a large boulder while I looked for fish and wondered what I was doing there. A foot-long shadow slid downstream and dropped into the boulder eddy with me. It was a rainbow. Then a second, third, and fourth fish came in. They were all rainbows. In a matter of minutes, the eddy filled with a dozen rainbows ranging from a foot to a foot and a half. They were wary, and each rapid movement or snorkel clear made them jolt, but they never scattered far and quickly returned. They tolerated me in the large eddy and stayed there working the current. The cold eventually penetrated through my drysuit and underlying fleece layer, and I started to shiver. I was thrilled that I had finally seen fish in the Loyalsock, and they were trout at that! I was too excited by the experience of swimming with so many large fish to be suspicious. I left the Loyalsock satisfied.

I struggled to unzip the drysuit because of the painful cold that weakened my hands but was finally able to wriggle out of it. I draped it across my car to drain. A man approached and asked, "What kind of waders is those?"

"Oh, that's a drysuit."

"So you was the guy snorkeling just downstream of where they was stockin'. See any fish?"

It all made sense, and I felt like a fool. I don't know why it didn't register that these fish were just stocked. Maybe I was too caught up in the excitement of snorkeling with a school of trout, or finally seeing fish in the Loyalsock, to see the clear evidence that the fish I was watching drop into the eddy one after the other just came from a tank truck.

"Yeah, a bunch of rainbows. Probably the fish they just put in."

"Yeah, probably."

This was the first day of the trout's wild existence, their first day out of the concrete-lined cell where they were raised. This was the first day they had to fend for themselves, find food, and avoid being eaten. Most rainbows don't survive the first few weeks in the wild. That's why it's called a put-and-take fishery: fisheries managers put them in, and fishermen take them out. However, every once in a while, I encounter a fish who had figured out how to evade capture and survive in the wild. Moreover, while these fish are stocked like the others, there is something different about them.

The White Clay is a suburbanized stream that flows through urbanizing southeastern Pennsylvania into northern Delaware. Most of its watershed is developed, so the stream suffers from heavy storm flows and excess nutrient and sediment loads. Sections of the stream corridor are protected and give the impression of being remote, though just beyond the immediate forested river valley, streets and lawns dominate the suburban landscape. I slid into a long pool at the transition between fall and winter. All the leaves were off the trees,

WHITE CLAY CREEK

Description: The White Clay Creek is an 18-mile tributary to the Christina River in Delaware, and it flows through a pastoral landscape in southeastern Pennsylvania and northern Delaware. Much of the river corridor is protected in state park and preserves, and 190 miles of the east and west branches, main stem, and its tributaries were federally listed as wild and scenic, a pretty incredible designation for a creek that runs through the middle of the northeastern megalopolis.

Access: GPS address: 208 Good Hope Road, Landenberg, PA. A small, dirt parking lot will be on the right as you travel east on Good Hope Road, right after crossing the bridge. There is a trail that leads down to the creek.

West Branch of the White Clay Creek.

and piles of waterlogged ones covered areas of bottom where the current had piled them.

A two-foot-long rainbow watched me from the downstream end of the pool 20 feet away. Its tail was down and in constant rapid motion; its pectoral fins twitched to keep its head up into the current. It was acutely aware of me before I even knew it was there. This fish must have been stocked at least since this past spring, and based on its size, I wondered if it hadn't survived for more than a year in the wild. This was a racehorse of a fish compared to the just-stocked Loyalsock trout. This fish was always prepared to bolt. Every muscle was tense and ready to fire. It was not trusting. Moreover, while the Loyalsock fish accepted me as part of the stream-scape, part of the background, this fish never did. It avoided capture in a heavily fished stream, so apparently, it had intelligence that enabled it to discern food from bait. This is the allure of and attraction to wild fish versus hatchery fish: their wildness, their wariness and fitness, their raw athleticism and wild intelligence compared to their hatchery-raised cousins.

I said a little prayer to the McKenzie as I hiked 5 miles upstream to my put in. It was more of a simple conversational homage. "I'm not here to conquer you or fight you or shred anything. I just want to watch and learn what you'll teach me. I just want to snorkel 5 miles of you, and I'd be much obliged if you would let me pass unharmed."

I was going to snorkel 5 miles on the McKenzie River, from Rainbow to Delta, Oregon. Everything in the Pacific Northwest is bigger than what I'm used to in the East: bigger fish, bigger mountains, and bigger trees. And, of course, bigger rivers. I did my due diligence the day before and asked a fishing guide who paddles a McKenzie River dory through here regularly if it was possible to snorkel this stretch. "Possible, yes. That doesn't mean smart." However, he confirmed there were no strainers or snags, "as long as you stay in the middle."

I got to the put in at Rainbow Campground, already tired from the fast-paced 5-mile hike upriver. It was going to be near 100 degrees in the Cascades today, being the first of August, but the McKenzie River still ran at 55 degrees. Volcano ice water, as my friend Jeremy Monroe taught me. The water in the McKenzie comes from melted Cascade snowpack that trickles through the volcanic mountains to reappear as the river.

I zipped into my drysuit and squirmed into my wetsuit on top of the drysuit. The drysuit and underlying fleece layer provided thermal protection. The wetsuit protected the drysuit from snags and tears. Once I was in the river, there were no options for getting out until 5 miles later. A flooded drysuit in this river for 5 miles would be bad.

Douglas firs towered 100 feet into the sky, supported by 8-foot-diameter trunks, and I wondered at what they had seen. What had they witnessed in their 400-year lives? The McKenzie rushed past unconcerned. Its aquamarine water foamed to white by a Class II rapid just downstream that I assumed would tail out into a nice pool for the rest of the ride. I was wrong. I tried to wade out to mid-channel but only got a quarter of the way there before the knee-deep water knocked me down and I was in the wash.

I couldn't really see the rocks approach despite the perfect clarity. They just appeared from the bubble curtain, and I had to fend off or veer around them, but mostly, I only had control enough to vault over them. The water formed cavernous holes on the downstream side of the rocks that sucked me in and compressed my chest with a breath-squeezing *thud* as the water rushed back into the void. This little Class II rapid was more than I expected.

The river spilled into a fast-moving deep pool, and there they were. My first wild, native rainbows. They looked and behaved so differently than our eastern

MCKENZIE RIVER

Description: The McKenzie River is a 90-mile tributary of the Willamette River in western Oregon. It originates from Clear Lake and drains part of the Cascade Mountains. It is fed by Cascade Mountain snowpack meltwater that trickles through porous volcanic bedrock and reemerges as clear, cold rivers like the McKenzie roughly 40 years later. Annual average water temperatures in the McKenzie run around 50 degrees. The McKenzie is a legendary cold-water fishery, famous for rainbow trout, steelhead, and salmon, and the river dories that are used to chase these fish. It is a fast-moving, cold river, so extreme caution needs to be exercised when snorkeling it. Locating still water on the McKenzie where you aren't constantly fighting current is a challenge, but slower water can be found along the shoreline and in side channels. Use caution to stay away from strainers. Brukart Landing is a boat ramp for white-water rafts and McKenzie River dories near the confluence of the main stem and South Fork McKenzie. There is some slower-moving water along the shoreline immediately upstream and downstream of the ramp.

Access: GPS address: 91530 Cougar Dam Road, Blue River, Oregon. From Eugene, drive 48 miles east on Route 126 to Cougar Dam Road. Turn right, and Brukart Landing Boat Ramp is on the right.

Above: McKenzie River.

hatchery-raised fish, I couldn't tell what kind of trout these were at first, even though I had seen hundreds of hatchery-born rainbows. They had even more athleticism than the stocked fish that hold over. They didn't have to work at it like the eastern fish I was familiar with. They just *were* that wild fish. They just knew that river since birth, and it was apparent. They knew that river from *before* birth. These fish were in their home waters, rivers where their first ancestors adapted to these conditions enough to be called a separate species. The McKenzie is in the central part of their historical range, which extends west of the Cascades, north to Alaska, south to Mexico, and east to Idaho and Nevada. Their range has expanded across North America since that time, since we started to tinker with fish distributions and have taken it upon ourselves to move fish into rivers where they aren't supposed to naturally occur, mostly for our benefit, with little regard to ecological consequences. However, these fish are the direct descendants of the rainbows that originated here driven by natural processes rather than hatchery trucks.

These rainbows fit here, like biologic puzzle pieces inserted into the physical environment for a perfect match. The habitat suited them. Trout need clear, cold water and habitat complexity: side channels, boulders, overhanging bank vegetation, pools that tail out into clean gravel flats. The one piece that was missing was large, woody material, such as entire old-growth trees with 8-foot-diameter trunks and 20-foot-diameter root wads. Woody material forms gravel bars in its lee, forces water into side channels, and, generally, creates habitat complexity. Large woody material was removed from rivers such as the McKenzie because it prohibited driving logs downstream and because early fish biologists perceived logjams to be impediments to fish migration. We now know better. Despite the lack of large, woody material, the McKenzie provides some of the best rainbow habitat anywhere. High-quality trout habitat has been reduced mostly because of soil erosion, which causes sedimentation in rivers and clogs the clean gravels they need for spawning. Eggs can't get oxygen when they are buried beneath a layer of silt. Ultimately, land-use practices cause sedimentation: logging, mining, suburban development, farming. What we have done on the land has greatly reduced the distribution and abundance of native rainbows. Water diversions, dams, and other impediments to migration, such as poorly placed and constructed culverts, have also contributed to the decline. Even though resident rainbows don't migrate to the sea like their steelhead cousins, they still need to move up and down rivers to spawn and send the next generation, and thus the species, on its way into the future.

Steelhead are genetically the same species as rainbows, but their life histories are very different. Resident rainbows will move up and down the same river to spawn but never head out to sea, whereas steelhead, or sea-run rainbow trout, spend most of their lives at sea and make epic, tenacious return trips back to their natal streams to spawn. Therefore, they are even more susceptible to migration impediments, and river damming has resulted in nine different populations of steelhead being added to the endangered species list.

Whether resident rainbow or long-distance migrant steelhead, both need the same thing to spawn: clean, sediment-free gravel. The female uses her tail to beat a depression, which is called a redd, into the gravel. This attracts the attention of nearby males. Sometimes, tail biting and circular chases occur before the female releases some of her eggs into the redd with a male by her side releasing sperm to fertilize the eggs as they fall into the spaces between the gravel the female created when she churned it up. She beats the bottom again, which sends a layer of gravel drifting downstream over the just-fertilized eggs to protect them and repeats the spawning process in the fresh end of her redd.

The pool ranged between 10 and 15 feet deep, and the bottom was boulder and cobble. It was a pool only in the sense that the boulders on the bottom were too deep to foam the water to white bubbles, but the current didn't relent, and I kept moving downstream as fast as I did while in the rapid. I struggled to swim for the shoreline to try to scout what awaited downstream and splashed over rainbows who seemed to effortlessly hold their position in the stiff current, especially compared to my flailing. They waited in the turbulence behind boulders for an unfortunate mayfly to get plucked from the bottom and flushed downstream by the current, or for a caterpillar to drop into the river from an overhanging branch. Their speckled silver bodies had a watercolor wash of reddish-purple down their sides, and they sparkled in the sunlight that easily illuminated the bottom in golden shafts through the aquamarine water.

I got to the edge of the river and tried to stand up, but the current kept pushing me farther downstream. Finally, I got to a collection of cobble in waist-deep water and stood. I was breaking every whitewater rule on this trip—heading downriver headfirst and standing up. The risk of heading downriver headfirst is apparent. The risk of standing up is foot entrapment. If the current were to push one of my feet under a rock, and I couldn't get it out, the current would fold my body over into the water, and I would drown. However, here I was standing up waist deep on a pile of cobbles, trying to figure out my next move. Five miles more of this didn't seem possible. But there was no way I could make my way back upstream. I was committed. Downstream was even more frothing river, and I could already hear the low hum of water against rock through my wetsuit hood. "Well, that was interesting," I said out loud, shrugged my shoulders, put my snorkel back in my mouth, and tried to relax as I headed for another Class II rapid.

Trout darted from underneath me, and even though I was working hard to keep my position in the river and avoid collisions with boulders, I still marveled at the power and grace and effortless beauty of these fish, which sparkled silver and crimson against a clear aquamarine backdrop. The epitome of wild. They were ever aware of the river and everything in it. They investigated everything, first with their eyes, and then, if the object looked enticing, they stalked closer until making the decision to strike with all their might. These rainbows were doing some kind of calculation, evaluating their options against some decision-making criteria. Maybe this was instinctual, maybe learned, or maybe both. Either way, there was thought as to whether the expected reward of a certain food item was worth the risk of pursuit.

I learned by watching the trout that if I just relaxed, paid attention, let the water take me, and let that water help move me to where I wanted to be in the river, it was a much more enjoyable ride. I came to appreciate the feeling of water compressing my chest when I landed in a hole and the hollow *ka-whomp* sound it made, like the sensation of a good cannonball jump into a pool. I appreciated these wild fish even more since I would soon return to the East, where wild rainbows are a legend.

In the East, rainbows are placed in even marginal suburban waters like the Gunpowder and White Clay. Those are streams that don't much look like trout streams. However, Riverlands streams, the streams that cut through the rolling hills of the lower Susquehanna Valley as they make their way to the Susquehanna, look like the quintessential trout stream, right out of a Rockwell painting.

I went to Riverlands preserve streams, which are protected by the Lancaster County Conservancy, looking for wild trout. Tucquan Glen is one of those. Tucquan Creek looks and feels remote. It cascades over schist shelves through a steep-sided valley of hemlock and rhododendron. I hiked into the gorge and slid into the water that was murky following some July thunderstorms. While the immediate valley of Tucquan is forested, much of its watershed, or the land that drains to it is farmed. Just the smallest shower sends tons of sediment into the creek and turns the water into something akin to chocolate milk. The shadows of larger fish stayed in view just long enough for my imagination to identify them as native brook trout, or breeding wild browns, but they never came close enough for me to confirm.

I returned to Tucquan on an early spring day when the water was clearer. Showers threatened as I suited up alongside the creek. The spring forest floor was covered in wildflowers: yellow and white mayapple blooms hung beneath bright green umbrella canopies, white toothwort flowers hung like pulled bicuspids strung together on an arching stalk, and, my favorite, the yellow bells of trout lily nodded a few inches above the leathery green leaves spotted with dark purple. It was easy to imagine the eddies and holes filled with trout nose up in the current waiting to pluck insect morsels as they drift by. I expected not only to see these fish but to capture their images since the last time I'd been there the murk made catching a shot of them impossible.

A tan shadow shot from under a rock to under a short falls. Was it a trout? I crawled upstream toward a chute that cascades water over a one-foot falls. The environment there was loud chaos. All I could hear was the rush of water that sounded like a train. Air bubbles blinded me. I pulled myself through the current

RIVERLANDS

Description: The Riverlands region is a landscape that runs along the last 40 miles of the Susquehanna River. It is characterized by rolling hills that are incised by clear, cold streams that cut through the underlying schist bedrock as they head to the Susquehanna. These form steep-sided, shaded, forested valleys and gorges that result in cool microclimates, so species occur here that are at the very southern edge of their range. The cool, damp climates of the valleys and gorges encourage the growth of rhododendron and hemlock forests, which further shade and cool the streams that form the valleys, and allow cold-water fish, such as brook trout, to occur in a landscape that is otherwise inhospitable for them. The Lancaster County Conservancy recognized the importance of these places and has worked to protect them. The Riverlands region is a National Heritage Area. Tucquan Glen, Fishing Creek, and Climbers Run are three preserves the Lancaster Conservancy manages that contain snorkelable streams. These preserves are being loved to death, so when you visit, please follow all preserve rules. Stay on the trails, park only in designated spots, and, if the parking lot is full, visit a different preserve.

Access: GPS Address: "Fishing Creek Preserve," "Tucquan Preserve," and "Climbers Run Preserve" will get you to the respective preserve. These three preserves are located in southwestern Lancaster County, Pennsylvania, roughly 30 minutes south of Lancaster, 1.25 hours north of Baltimore, and 1.5 hours west of Philadelphia.

Above: Tucquan Glen, a Susquehanna Riverlands preserve.

to behind the chute and witnessed the force of the water as it carved smooth holes in the sparkly, silver-orange bedrock. I didn't see any fish. I drifted with the current back downstream, let myself experience the freedom of getting spun in an eddy, and looked under a lone rock in the middle of a pool. There, hidden in the shadow, was a brown trout that stared back at me for a second, then rocketed out of the pool with one powerful flick of its tail, and it was gone for the rest of the day.

The next winter, I returned after an ice storm glazed everything, including the forest floor. The mile-long hike in was tricky, and I wished I'd worn crampons to navigate a few steep and slick sections where I crawled over the trail to keep from falling into the chasm the Tucquan Creek carved through the bedrock 20 feet below. Most of the river was frozen over except where the water moved especially fast. The plunge pool below a 5-foot falls had open water, so I sat on the ice, slid over the sheet to the edge, dangled my legs in the stream, then slid all the way in.

The water stung but was clear, and I instantly saw two large brown trout lying on the bottom of the 5-foot-deep pool. They sped upstream into a void carved behind the waterfall when I got too close. I worked hard to swim against the current as I followed them into the falls. I could probably stop myself before I got swept under the downstream ice, but I didn't want to find out. I was blinded by the bubble curtain coming off the falls and deafened by the noise. The upstream eddy current grabbed me and pulled me in, which was equally unnerving as the thought of getting swept under the downstream ice sheet. Just as I emerged from the

Wintertime Tucquan Creek.

PISGAH NATIONAL FOREST

Description: Pisgah National Forest encompasses 500,000 acres of forested land in western North Carolina. Because of the forests here, Pisgah also contains more than a thousand miles of cold-water wild trout streams.

Access: GPS Address: 1401 Fish Hatchery Road, Pisgah Forest, North Carolina. From Brevard, North Carolina, take Route 276, Pisgah Highway, which follows the Davidson River. There are multiple pull-offs and opportunities to get into the river. Two of the notable spots with easy access are the Davidson River Recreation Area and the Pisgah Center for Wildlife Education. A trail runs downstream of the education center, and access to the Davidson can be made here.

Davidson River in Pisgah National Forest.

turmoil of the main flow into the calm beside the falls, I saw a school of a half dozen different sized browns hiding in the lee. Maybe it was the barely above-freezing water that made the fish less active. Or maybe the chaos of the falls, the air bubble curtain, and the constant noise all provided camouflage. However, for whatever reason, the brown trout stayed at the bottom 4 feet below and let me admire their beauty, specifically their yellow-haloed black-and-red dots and golden pectoral fins as they watched me back before launching for the downstream side of the pool and disappeared under the ice.

This wasn't my first encounter with brown trout, but it was my first encounter with so many. The first time I saw a brown trout, I was looking for hellbenders in Pisgah National Forest, North Carolina, in early December.

I was in a deep pool a hundred yards downstream of a 50-foot waterfall. The creek on the left shoaled to a foot deep where gravel accumulated and steeply sloped to a bedrock-lined 6-foot-deep pool on the right side of the stream. I enjoyed the crystal-clear water and swam against the current, intent on seeing a hellbender. A recently fallen oak tree lay across the entire stream just above the water's surface, and one of its thick branches was completely submerged.

My snorkel rubbed against the underside of the tree as I passed. I looked to my left, and a 2-foot-long rotund brown trout stared back at me from his position on a clean bedrock shelf right under the large branch. Its plump, yellow belly glowed against the red bedrock. We watched each other for a few minutes, the trout unsure of what to make of me, until it finally had enough of my presence and rocketed to deeper water. The large butter belly was a total surprise and thrill, even if it is a nonnative fish.

Brown trout, originally from Europe, are also stocked and have established widespread wild-breeding populations. They often replace native brook trout. I'm pretty certain the browns I saw in Pisgah and Tucquan were wild-breeding populations, and while not native, these wild-bred fish challenged my skill to stalk and observe and were almost as exciting to watch as natives.

We can't fully know, appreciate, and love our freshwater life without watching and experiencing it on its own terms in our rivers and streams. One of those fish we need to get to know on its own terms, where it lives in all of its aquatic glory, is the native brook trout. There isn't much that is more thrilling than watching native brook trout in their element: clear, cold streams.

Brown trout in a Pisgah National Forest stream.

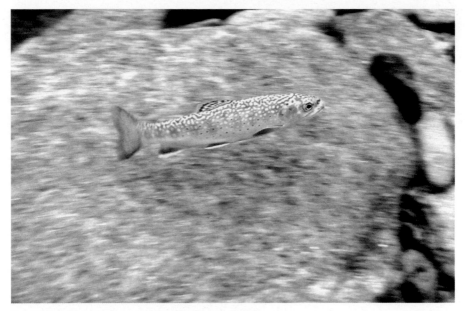

Brook trout in a Susquehanna Riverlands stream.

Climbers Run is another Susquehanna Riverlands stream protected by the Lancaster Conservancy. It looks like it belongs in the mountains of western Pennsylvania more than in the farmlands of Lancaster. Climbers Run tumbles clear and cold over schist shelves through a hemlock-lined gorge, and the first time I got in, I instantly saw a brook trout.

Brook trout are one of our most beautiful native fish. They have red bellies, white-fringed, red pectoral fins, and red tails with orange and yellow spots on a crimson-sided body that grades to dark, tiger-striped green above. Dappled sunlight penetrated the water of Climbers Run to make the fish I was watching blaze sky blue with brilliant red fins as they hunted food from the swift current. In fall, brook trout spawn and put on spectacular breeding colors. Their undersides glow golden reddish orange, and their fins become brilliant scarlet. They match the yellow-and-red autumn maple and oak leaves that float on the surface of the stream.

I hid behind a bedrock slab just out of the main current. The cool water washed away the July heat as a half dozen brook trout flashed and danced a wonderful ballet defending prime feeding spots and snatching food from the current. I drifted downstream away from the slab, and the trout scattered as soon as I came into view. I stopped short of the end of the pool, where a large branch had lodged. Two juvenile brook trout used the twigs for protection while they fed. It looked as though translucent, vertical gray bands, known as parr marks, were stenciled over the classic brook trout red-spotted and tiger-striped patterns.

Brook trout parr.

These ferocious little trout, just inches long, were masters of their end of the pool, just as the adults were masters of the upper part. They treaded the current and waited until just the right moment to precisely strike away from the safety of the submerged wood and nab food that drifted by. It is encouraging to see the next generation, especially in a species that is declining.

Brook trout require cold, clear water with little sediment. Therefore, the streams they inhabit have forested watersheds, which are vanishing. Brook trout have already been extirpated from parts of their range due to the loss of forested watersheds, which equates to the loss of clear, cold water.

I grew up on the Pumpkin Patch, which is one of those streams that used to run clear and cold but now runs warm and clouded. It used to hold brookies. The Pumpkin Patch is a tributary to the Rahway River, which is the major river entering the Arthur Kill, which in turn forms part of the Hudson Raritan estuary complex. I visited the creek daily, in all weather. The Pumpkin Patch was where I was a master crayfish fisher and knew their life cycle by being a part of it. The Pumpkin Patch, at least my section of it, started from three storm sewer outfall pipes at Public School #22, flowed through the last remaining patch of woods in a suburbanized part of New Jersey, and trickled over a concrete-lined and channelized section where algal mats grew thick.

Mrs. Ruth Beck lived across the creek in a Tudor-style house that she and her husband Karl had built from materials they harvested from the local forest and creek. Ruth and Karl had escaped Nazi Germany and were the first to build in the woods off of Inman Avenue before my street, Hawthorne Avenue, was even a muddy smudge. The fireplace and chimney were made from round, water-smoothed red-, gray-, brown-, and rust-colored rocks they collected from the creek. All the lumber, the plank paneling, exposed beams, and hardwood flooring had been milled from oaks they cut in the course of clearing their homesteading site. Mrs. Beck's description of the area when they first arrived captivated me—there were no other houses, and Inman Avenue had been a pothole-filled dirt road. However, what really grabbed my interest were her stories about the creek. Mrs. Beck's blue eyes sparkled behind her small, gold-framed glasses as she described how the creek had run clearer, colder, and deeper back then. She told stories of how she and Karl had fished as many huge brook trout out of the cold water as they could possibly eat and took pictures of Karl holding stringers full of large, round-bellied brook trout down from the mantel to show me examples of the bounty that once was. I could barely imagine the area covered in forest, with her house and one-half-acre garden patch the only clearing instead of all the houses, streets, and lawns of my day. I couldn't imagine that kind of bounty coming from the 1970s Pumpkin Patch. The best I could do was catch 4-inch crayfish and foot-long suckers. That's all that was there, and I considered this to be abundance, but I still dreamed of a day when the Pumpkin Patch would be restored. A time when the water ran clear and cool and native trout again topped the food chain. I didn't understand the significance of those photos then, but I do now, and I seek out native brooks to watch and learn their ways and to try to capture their beauty and intricacy in photos.

The Bushkill is just about as close to pristine as streams come in the East. It is located in the Pocono Mountains of eastern Pennsylvania, and for only being a few hours from both New York City and Philadelphia, it offers a rare glimpse into the life of a minimally impacted stream relative to other creeks in the eastern megalopolis. I was headed to a contentious meeting about the fate of the upper Delaware River and the fight over its water. I planned extra time into the trip to get into the Bushkill.

There were still a few pockets of April snow tucked under the deep shade of hemlock as I drove along the Bushkill on the gravel Pine Flats Road. Tannins stained the water as it percolated through the peaty organic-rich soil so that the stream was the color of strong tea. I couldn't see the bottom of the 5-foot-deep pool from my red shale bedrock shoreline outcrop as I zipped into my drysuit. The snow still on the ground meant this was going to hurt, and since I wasn't able to see anything through the tea water, I wondered if the cold pain would be worth it. I slid in and instantly was hovering above hundreds of white-fringed pectoral fins. I was swimming with the largest school of brook trout I had ever seen. Foot-long trout warily darted out of my shadow on the bottom, but there were so many of them, and they really had nowhere to go, so they nervously shot around. I tried to remain motionless, to blend with the creek, and as I relaxed, so did the trout. Sunlight dove through the water in lines of orange beams and made

Large brook trout school in Bushkill Creek.

the backs of the trout glow when they swam through them. I floated motionless in amazement as white-edged pectoral fins flashed so that it was hard to differentiate individuals. I was watching a large mass of yellow squiggles and red dots and red fins all moving in unison. I knew this was an awesome sight, to see so many brook trout in the same place in the creek. It is possible these were stocked, but the stocking records didn't include this location. Maybe the fish stocked elsewhere in this system moved a few miles to gather in this pool. Or maybe this is where brook trout overwinter in this stream, in this pool slightly deeper than the rest of the shallow stream, and they hadn't dispersed from their winter gathering yet. Regardless, I was mesmerized by their abundance and beauty, and all of this magic was completely hidden from view from the surface due to the tannin-stained water.

Brook trout in streams such as Climbers Run and the Bushkill means we are doing something right to protect pockets of the environment in the rapidly developing East. This becomes even more critical in light of a recent Environmental Protection Agency (EPA) report that predicts there will be no native trout east of the Mississippi in 80 years (the year 2100) due to climate change. This may be within my children's lifetime and is definitely within my grandkids' lifetime. This frightening forecast is a strong warning, and it makes unexpected places such as Climbers and Bushkill all the more special.

However, unlike Climbers and Bushkill, where I didn't expect to see brooks, I went to Shades Creek with the intent of swimming with brook trout. Shades Creek is in the Pocono Mountains in Eastern Pennsylvania, and the Bear Creek Preserve, where Shades is located, is part of a complex of preserves that protect the headwaters of the Lehigh River. The Lehigh is a major tributary to the Delaware. The Shades Creek watershed is almost entirely forested, and it is remote. Black bears are commonly sighted along Shades. I humped my 30 pounds of snorkeling and camera gear through a sea of soft light green ferns that covered an unforgiving rocky terrain all in the shade of mature hickory and oak trees. Huge rhododendrons lined Shades Creek, beneath a hemlock canopy.

The creek is small: classic brook trout habitat. I crept along the trail that paralleled the stream and peered through the thick hemlock and rhododendron cover to look for a pool that was large enough to snorkel and that looked promising to hold brooks. Long grasses arched from their bankside clumps to just kiss the water. Red cardinal flower spikes pierced the green. I gently slid into the clear, cold, shallow water and slithered upstream, scraping over rocks, and got into the the pool. A trout shot out of view as soon as I entered. I couldn't identify what kind it was: native brook or stocked brown or rainbow. I crept through the creek on tiptoes and fingertips, hoping for a brookie. I scanned the pool ahead to try to see them before they sensed my presence, but these fish were too smart for me, and the waves I made reached all parts of the pool long before I did. I saw nothing but beautiful stream architecture of smoothed cobble covered in bright green moss, overhanging mountain laurel, and hemlock.

I reached the head of the pool and turned back downstream disappointed. I looked into the shadow of a root wad, and there, nuzzled beneath the tangle of

Brook trout in Shades Creek.

wood, was a beautiful brook trout. Brilliant yellow-and-red dots glowed from the shadows. The fish knew I was there and followed me with its eyes. However, it didn't dart from its hiding spot. It must have known that its best chances of not being detected or caught were in the maze of submerged roots of this upturned tree. I watched the trout for a half an hour, wondering if I was looking at one of the last of its kind. I just absorbed its beauty. I tried to burn it to memory for the day when these fish are no longer here.

However, Shannon White, a PhD candidate at Penn State, thinks that the predictions of brook trout extinction are overstated. "We will see continued declines, but extinction is unlikely," Shannon says, based on her extensive research on Loyalsock brook trout. The Loyalsock watershed is largely forested now, though it was clear-cut in the heyday of logging in Pennsylvania about a hundred years ago. "And brook trout survived that," Shannon reminds. One of the goals of Shannon's Loyalsock brook trout work is to determine the impact climate change might have on these beauties. Her work has resulted in some new knowledge that counters long-held assumptions, and hopefully, this will lead to better management of these gorgeous, troubled fish.

It has been long assumed that most brook trout populations are sedentary in smaller headwater streams. Moreover, they are managed based on that assumption. Shannon found that brook trout travel farther than we thought. As soon as they spawn in the fall, 20 to 40 percent of some brook trout populations move out to the main stem and overwinter and then move back into small tributary streams in the early summer. Shannon calls these fish "risky movers." Increasing genetic connectivity increases brook trout chances for survival. Sneaky movers maintain population health. However, barriers to sneaky mover movement decrease genetic connectivity. Culverts, high and low river flow, sediment and gravel from roads, and improper logging practices reduce brook trout movement. Since movement is the key to survival for brook trout, there is hope that we can control a lot of these barriers. We can redesign culverts to allow brook trout passage. We can mandate logging practices that protect water quality, and we can reward logging companies already implementing those practices. We can manage road construction to minimize sediment and gravel inputs to streams.

Shannon's next finding is a little more troubling. We have less control over the climate warming spiral our dependence on fossil fuels has set the Earth on. Though we can take action now to curb the warming trend, the planet is already warming, and so are brook trout streams. She measured heat shock proteins in brook trout. Heat shock proteins are produced to protect cell walls from breaking down when they are heated. Without these heat shock proteins, cells would fail and the organism dies. We historically thought the warmest water brooks could be in without getting stressed was 65 degrees. Shannon's work with measuring heat shock proteins in brook trout indicates these fish thermally stress at temperatures between 48 to 50 degrees, quite a bit cooler than 65.

The question that remains is whether brooks will adapt to warmer temperatures. While Shannon feels the EPA report might be pessimistic, her stance depends on small-scale habitats that might allow fish to survive if populations are allowed to move around. It is up to us to eliminate movement barriers. I hate to think that our grandkids wouldn't be able to enjoy the exquisite allure of these beauties of our eastern forest streams. The work of researchers like Shannon gives me hope that brookies will endure the approaching climate-driven changes, as long as we use that research to make the right choices. The worst-case scenario is they will survive where they aren't welcome.

Just like rainbows aren't native to the East and change the ecology of our streams, brooks aren't native to the West and do the same to those streams. They especially impact the native cutthroat trout populations. I went to the Calapooia River, which originates in the Cascades and flows across the Willamette River floodplain in northeastern Oregon in the hopes of seeing some native rainbows while I scouted to establish a new student snorkeling program. I entered into a pool that was surrounded by clear-cut forest and was instantly immersed in a school of at least twenty rainbows. There were all different size and age classes, from monster 16-inchers who ruled the pool with their years of wisdom and experience, to the young of the year just starting to figure out life.

They all swam along the bedrock bottom smoothed and fluted by eons of water rushing past. Ahead of this thick school out in front of the pool by itself was a cutthroat. A coastal cutthroat, and the first one I had ever seen. I didn't know what it was at first; I just knew it was different than the rainbows. Its spots were prominent, and Erick Larkin, a fish biologist from the Willamette National Forest who was scouting with me, picked his head out of the water and excitedly said, "Hey, see that cut?" He then put the snorkel back in his mouth and went back to watching all in a single breath. That confirmed my hopeful suspicion. The fish held at the head of the deeper pool. It seemed to have a more relaxed demeanor than the rainbows; it seemed less nervous, more assured. While a pretty fish, it was rather drab in coloration, and it lacked the blood-red swatch on its operculum and under its lower jaw, which makes them look like they have a cut throat, hence their name. However, this fish and its ancient tie to the river held my attention and curiosity. It is always a thrill to see a life-list fish.

I headed to Cummins Creek a few days later on the beautiful rocky Oregon Coast to look for more coastal cutthroat and to experience a stream out of time. The coastal highway bridge was like a time portal as I hiked up the creek away from the beach and the pounding Pacific surf behind me. Wisps of fog blew in from the ocean through the pines whose canopies were pruned flat parallel to the steep terrain by nonstop wind and salt spray into the old-growth forest that Cummins flows through. A scramble of logs and bull kelp, which looked like the amber-green tentacles of some sea creature, were piled in the streambed at the first curve where Cummins runs away from civilization and loses itself beneath

CUMMINS CREEK

Description: Cummins Creek flows through an old-growth remnant in the Coast Range before it spills into the Pacific. It is part of the Siuslaw National Forest, and the Cummins watershed contains the only Sitka spruce old growth in the Oregon wilderness system. It is truly a gem that gives a glimpse of what the entire Oregon Coast was like before development and logging dominated. Steelhead, cutthroat, coho, chinook, and sculpin are all common. We need to stay vigilant to ensure that places such as Cummins remain protected.

Access: Cummins Creek is located 4 miles south of Yachats on Coastal Highway 101. There is a parking and picnicking area just south of the Cummins Creek Bridge on the right as you are traveling south (left if traveling north just before the Cummins Creek Bridge). Follow the trail down to the creek bed and hike upstream to reach the first pools.

Above: Cummins Creek, Oregon.

a 300-foot canopy formed by 500-year-old Douglas firs. Six-foot-tall ferns covered the forest floor and overhung into the stream. I expected a Sleestak around each bend.

At some point, the tide came up high, 200 yards from where the ocean currently rolled up onto the shore. I rounded the next bend in the stream and was transported 1,000 years into the past to a time before we cut trees, dammed rivers, and fished out all the fish. This is what the coast range was like pre-European settlement, and this is what it should be like now. Tree trunks the length of school buses and half their diameter spanned the creek. Root wads bigger than SUVs forced the water in Cummins Creek to plunge, which created deep scour holes with clean gravel mounded on the downstream end. Juvenile trout and salmon danced in the current that upwelled on the downstream end of the hole formed by the massive wood. I couldn't tell which one was what species, except for the coho, because of their brazenness and flashy, white-edged red fins, but that didn't matter. The important thing was they were there, and I was in the river with them, watching them. These fish were here of their own volition. They got here from parents who weren't hatchery stock. They got here without being trucked around a dam. They got here naturally, without human meddling. And I watched them dance in the current, plucking pieces of food I couldn't see from the current as they flashed silver and gold and red in the sunlight dappling through the ancient forest canopy above.

After a few miles of an upstream pool-hopping hike and snorkel into the wilderness, into the old growth, into the past, I cautiously floated back downstream toward the ocean through logjams tossed into the stream like pixie sticks. The chances of getting caught in a strainer, an obstruction that lets water through but pins lager objects like me to the submerged branches so that you can't get a breath and drown, were real. I had to take off my dry bag pack and push it ahead of me to make it under many of the logs. I was constantly vigilant, always looking for straining branches plunged into the creek. I wriggled through the last woody jumble, and let the current spit me out of the scour hole into a deep pool. Steelhead parr nabbed food from the water beneath me with sharklike aggression. And then I saw two coastal cutthroats holding in the pool in 5 feet of water, 10 feet downstream of me. As soon as I swung my camera into position to get a shot, they disappeared with one flick of their caudal fins. And they were gone. I saw them just long enough to appreciate their freckled spots. They are the dalmatians of the trout world. Their bodies are a clean golden above before fading to a pink belly. There are resident coastal cutthroats and sea-run who swim between the creeks and sea. I'm pretty sure these were sea-run fish due to the proximity to the ocean and lack of barrier to keep the fish from getting there. Coastal cutthroats are considered a secure cutthroat subspecies, though there has been a general decline in sea-run fish during the last century. Their current abundance is unknown but seems to have stabilized after a significant decline since the 1950s. I feel privileged to have witnessed a subspecies of one of the most iconic fish of the West. Cutthroats are the only trout native to the Rockies, just as brooks are the only trout native to the East. Moreover, cutthroats are in trouble partly due to the introduction of brook trout and other fish. Brookies compete with juvenile cutthroat for food, and once brooks are established in streams, cutthroat rarely make a comeback. Cutthroat subspecies are hard to separate based on morphology. The advent of DNA testing has set what we thought we knew about cutthroat subpopulations and their distribution on its ass. However, we know that cutthroat are in decline and that we have already lost two subspecies: the yellowfin from the Arkansas River drainage due to hybridization with introduced rainbows, and an unnamed cutthroat that was identified through genetic testing of museum specimens. Habitat destruction is another threat to nonnatives. Cutthroat have complex life cycles that require them to move up- and downstream through river systems. Blockages such as dams and improperly placed culverts impede those necessary movements. Land uses that contribute sediment, such as mining, clear-cutting, and agriculture and suburban development, also contribute to the decline. Nine genetically distinct subspecies remain, and each is waning in range and abundance. For example, it is estimated that one of those subspecies, the westslope cutthroat, only occupies between 19 and 27 percent of its historic range in Montana and 36 percent in Idaho.

Watching the coastal cutthroat in the Calapooia River and Cummins Creek inspired me to explore these fish more. I set off to see if I could watch some cutthroat in the Colorado Rockies.

"Head to high-altitude lakes if you want to see cutthroat," Jeremy Monroe, director of Freshwaters Illustrated, advised when I asked him what my best chances were of encountering these mythic fish. I went to Emerald Lake in the San Isabel National Forest. I knew cutthroat were a long shot here due to the stocking of nonnative trout such as rainbows. However, cuts were possible. Emerald Lake sits at 10,000 feet at the base of the highest mountain in Colorado, which is Mount Elbert. It's a fitting name for this place, Emerald Lake. Though, it could have been sapphire. Essentially, it is a large aquamarine collection of snowmelt water puddled in an alpine basin. Bare gray granite peaks touch the sky in the immediate distance, and an emerald ring of lodgepole pine tree separates the lake from the peaks. The water is clear and grades from emerald-green near the shore to blue-green where it gets deeper. I donned my drysuit in this alpine splendor and floated away from the shore, hoping for cutthroats. Even if there were no cutthroat in Emerald Lake, just being here was reward enough.

The bottom was covered in Canadian waterweed, an underwater plant that forms peaks that mirror the terrestrial geography. Curious rainbows came out of the depths to explore the intruder to their home. Sunlight dappled their backs and the underwater grasses so that they would have blended in if they weren't moving. This was constructed ecology. While the Canadian waterweed is native, the trout are not. They were stocked and likely drove the cuts out.

However, the artifice didn't matter. The experience was real. It was a special, humbling experience snorkeling through this emerald gem at 10,000 feet while curious rainbows came in close to examine me above a bed of emerald city grasses, native or not. But still, I wanted to see cutthroat.

Straight Creek is a small stream that runs parallel to Interstate 70 in the shadow of the Eisenhower Tunnel, which pierces the mountains that form the

EMERALD LAKE

Description: Emerald Lake is an alpine lake at 10,000 feet located within the San Isabel National Forest. It is heavily visited in the summer and fished year-round. While there aren't native trout in this lake, the stocked rainbows are beautiful and provide an opportunity to watch trout behavior. The underwater scene in total here is ethereal, and the setting, combined with the underwater architecture, make the trip worth it. Water is deeper here than the usual river snorkeling location, and the water is cold, so use extra caution.

Access: GPS Address: Emerald Lake Picnic Area, Leadville, Colorado. It is located immediately off Route 110, 10 miles southwest of Leadville, Colorado.

Emerald Lake.

Continental Divide. The water drops through a series of rock stairsteps and wood jams that form pools barely sufficiently deep to float. The pools weren't big enough for my whole body to fit, so my legs awkwardly hung over a log, rock, or other anchor on the bank while my head and torso craned at an unnatural back-and-neck-arching angle to see if there were cutthroat in the length of the pool. I had my doubts, and after examining just two pools, I was ready to quit. However, Mark Hare, a fisheries technician with the Forest Service, said cutthroat were here, so I pressed on.

"If you want to see cutthroat, you either need to go way remote or go to the urban interface," Mark said. The key to cutthroat being in the urban interface streams are the same poorly designed culverts negatively impacting brook trout in the East. Here, these movement-limiting culverts are keeping brook trout out of cutthroat streams. Moreover, Straight Creek was in that interface, just on the outskirts of Dillon, Colorado, between the town limits, a water treatment plant, and a landfill. So I kept working upstream.

I was exhausted by the fourth pool from walking in a drysuit with fleece layer underneath in 85-degree sunlight and then immersing in 52-degree water. I was sweating hot one minute, freezing cold the next. Plus, I was carrying 20 pounds of gear on my back and the 10-pound bowling ball of a weight that is my camera over steep terrain on unstable, slippery boulders. The only thing I saw were brook trout, and I figured the cutthroat were all gone, that this was largely a waste of time and energy. I was about to give up as I had a hard time catching my breath. My body was still acclimating to 10,000 feet.

But then there they were. Two cutthroats with soft peach-and-pink-colored fins and sides with a darker pink cut, their namesake. They were similar to two soft pastel sunsets gently waving in the current holding their positions in the pool. They took my breath away, and I shook at first. I was so in awe of seeing these fish. I had to work to stay composed. I wanted to whoop through my snorkel. I inched slowly closer and shot picture after picture, working hard to capture their image before they shot off upstream into the camouflaged and secluded security of a bubble curtain where water poured over a 4-foot-tall wood jam. At the same time, I just wanted to be with these fish, not working to capture their image or notice behavior. I just wanted to be with them. Experience the creek on their terms, respect them as the owners of this pool, and just watch them

Straight Creek cutthroat trout.

Straight Creek, Dillon, Colorado.

STRAIGHT CREEK

Description: Straight Creek is a small stream that flows parallel to US Route 70 sandwiched between the highway and the town of Dillon. A water diversion supplies drinking water from Straight Creek to the town of Dillon. As small as it is, and never out of range of Route 70 traffic noise, Straight Creek provides some excellent snorkeling opportunities, even though quarters are tight due to its small size. You are likely to see brook trout and cutthroat here.

Access: GPS Address: Laskey Gulch, Dillon, Colorado. From Denver, take Route 70 to the Silverthorn Dillon exit. Turn left onto 6 East, turn left onto Evergreen, and an immediate right onto Colorado Road 51. This turns into a dirt road. Follow this to the end. Hike upstream past the water diversion.

without disturbing. And I did that for a few minutes. However, the drive to document them because I may not get back there, and if I do, they may not be there anymore, drove me to spend more time pulling the camera housing trigger than just watching and being.

Based on the work of people like Shannon White, we are learning that if we give brooks a chance by removing barriers to movement, they will probably survive in their native range, though in reduced numbers and restricted geography. Cutthroat may not. The worst case for brook trout is that they would be eliminated from their native range but will survive as a species where they don't belong. The same doesn't apply to cutthroats. They aren't establishing new populations in new geography like the brook trout. Once brooks are gone from the East, they are

GORE CREEK

Description: Gore Creek runs through the town of Vail, Colorado, and is easily accessed at the Ford Park and Amphitheater, named for the former President and First Lady. Mark Hare and I went to Gore Creek to see if we could find cutthroats and to see if this would make a good location for a student snorkeling program. We hiked to the edge of the stream in this easily accessed, idyllic setting, with large lodgepole pines lining the shoreline. We slid into the creek on the downstream end of a deep stretch and instantly watched two dozen trout feed at the head of the pool, 30 feet upstream. The water was clear and cold, and the bottom of this 10-foot-deep section was covered in a jumble of boulders. A pedestrian bridge crosses the creek here, and we got some odd looks as we slowly worked our way upstream under the bridge to get a closer look at the trout, hoping some of them were cuts.

The fish plied the complex of currents deflecting off the boulders at odd angles with ease and expertly nabbed prey from the water column. I was mesmerized by the athleticism and awareness of these fish and found a rock just deep enough for me to lay on without getting pushed downstream by the moderate current.

White-edged red pectoral fins of brook trout flashed, and purple-red sides of rainbows glowed from the shadow of the bridge. Speckled silver tops and crimson sides of cut bows, hybrids between stocked rainbows and cutthroat, another cutthroat threat, flashed on the bottom. There wasn't anything native in this pool. I didn't see anything that was here in Gore Creek long before the ski slopes and amphitheater and I-70. Everything I saw replaced what should have been here. However, this cacophony of nonnative trout was beautiful just the same, and this is a special little snorkeling hole worth a visit.

Access: GPS Address: Ford Park, Vail, Colorado. Take I-70 West from Denver to exit 180. Follow Frontage Road for about a mile. Ford Park will be on your left. Follow the walk downhill past the amphitheater to the pedestrian bridge over the creek and take a trail on the right just before the bridge to access the stream.

Above: Gore Creek at Ford Park, Vail, Colorado.

gone from their native range, but the species will still be on this planet. Once cutthroat are gone from their native range, they are gone as a species.

I am biased in favor of brook trout because they are my home fish. They are part of my history. However, I am more worried about cutthroat, and I feel like

I just witnessed one of the last. At the same time, the fact these fish are in an urban interface stream, and apparently holding their own against the brook trout invasion, gives me hope that maybe they just might make it if we give them half a chance.

One species that is trying to make a comeback because we are giving it half a chance is the bull trout. I first encountered this fish snorkeling the South Fork of the McKenzie River with Kate Meyer, a fish biologist working at the Willamette National Forest in the Cascade Mountains, Oregon.

I first met Kate at the Washington DC Environmental Film Festival, where Jeremy Monroe's film *UpRiver* was shown. The movie has a segment that features Kate supervising a heli-logging operation to restore large, woody material—large as in an entire hundred-foot-long Douglas fir large—to the McKenzie River. She is a no-holds-barred fish biologist when it comes to restoration, as evidenced by this enormous operation as well as her latest project that reconnected 600 acres of floodplain to 5 miles of the South Fork of the McKenzie.

The construction of Cougar Dam and downstream levees in the 1960s starved the lower part of the South Fork McKenzie of sediment and wood and confined the river to one fast-moving channel, which completely changed what was once a complex habitat system of braided channels and wetlands. The effort to restore habitat complexity to this floodplain was an ambitious project where Kate led a team of partners to divert the water flowing out of Cougar Dam into a historic channel of the South Fork while the rest of the surrounding land along the four and a half-mile stretch of river was graded essentially to the same elevation with what would be the water surface when they diverted the flow back onto the restored floodplain. The team left a few hummocks and large woody material, but essentially, they let the river go where it wanted, forming side channels, wetlands, holes, and logjams and all the complex habitat that rainbows, chinook, and bull trout need to survive. We simplified rivers in the course of using them for our gain. We know better now, and biologists like Kate are working to reverse a few centuries of habitat simplification and destruction.

I met Kate and her crew at a nondescript pull-off, which was barely wide enough for our trucks, before the land fell steeply away to the South Fork. We donned our fleece layers and drysuits at the trucks and bushwhacked down the slope that was spongy from decades of Douglas fir needle accumulation until we reached a large pool on the river. Sweat dripped into my eyes. The fleece beneath the drysuit was overkill for the 80-degree late-September day, but soon it wouldn't be enough protection against the cold Cascade Mountain river. This was all new to me, and I didn't want to look like the novice I felt I was. I had snorkeled hundreds of rivers thousands of times. But never here, in these remote and rugged conditions. Each river is different, and this was foreign. This was my first immersion into Cascade water, my first underwater exposure to Cascade mountain streams. I didn't know their character, their flow patterns, or their underlying geology and how the water responded to it and how life responded to the water. I didn't want to slow Kate and her crew down. They were here to survey for bull trout and were gracious enough to allow me to tag along.

We slid into the water between Volkswagen-Beetle–sized boulders into a 15-foot-deep pool in this small stream that was almost deeper than it was wide. We were at the tail end of the pool where the cobbled bottom came up to within arm's reach. It stretched 40 feet upstream where the river tumbled over a short cascade. The water was crystal clear and freezing cold, which was a welcome relief from the heat as it penetrated my neoprene gloves and hood and compressed the fleece through the drysuit, at least at first.

Bright Irish-green mosses covered large boulders that framed the sides of the pool. Three-foot-long chinook salmon patrolled back and forth at the head of the pool, black silhouetted against the turquoise backdrop. We explored pool to pool, downstream to up, looking for chinook and bull trout, which are both federally listed species. It wasn't long before the cool relief the waters provided turned to

Kate Meyer surveying the South Fork of the McKenzie for bull trout.

chilly discomfort. We reached the farthest upstream pool for the survey. We still hadn't seen any bull trout, though we had counted a few chinook and rainbows.

The river here was 30 feet wide and 20 feet deep. The right side was a bar of softball-sized cobble that sloped down to the bedrock bottom 20 feet below opposite a wall of volcanic bedrock that continued above the surface as a cliff that formed the facing shore. A gravel ridge spine stretched downstream in the eddy of the bedrock cliff. The four of us lined up beached on the gravel bar and watched the depths of the pool, hoping for a bull trout. A large cigar shadow appeared on the bottom, and it casually but confidently swam to the head of the pool. Smaller rainbows got out of the way of this shape. This fish swam up the slope, turned, and allowed the current to push its body back downstream on our side of the river as the 2-foot bull trout looked into each one of our masks, with no indication of fear, but rather with an air of indignation. This was his pool. This bull trout owned this part of the river, and he knew it. Our presence was a mere curiosity. Satisfied we weren't a threat to his dominance, he went back to his throne on the bottom.

This was my only encounter with a bull trout. They used to dominate rivers such as the South Fork, and while this individual was fearless with a "bring it" attitude, they aren't invincible against tiny increases in sediment and temperature. They need the cleanest, coldest water, and so they have been lost from much of their range.

Bull trout last occupied the Clackamas River in Oregon in 1964. They were extirpated due to pitiful approaches to watershed management that clouded and warmed the water. However, we have atoned for our past sins of poor logging practices and crappy road construction that drive sediment to rivers, and the Clackamas now contains water of high enough quality and low enough temperature to support bull trout. The Oregon Department of Fish and Wildlife and the US Forest Service gave the Clackamas a nudge with the reintroduction of bull trout hatched from fish that still run wild in clean waters, like the South Fork McKenzie. The stocked bulls are producing more bulls, and the beginnings of a naturally reproducing bull trout population are now the kings of parts of the Clackamas.

So I went to the Clackamas in August to see if I could encounter bull trout. These Clackamas fish represent hope. I went to the Clackamas to see hope. A large sign with a 5-foot bull trout illustration advised anglers to know how to identify these fish, because they are back in the Clackamas, and it instructed them to throw bull trout back if caught. It was a good omen, I thought. I got to the edge of the River, which looked so much smaller from the road above. A huge eddy slowly churned over water-worn bedrock. The surface of the river was a mirror barely dimpled by swirls of current. However, beneath the deceiving veneer, the river flowed full and fast. The bottom was a little too deep to force the water up to do much more than just wrinkle the surface. The nearshore bottom was large cobble that dropped out of sight to an unknown depth. A Class II rapid roiled immediately downstream.

I got in and sheepishly left the protection of the shallows and sight of the bottom as I swam out over big, deep water. Visibility was at least 30 feet, so I know the bottom was deeper than that as it faded from sight. I wanted to make my way to the upstream end of the pool, where the full force of the Clackamas dumped into this bowl and slowed. If bull trout were here, they were likely holding at the head of the pool, just out of the main force of the current, stalking the water that would deliver unsuspecting food to their hungry mouths. I swam into the main eddy flow and was swiftly pushed upstream. It was unnerving to be in such a huge swirl of water. It reinforced the knowledge that the river was in charge. All I could do was respond to it, and if I responded correctly, I could stay in this pool and not get swept downstream. If the force of this side eddy current was this strong, I didn't want to learn of the power of the downstream current. Moreover, I was circulating rapidly upstream on my way to getting spun out into that main river stream. I was counting on an opportunity at the head of the pool to peel out of the flow and hide from the current behind a rock. There was still no bottom in sight, so I was gliding over at least 40 feet of water. There may have been bull trout on the bottom hunting, waiting, stalking, but there was no way for me to tell. I was too buoyant in my drysuit to surface dive to the bottom.

CLACKAMAS RIVER

Description: The Clackamas River is legendary among whitewater boaters and fishers. It originates on the Olallie Butte in Hood National Forest and flows for 83 miles before emptying into the Willamette River in northwestern Oregon. Parts of this river are deceiving and look placid with little current, but in reality, the Clackamas flows at a good clip. It is a large, pushy river with cold water, so use extra caution and know your limits. There are numerous access points for the Clackamas along Route 224 out of Estacada. One of these locations is the Big Eddy Day Use and Picnic Area. The river widens here, and a large eddy current circulates upstream. The near shore is shallow and the bottom slopes to deep water toward the center, so there are options for snorkelers of multiple skill levels, but pay attention. The eddy current can be sneaky.

Access: GPS Address: Big Eddy Day Use Picnic Area, 224 Clackamas Highway, Estacada, Oregon. The Big Eddy Day Use area is located 14 miles from Estacada, Oregon, on Route 224 East. The parking area is a very wide shoulder on the right. Follow the trail to the river.

Above: Clackamas River at the Big Eddy Day Use Area.

The rock I saw from the shoreline that I was counting on as my refuge worked out, and I was able to get out of the main eddy flow to enjoy the protection it provided. The bottom was shallower here, maybe about 10 feet, and I could see multiple fish feeding. All rainbows. There weren't any bull trout here, at least none that I could see. I enjoyed the calm behind my rock as the Clackamas whizzed by, and I waited and hoped for a Clackamas bull. However, none appeared.

Instead, I was intrigued by mountain whitefish. These fish are members of the salmonid family, the same family as trout and salmon. They don't quite resemble the trouts. A mountain whitefish has a deeply forked tail and a downturned mouth that almost looks like a snout, and they remind me of Don Knotts's character in the movie *The Incredible Mr. Limpet.* They are one of the most widely distributed salmonids in the western United States, occurring throughout Washington, Oregon, Montana, Idaho, Wyoming, Utah, and Colorado. Unlike bull trout, mountain whitefish are abundant, and populations appear stable.

Mountain whitefish.

The silver flash of one individual is what first caught my attention. The scales acted as prisms so that they had a clean, white-silver look with a rainbow sheen. This fish used its pointed snout to intentionally and methodically probe

Mountain whitefish school.

MOLALLA RIVER

Description: The Molalla is the largest undammed Willamette tributary and flows 51 miles before joining the larger river. The stretch around the town of Molalla has numerous fluted bedrock tables and outcrops that form parts of the riverbed. Deeper holes contain trout and whitefish while the cobble-bottomed shallows contain dace, sculpin, and trout and salmon parr.

Access: GPS Address: 16185 South Freyer Park Road, Molalla, Oregon. Freyer Park is a Clackamas County park located 3 miles southeast of the town of Molalla. It has easy access to the Molalla River.

Molalla River.

between rocks for food. A few days later, I was snorkeling the Molalla River in Molalla, Oregon. A large shelf of bedrock extended to the edge of the water. Tom Derry of the Native Fish Society says this is normally covered, but it's been a hot, dry summer for Oregon, and river levels are down. I sat on the edge of the bedrock and admired the potholes scoured into it, then I slid in as if the bedrock shelf were the stern of a boat. I was in 15 feet of water and didn't see many fish, so I shot across the swift current to the cobble shallows on the opposite bank. I crawled my way upstream to the head of the pool where the river drops over a 2-foot boulder riffle into this pool. A few speckled dace fed in the calm behind one of the bowling-ball-sized rocks, and a few rainbow trout hunted from the eddy on the opposite side of the chute. It was as loud as snorkeling near big riffles and rapids usually is, and I was blinded by curtains of bubbles that happened to swirl farther to the left than the rest. I noticed some whitefish at the base of the boulder slope and decided to surface dive to the bottom and glide.

I took a hard breath and drifted to the bottom, where the current whisked me along a 15-foot wall of fluted and worn bedrock. A large school of thirty to forty mountain whitefish appeared, unsure of what to make of me, but they were certain they didn't want my company, so the school split down the middle as I drifted along the beach-ball-sized cobble bottom.

I wanted to experience these fish more than just disrupting the school, so I did another surface dive and grabbed on to one of the boulders on the bottom to keep my position in the river. The fish initially parted and then gathered back together so that I was completely encased in the school. They looked clean and golden brown with silver flecks from this perspective, and white silver sides occasionally flashed as individuals rubbed against the bottom or nuzzled between boulders for food so that the sun hit their sides straight on. I was so engrossed by being enveloped in the school that I forgot I was underwater and almost took a breath before letting go of my rock and reaching the surface.

Whitefish are examples of the variety of forms and behaviors represented in the salmonid family. And while the whitefish and trout are beautiful, complex and intriguing to watch, their migratory cousins, the salmons, are even more so when I consider the ordeals these fish must endure during their thousand-mile treks to and from the sea.

CHAPTER 2

Salmon

COHO

I could see a silver thread of water through the branches of a couple hundred-year-old Douglas firs that looked a couple hundred feet tall. However, I can't look too long, or I risk crashing into one of the multitude of cars parked on the Historic Columbia River Highway, or their pedestrians. People flocked to the falls. I couldn't understand the draw at first, but as the falls came into clearer view, I got it. They are an impressive sight. But I was here for something else. I head downstream away from the falls, against the current of humanity.

It was wet and cool under the trees but hot and dry where the sun pierced through gaps in the canopy, and people waded in the creek, which ran adjacent to the paved path that led to the falls from the I-84 parking area, to cool off. Many did not recognize the significance of what was happening beneath the surface. I took a left off the path, weaved through some seated tourists, hopped over some concreted riprap designed to join the stream and path in perpetuity and keep the stream from wandering the way streams are meant to, and waded through some thigh-deep cold water to get to a gravel bar that resembled, more or less, a natural wild stream. Though, in reality, it was probably far from it.

I leaped from gravel bar to gravel bar trying to keep out of the water as much as possible as I made my way downstream, away from the tourists, so as to not stir up the bottom, but also so as to not disturb the fish and snails who made their homes there. I kept hopping sandbars downstream until I was out of view of the crowd, just around a bend in the creek, pulled my mask and neoprene jacket out of my gear bag, and slipped into the water. Two million people visit Multnomah annually, all to see the falls. Yet the real drama is occurring beneath the surface of the creek they stomped in to cool off.

The stream was tiny, not much wider than my body length. It was shrouded in a thin covering of trees that shielded it from full view of the railroad on one side and I-84 on the other, though they did little to reduce the traffic noise and nothing to reduce the rumble of passing trains. Invasive blackberries formed a tangle along the banks, and viburnum shrubs overhung the creek. A cluster of four 3-foot-diameter alders had yellow caution tape around them since an ambitious beaver partly gnawed through the trunks. The cold water took my breath away as it crept between the neoprene layer of the jacket and my skin. Beneath the surface, there was a constant murmur of moving water in the background, except for when a train passed, when the grind of the engines dominated. I settled into the creek and let the feeling of weightlessness settle in. I inadvertently kicked up a ruddy brown flocculent off the bottom as I got in, and I watched the current wash the little silt cloud downstream. The cool water and aquatic silence gave a temporary reprieve from the heat and chaos that tends to accompany humans.

A whole new world came into view. Logs spanned the width of the stream on the bottom and formed different habitats. On the upstream side, the logs held back gravel, so the creek was a foot deep and surprisingly powerful given its tiny stature. Downstream, the water carved a plunge pool where it cascaded over the log. The bottom dropped to 4 feet, and the current slowed in the deeper water. I looked horizontally downstream through the aquamarine water and watched a school of juvenile coho squiggle upstream from the bigger pool against the flow. They looked like a swarm urgently moving to investigate me, this new thing in their world. They gained speed and used their momentum to vault over the log embedded in the bottom to figure me out. One after the other, they swam up to my mask and flashed white-fringed, brilliant-orange dorsal and anal fins similar to large flags relative to their tiny bodies as if to announce something, or maybe to challenge my presence.

The significance of these small fish go beyond their beauty and pugnacious response to me being here. It goes to their numbers. The Columbia River coho

Coho parr upstream.

is a fish species struggling to survive, maintaining at historically low numbers thanks to dams that block their parents' path to traditional spawning grounds as well as overfishing. They were listed as threatened in 2005 and still remain threatened 15 years later. The fact that these juvenile fish were here in Multnomah Creek meant adult coho were here this past November and successfully made the next generation of fish. Granted, there were only maybe 100 coho fry here, but that's significant for a species barely hanging on.

There was other life here too. Big mouthed sculpins look like they wore the desert camo pattern that was issued when I went to Saudi Arabia for Operations Desert Storm and Calm, and their mottled gray-and-tan bodies blended with the gray-and-tan rounded rock bottom. Their orange eyes gave up their positions while their oversize, stiff-rayed pectoral fins fanned out over more bottom than it looked like they should, given the small size of their bodies.

Snails clung to the half-buried logs, and all pointed in the same direction, like flags in a breeze. Their shells glowed green at the opening and graded to a warm amber and deep chestnut as the shells got narrower toward the older part where it was worn white at the pointy tip. Twenty-five of them grazed lunch off the log.

Some guy pissed into the creek just upstream of me on the other side of a bend as I got out. A wise-ass grin covered his face when he realized he was essentially pissing on me. I felt sorry for him. He didn't understand what he was really doing. He didn't understand what he was missing. He urinated on an entire community of incredibly beautiful and intricate and complex fish, and I think if he knew what was there, he would have pissed in the woods somewhere. Or in a toilet conveniently provided a hundred yards away in Multnomah Lodge.

I was completely energized and connected to this place when I got out despite this human encounter. The fish and snails and clean bottom cobble, along with the aquamarine color of the water when I glanced downstream, formed an enchanting aquatic world. The total community and scene were hidden from view and consideration of thousands of visitors per day. People didn't know what they overlooked as they hustled past, to or from their selfies with the falls in the background. A few splashed in the stream, but no one looked beneath the surface. No one witnessed or understood the sophistication and splendor this tiny creek contained. I sloshed back to my car.

Then the fires hit.

I watched from 3,000 miles way as places that I had instantly connected with, and felt at home in, burned. Multnomah and much of the Columbia Gorge was on fire. I called a friend as Portland was shrouded in smoke. She said it was as if Oregon residents lost part of their identity. The Eagle Creek fire descended on Multnomah and threatened the historic lodge. Firefighters held it off, and the lodge stands today. However, the area was closed for fear of landslides. I wondered how the residents of Multnomah Creek—the coho and sculpin and snails—made out. Fires negatively affect streams for months, sometimes years, after the fire is out due to increased sedimentation. All that clean gravel the coho, snails, and sculpin depend on might be buried by the residual fire effects.

I flew into Portland 4 months later, over a lunar landscape. What had been vibrant, green trees were now charred matchsticks poking out of a brown backdrop. The forest looked like week-old gray beard stubble on a hard-worn and weathered face. While everyone else was worried about the lodge, I wanted to get back in Multnomah Creek to see how that community fared. However, the whole region remained off-limits. I called on a friend in the Forest Service to introduce me to the regional fish biologist, hoping to use my relationship to get access where others couldn't. It didn't work that way. "Sorry, we are worried about landslides. That's why the area is closed. It isn't safe," the fish biologist warned. "And those fish are likely stressed due to the increased sediment load coming off the burnt areas. You getting in the creek with them will add to their stress." Additive stressors in ecology and people lead to poor health.

Normally, I would just sneak in and carry out my initial plan. We live in a litigious society, though, so all the landslide concerns were really legal in nature. On the off chance that an errant boulder or collection of them might hurtle down the mountain and get lucky enough to hit me, the Forest Service didn't want to get sued. I wasn't worried. The threat was there but likely overstated, out of concern for lawsuits by people who should know their own risk. However, the regional fish biologist got me on his second point. These fish were already dealing with crappy fire-induced conditions, and I didn't want to contribute to their struggle. I would just have to wait. As I flew in over the burnt mountains, I wondered what happened beneath the surface of the creek and ached to get in.

A year later, stripes of brown and green, burned and unburned, flowed down the mountain. The tops of some charred trees were greening back up. I caught the occasional faint whiff of burnt forest, interspersed with the faint whiff of hot dogs on the Multnomah Inn grill.

I was surprised and happy to see clean gravel when I first stuck my head in the water. Snails ambled along the bottom. Some bulldozed coarse sand, some grazed on larger rocks, and some wandered through sunken logs. Sculpin blended into the substrate. I didn't see any coho at first, and I was worried that the fires eliminated this population. However, just then a small school emerged from the background in an upstream eddy. Then a larger school twirled downstream like pixies. These fish recently transformed from fry to parr. They were still small and dainty compared to the robust parr who challenged me a year and a half ago. These young fish were more eye than body, and like their kin last year, they came right up to my mask and camera.

The coho energetically wriggled against the current and looked like it was more for show than effect, since for all their wriggling, they didn't make it very far upstream. Schools of the new parr stayed in the relatively slower water on the stream edges, where fine red and amber roots slow it all down and give the

Coho parr in the protective cover of a root wad.

baby coho a chance to swim against the current. Sunlight streamed through the water and lit up the roots, and the coho looked like they had a strobe on them as they wriggled through shafts of light. Just downstream, on the other side of a log that held back a ton of gravel, the larger year-old fish stay hidden in a tangle of shrub branches that arched to the bottom of the 3-foot-deep hole. Coho juveniles become warier as they age. They learn to not trust in their first year. It looks like Multnomah Falls, the Inn, *and* Creek all survived. At least this time.

Friends tell me not to worry. Ecosystems are resilient. So are rubber bands. Stretch them, and they return to their former shape, to a point. Stretch them too far and they snap. For now, however, the next coho generation is in Multnomah, after the fire.

CHINOOK THE KING

I was careful not to disturb them. Jeremy Monroe shot video from a drone hovering above the water, and I floated under arched grasses and leafless shrubs along the shoreline to shoot stills on this overcast chilly and damp early November day. The chinook didn't care that we were there. Their singleness of purpose demanded all of their attention. But, still, we were careful.

These were spring-run chinook salmon, which are in danger of going extinct. They are listed as endangered in the Upper Columbia River and threatened in California's Sacramento River and coastal streams, Puget Sound, Lower Columbia, and the Upper Willamette, where Jeremy and I snorkeled today. As I watched these 4-foot-long bulky fish beat the bottom into a depression and

Chinook male at the end of his life.

perform their ancient mating dance, I felt their timeless connection to the ocean 300 miles away and the life they led there.

Southern resident killer whales, or orcas, live off the Pacific Northwest coast. They are critically endangered, with only seventy-eight left in 2019, and they are likely to go extinct in my lifetime. There are three primary reasons for their decline. First, they depend on chinook for their diet. As the number of chinook has declined, the orcas have a harder time finding food, which means they are burning fat. Fat that has accumulated toxins over the years. This is a second contributor to their decline. The third, boat noise, interferes with their ability to communicate with each other and locate their dwindling food supply. With only seventy-eight individuals left, I expect these beautiful animals won't be around for much longer. Dams aren't just responsible for the possible extinction of chinook salmon. They are also responsible for the loss of southern resident orcas. The relationship between these fish before me that I watched work so hard to perpetuate their species, as well as a group of seventy-eight remaining whales 300 miles away, emphasizes the importance of recognizing that all life is truly, intimately connected.

This was the end of their run and lives, and the last bits of energy they had left they invested in making the next generation. Huge redds, 10 feet long and 5 feet wide, dominated the bottom, and I was careful to stay away from them. I didn't want to dislodge any fertilized eggs that had settled into the newly churned gravel. A large mound of freshly tossed pebbles was at the downstream end of each redd, which forced the water into a small wave. It looked like someone had rutted the bottom with a four-wheeler. This rearrangement of stream bed would be the only noticeable remaining monument to their existence, until the fertilized eggs they left behind hatched and the fry started to swim.

I slowly and quietly slid into the water from the bank and held to the shore, so as to not disturb the fish or their redds. The spawning chinook didn't notice or care that I was there. Males with overbite snaggletoothed jaws fought for position over redds beaten into the bottom by the females. They had incredible energy for fish that were rotting before my eyes. Their fins were white and frayed. Their bodies were tan blotched, and their backs were white, where the skin had already fallen off. The only chinook that paid any attention to me was a female who drifted almost lifeless downstream into the eddy formed behind my knee. She was done; her life was spent. She rested in the stillness my leg created from the current, and took her last few breaths, passed water over her gills for the last time. Her tail was completely white, tattered and frayed from beating softball-sized cobbles out of the way as she formed her redds. Her body was dark and dull, with patches of skin rotting off. She had been decaying alive for weeks, and now, the process was complete. She had run her course, done her job. She contributed to the next generation of chinook, did what she could to ensure the continuance of her kind, and now, she was done. She moved water over her gills one more time, then the last bit of life flickered from her eyes and she drifted downstream, lifeless. She was lifeless, but her role still wasn't finished. Her body would provide critically important nutrients to the Elk Creek ecosystem.

When we think of watersheds, we often think of them as one-way flows of materials and energy. It all flows downstream. We forget these are two-way exchanges. Migratory fish, such as chinook, perform numerous functions that are essential to the health of rivers. One of those functions is their death and the nutrients their bodies provide to the river after they die.

Salmon die after spawning and provide nutrients to the river postmortem.

ALSEA RIVER AT CLEMENS PARK

Description: The Alsea River flows for 48 miles from the Coast Range to the Pacific. Clemens Park is a Benton County park and includes a half mile of Alsea River frontage. The Alsea contains a variety of habitats here, from deep pools to shallow, swift riffles.

Access: GPS Address: Clemens Park, Alsea, Oregon. Clemens Park is located 21 miles southwest of Corvallis on highway 34. From Corvallis, take highway 20 west to highway 34 west. Stay on 34 for 14 miles. Turn left onto Seeley Creek Road. Seeley Creek Road ends at Clemens Park.

Alsea River at Clemens Park, Oregon.

A few days later, I snorkeled the Alsea River at Clemens Park in Oregon. The Alsea River turns left in a sharp curve around a peninsula of coast range rain forest. Lush, dark green ferns covered the forest floor, and olive sponges of moss dripped from tree branches. A tan chinook carcass was beached on a shallow gravel bar. The body was mostly rotted away. Remnants of the gills, head, and some of the flesh gently swayed with the small wavelets formed from the rapid upstream, and a fine dusting of silt had gathered on the remains. A few adults still swam the 5-foot pool behind me, but my attention was on this dead one. This fish had fulfilled its purpose in life and was now fulfilling its purpose in death by giving the energy and nutrition contained in its body back to the stream and forest. I felt a twinge of sadness for this chinook as I tried to imagine its life and the adventures it experienced while traveling a few hundred miles from this river to the ocean as a juvenile salmon, then coming back as an adult to spawn. However, a feeling of contentment took over. This creature lived the life it was supposed to. We should all be so lucky.

I returned to Oregon the next year during the fall spawn in the hopes of snorkeling with chinook again. Erick Larkin and I slid into the water of the South Santiam 16 miles upstream from Foster Dam. Erick is a fisheries biologist who works on the Willamette National Forest and intimately knows the rivers and forests in this region.

The South Santiam is one of the most intriguing rivers I have ever been in. The short two-and-a-half-mile section Erick and I snorkeled traversed three distinct geomorphologies. We started 2 miles upstream of our planned take out, where a bedrock outcrop plunged to the bottom of a 10-foot-deep pool. The water was clear and bracing cold, though we were both pretty well protected in our drysuits. There weren't any fish here, but the new river, remote setting, and stream architecture made up for their absence. The river from here spilled through a series of boulder-packed pools. Some weren't deep enough to float through while others had plenty of water initially but tailed out into a cobble bed where the river dove below the slick rocks. The trick was picking the right route and line. There were a few skittish rainbows through here, but I was so focused on picking my way through the river that I didn't really watch these aquatic athletes. We had to get out and walk a few of these sections, and it was tough going.

Round, unsteady rocks, slick with algae, are some of the most difficult walking there is. But it was beautiful. Tall grasses grew in arching clumps, which made walking even more difficult since we couldn't even see the unsteady, slippery rocks. We took our time snorkeling when we could, called out fish when we saw them, and just enjoyed being in the river. However, we were tired and hungry before we even hit the midpoint of what was supposed to be a short snorkel.

The Santiam grades from a cobble-bottomed river to water-carved and fluted-orange bedrock, marbled with white, which forms smooth-walled chutes and flumes. It was what I picture snorkeling rivers carved into glaciers to be: smoothed walls that both shoulders touch as I zipped through, which empty into occasional bowls carved into the rock, and spill out into another flume. It was like snorkeling through a Creamsickle waterslide. These channels were carved into a flat, orange bedrock table, and they occasionally got too braided and small for us to pass, so we hiked over this very different geography until we hit carved channels big enough to swim. This abruptly transitioned to yet a third vastly different geography: steep bedrock canyon walls that plunged deep into the river punctuated by waterfalls that had to be difficulty portaged on slick, steep rock. We scouted downstream to determine whether short waterfalls were runnable, and we got bruised in the process of trying a few. The Santiam here was deceiving. We could just about touch both walls yet were snorkeling in water 30 to 40 feet deep. We dove for the bottom and hung on to immense logs lodged under giant boulders to watch huge rainbows hunt. This was truly an epic journey, though only 2 miles long, it took the better part of the day.

It was worth every exhilarating minute. However, we came here to look for, and hope for, chinook. I came upon a dead one that eerily glowed whitish gray through the clear water as it floated nose up to the surface. Its tail had been cut off, and a clean, round stump that remained where the tail was removed drug on the bottom. The only chinook we saw that day were these tailless dead ones strewn about the easier access points.

"We put those there," Erick explained, "to bring the nutrients back to the river that would have been introduced if chinook were spawning in the number they should." He went on to explain that these were hatchery-raised chinook, evidenced by the lack of an adipose fin, which was clipped off before being released. They are raised at a hatchery at Frasier Dam and others, as part of a plan to mitigate the effects of dams on migratory fish.

Hatchery chinook are captured at the dams when they return to spawn to prevent them from contaminating the genetic pool of the native, non-hatchery chinook who are trucked above the dam and re-released into the river through a 30-foot-long, 12-inch-wide fish tube. The eggs and milt of the hatchery fish are stripped to make the next batch of fish we don't want to return to the South Santiam above Frazier, and they are killed. Their tails are chopped off to differentiate their carcasses as hatchery-seed fish and are turned over to Erick's crew, who reunite the dead fish with the Santiam upstream of the Frazier Dam to ensure the river still receives the nutrients from the rotting fish. Eighty-eight native, non-hatchery, spring chinook were trucked around Frasier and released in 2018.

I went to the Salmon River Cascade Stream Watch at the Wildwood Recreation Site. I hoped I would see some chinook just starting the last phase of their final journey rather than watching the last bits of it. I hoped being here in mid-October would work out so that I was early enough the see these fish before their rotting flesh was dripping from their skeleton but not so early that they hadn't started to spawn yet. I saw a white, oblong glow from an eddy at the base of a short rapid. It was a dead female, and I worried that I mistimed this visit. However, at least I had evidence that chinook were here.

I entered the Salmon at the head of a 50-foot-long, 10-foot-deep pool and let the current drift me rapidly downstream. Most of the current was in the center and the far side of this elongated pool that extended 20 yards downstream. A sand, gravel, and cobble beach formed where I got in. The other bank was a steep volcanic bedrock wall that plunged to the bottom. Douglas fir boughs arched over the water and were decorated with thick clumps of olive-yellow moss. The bottom was a collection of desk-sized boulders arranged with plenty of space in between for sand, branches, and sticks to gather. A mound of twigs, seeds, and small Douglas fir cones, blackened by partial decay, swirled on the bottom in a large eddy that peeled off the main flow and shot back upstream. It felt odd

SALMON RIVER

Description: The Salmon River is a wild and scenic designated river for its entire 33-mile length. It originates in the Cascades where it drains the southwest side of Mount Hood and flows into the Sandy River, which is a tributary to the Columbia. The Cascade Stream Watch Trail runs along the Salmon River and was developed by Wolftree, a nonprofit environmental education organization, the US Forest Service, and the Bureau of Land Management. Cascade Stream Watch is part of the Wildwood Recreation Site, near the town of Welches, Oregon. This is the best interpretive display about a river I have ever seen. It includes multiple art installations, interpretive signs that detail river and salmon ecology, and an underwater viewing chamber. It also includes a few access points where people can get into the river to swim and snorkel. Follow the trail until you reach one of those access points.

Access: GPS Address: Wildwood Recreation Site, Welches, Oregon. The Wildwood Recreation Site is 1 hour from Portland. Take I-84 East to I-26 East. The Wildwood Recreation Site will be on your right. Follow the entrance road to the Stream Watch parking area, which is on the left. There is a $5 per car entry fee. It is well worth it.

Above: Salmon River at Cascade Stream Walk, Wildwood Recreation Area, Oregon.

to have to swim to make downstream progress. I could see 30 feet horizontally through the water. Mountain whitefish darted from my path as I scanned far ahead of where the pool tailed out into a riffle to try to see any chinook that might be there before they detected me. A group of a half dozen fish held where the bottom came up and the water shallowed to 2 feet. They pointed their noses into the current as their tails beat to keep them in place. I tried to drift toward them slowly. I didn't want them to spook and was hoping they would just accept me as part of the river, as something drifting downstream. No threat. I think it might have worked if it wasn't for the large dome port that covers the lens on my camera housing. It looks like a big eye, and as soon as I pointed the camera in their direction, they moved to a different spot on the river. Maybe it reminds them of an orca eye. They were still within sight, almost as if to tease. However, I knew I wasn't important enough to them at this point for them to put any thought into me, other than keeping a safe distance between us.

The males chased the females in tight circles, and the females beat the bottom with their tails to make their redds. I followed a male upstream. He could have easily put plenty of distance between us. Instead, he tried to ditch me by weaving between boulders, threading through a tight gap, and completely breaching from the water, like an orca, a species that depend on these fish so heavily for survival.

These chinook were animated and vibrant, and while they had started their living decay, they still had more life than death. I watched a female push upstream and wondered if she knew she was going to die in the next few days. I wondered if she felt her body failing. Her fins were starting to rot and fall apart. However, her tail was still intact. A male chased her, and the two paired off. The sun set as I watched this school of half a dozen fish court each other. Dorsal fins and tails sheared the surface in a shaft of orange glow that escaped the forest canopy from the setting sun.

I returned to the Salmon River the next day. The pool where I had watched the chinook was quiet. As I wondered where they went and debated what river I should check next, I heard splashing downstream and saw tails and dorsals of a dozen fish splashing out of the water. One leaped. I hustled downstream on the bank and slowed my pace to get into the river as gently as possible. I snuck out towards deeper water as stealthily as a 5-foot, 10-inch blob could. I hid behind a laundry-basket-sized rock out of the current so that my toes on the bottom propped me in the river, which left both hands free to work the camera. I stayed behind that rock, and a male and female pair explored each other 10 feet away. They came closer until the male noticed me and the lens dome pointed at him. He switched his attention from the female to me but kept slowly approaching to determine whether I was a threat. I snapped photos as fast as I could without moving more than the finger on the camera housing trigger. He seemed to get used to me and ignored my presence more but not completely.

They are called king salmon for a reason. They are massive, and they know it. They remind me of the bull trout's air of dominance. The male got close and hung out, watching for females as well as watching me. We were 2 feet from

Spawning male chinook salmon.

each other. I could see wisdom and knowledge in his eye. I could almost see his journey, and I imagined the things he had seen and experienced. His stippled body matched the colors of the cobbles beneath him: reds, dark-slate blues, and shades of white. His snout matched the olive/aquamarine bottom reflected on the quicksilver underside of the surface.

The male stayed with me for what felt like a long time, but I wasn't keeping track. I was lost in his sleekness, his power, and I was lost in his eye, which knowingly evaluated me. A female was just upstream of this male, and he kept a protective watch over her as she made a redd. He decided she was more important than me and shot upstream to join her. She was powerful enough to move softball-sized cobble weighing between 5 to 10 pounds. No wonder her tail was beaten white. Not only did she have the energy and wisdom to run the gauntlet between the ocean and here, she still had the vigor to move substantially sized rocks. Hopefully, that tenacity will ensure the continuance of her kind. However, a lot of that depends on us. It is hard to imagine this river full of chinook the way it should be, but I like to picture the day such a vision isn't a dream. I like to dream of a river filled with salmon shoulder to shoulder and bank to bank, rather than just a group of a dozen in a tight formation. I like to believe that we can restore our chinook, and all salmon runs, to what they once were. It will take our collective will to drive politics and policy to make that dream a reality. I stayed downstream and watched them from a distance. I didn't want to disturb them any more than I may have already. I inched out of the river as stealthily as I had entered.

DOWNEAST SALMON

They didn't know what to do with themselves, much the way I imagine prisoners find themselves when they are finally free. Some maintained the school they became accustomed to while living the first 9 months of their lives in black-painted, 400-gallon tanks at the Peter Gray Hatchery. I watched them take their first disoriented breaths of freedom, back in the East Machias River, where they belong. Some dove for the bottom and nuzzled into the stringy algae that covered everything. They seemed to be confused by this new substrate but knew enough to burrow underneath for protection. Most quickly found their way to a stand of pondweed just downstream of the release site and hid in the fronds. I knew they would be OK when they started to dart from the protection of the pondweed to the surface to nab some insect morsel of food. They would be as all right as Atlantic salmon parr could be. Most of the 14,000 fish I watched get bucketed from the US Fish and Wildlife Service truck to the stream by students from the University of Maine at Machias would not make the return trip to spawn. They are consumed by an array of predators as they metamorphose in the East Machias to smolts. Once they are smolts, they migrate out to sea where they are exposed to a new suite of predators in the ocean. However, these river and marine predators are natural threats their ancestors successfully navigated for eons. These youngsters also need to learn how to survive more recent, human-made threats of warming stream and Gulf of Maine waters, as well as other less obvious impacts of climate change.

Release of Atlantic salmon parr raised in the Downeast Salmon Federation Peter Gray Hatchery.

Capelin are an oily fish that salmon feed on. They now contain half the energy content they once did. Changes in ocean chemistry driven by global warning have resulted in a change in the zooplankton that used to make up the majority of the capelin diet. This translates to a 50 percent reduction in energy content going to the salmon.

Atlantic salmon used to range as far south as Connecticut. Now it's just Maine in the United States. These fish are victims of climate change, one of the factors driving their demise. "But there's not one single cause," Zach Sheller cautions. Zach is the manager of the Downeast Salmon Federation's Peter Gray Hatchery. "It's multiple things: dams, pollution, and climate all play a role. Past overfishing and even the historic practice of removing boulders and logjams so that logs could be driven down rivers still has lingering effects due to a loss of habitat complexity."

The Downeast Salmon Federation is the organization that operates the Peter Gray Hatchery. Three people run the hatchery and are assisted by more than 300 volunteers annually. These people stand in the breach every year, staving off extinction with each parr release, one more time, one more year. The Peter Gray Parr Project began in 2012 on Maine's East Machias River. The project is based on successful salmon restoration methods used by Peter Gray on the River Tyne in England. Unlike the majority of hatchery-raised fish, these Atlantic salmon are cared for in a way that brings them as close to wild-produced fish as we know how in captivity. The goal is to restore wild, naturally reproducing Atlantic salmon populations to the East Machias River in Maine. "We are trying to produce fish that are going to reproduce, not just fish that are going to get fished out," Zach said as I watched the young crew work quickly to load 14,000 parr into 250-gallon tanks outfitted with oxygen bottles, strapped to US Fish and Wildlife Service flatbed trucks. They were well-practiced, and the process of netting the parr out of the hatchery tanks, weighing them into waiting 5-gallon buckets, and transferring them to the transport tanks 5 to 10 pounds at a time was flawless.

The parrs' adventures started in January when they were delivered to the Peter Gray Hatchery as eye eggs, two black spots on a salmon-colored bead. Before that, they were milt and eggs stripped from Atlantic salmon raised at the Craig Brook National Fish Hatchery. Craig Brook Hatchery is run by the US Fish and Wildlife Service and was established in 1889 to raise and release Atlantic salmon.

River-specific populations of Atlantic salmon from the Dennys, East Machias, Machias, Narraguagus, Pleasant, and Sheepscot Rivers were declared endangered in 2000. Juvenile salmon are collected from each of these rivers and are raised to adulthood at the Craig Brook Hatchery. Some of these adults are stripped of their eggs and milt to make the next generation of eye eggs. Others are released as gravid adults. The eye eggs from East Machias salmon are given to the Peter Gray Hatchery to raise to the parr stage. Each of the rivers has specific genetics, so the fish from the different populations are kept separate.

The eye eggs are placed in heath stacks—trays where the water cascades down from the top, bathing the eggs, which are protected beneath fine mesh screens. Once the fish hatch, they are placed in substrate incubation boxes, something that sets the Peter Gray Hatchery apart. Here, the alevin, or sac fry, wriggle down into an artificial substrate that mimics the gravel they would have been born in, carting their large, still-attached yolk sacs with them. They emerge on their own accord a couple months later, yolk sacs absorbed, swimming up and out of the substrate incubation boxes, dropping into 400-gallon, round, black tanks where they mature into parr. Along the way, hatchery staff does everything they can to raise wild fish, from pumping raw East Machias river water directly into the tanks to collecting benthic macroinvertebrates from the East Machias to feed to the parr, so they can get used to hunting wild food. "The parr learned they didn't want to tangle with hellgrammites," Rachel said, one of the three people who run the hatchery.

This is the seventh year of operation for the Peter Gray Parr Project, situated on the banks of the East Machias River, in the former powerhouse building of Bangor Power just downstream of a dam removed in 2000. This is fitting reuse because dams are one of the reasons for the demise of Atlantic salmon. Zach and I commiserated about the lack of Federal Energy Regulatory Commission requirements for fish passage, and I felt tears well up as the last bucket of fish was emptied into the truck. This was the millionth fish estimated to have been produced by the Peter Gray Parr Project's Peter Gray Hatchery in its 7-year lifetime. However, the emotion I felt came from more than this milestone. It was the frank understanding that these tiny fish represent the last chances for an entire species, and the dedicated people of the Downeast Salmon Federation are giving them their last stand. "This is our last best chance to save wild Atlantic salmon from extinction," Zach said as he climbed into the cab of one of the trucks while a steady, cold rain fell. More than 14,000 parr were going to the East Machias River at Pokey Dam. Another 9,000 were going to the East Machias River just upstream of the hatchery, at the former dam site.

I felt privileged to float in the East Machias River just downstream of the Pokey Dam to witness the parrs' release, to see the end of this part of the parrs' journey. Initially stunned, the fish quickly oriented and headed for the bottom or shoaled. However, most eventually swam for the protection of a pondweed bed immediately downstream of the release site, and my focus transitioned from their moment of release to their first 15 minutes of recognizing freedom and insects. Individuals emerged from the protection of the weed bed to nab insects from the surface. The clouds parted as the last bucket was emptied.

I watched individual parr look toward the surface for food, pick out an individual particle, target it, burst towards it, and break the surface as the fish nailed whatever it pursued. The power in these just-released fish was unexpected but undeniable. Fish after fish hunkered in the pondweed patch, watched the surface,

Recently released Atlantic salmon parr in the East Machias River, Maine.

and burst towards it. They looked like golden lightning strikes from the pond-weed to the surface. I'm sure their behavior was different than a parr raised from the gravel of this stream. Problem is, there aren't any of those left.

In 2016, sixteen fish came back to the East Machias. A 1.6 percent return on investment. Last year, nine adults came back, a 3.5 percent return on the numbers stocked, which is huge. Normal returns are less than 1 percent. We have decimated this fish so much that it is questionable whether a normal return will bring them back from the extinction cliff. Once they are gone, they are gone forever. It is a disgrace that their extermination may occur in my lifetime.

I met Zach the next day at the hatchery to confirm a few details. The hatchery was shutting down. Megan, the third member, pressure washed the tanks while Rachel pulled up the iron covers on the drain troughs in the floor and Zach cleaned them out. It's a lot of work, raising 100,000-plus eyed eggs to parr, and they were preparing the hatchery for their next load of eyed eggs due to arrive in January.

The odds are against the recovery of Atlantic salmon, and the success of the Downeast Salmon Federation in achieving their goal of restoring a viable sport salmon fishery. Adult salmon returns remain chronically low, and many of the threats salmon face, such as climate change, aren't going away. Zach acknowledged the odds but gave it some perspective. "It's at least a 4-year return on this year's efforts, and we aren't going to reverse centuries of loss in a season. This is a long-term care plan. As long as we can get the trend line going in the right direction, then maybe we can get naturally reproducing fish back in the East

EAST MACHIAS RIVER AT POKEY DAM

Description: Located at the headwaters of the East Machias River, the Pokey Dam is 9 feet tall at the outlet of Crawford Lake, which looks similar to a large beaver pond, and was constructed to regulate water for residential and recreational uses of the four lakes above Pokey. The failing Pokey Dam fishway was replaced in 2014. The new fishway made critical spawning habitat available to alewives and blueback herring, two kinds of migratory herring, and overwintering habitat available for salmon. The reconstructed fishway allows over a million river herring to reach 4,500 acres of spawning habitat and as many as one billion juveniles to pass back downstream to the ocean.

The East Machias River downstream of the dam has a variety of habitats, from soft sediments to cobble bottom and underwater vegetation beds. The varied habitats support a variety of life, from sponges and mussels, to stocked salmon parr and migrating river herring in the spring.

Access: GPS Address: Pokey Dam Road, Crawford, Maine. From Machias take 192 North to 9 East, Pokey Dam Road is a labeled dirt road on your left in 6 miles. Follow Pokey Dam Road until it ends at the dam. Follow the trail downstream to access the river below the dam.

Above: East Machias River at Pokey Dam.

Machias. We are slowly moving single-digit returns to double-digit returns," he said. "The Downeast Salmon Federation was started in 1982 by fly fishermen who noticed what was happening to Atlantic salmon and wanted to do something about it, so they started this grassroots effort to try to bring the salmon back. If we don't do it, who else will?" Zach asked. And they are, in fact, slowly bringing the salmon back, despite the tough odds.

Stream sampling shows a 181 percent increase in juvenile salmon densities between 2013 and 2016, going from 5.3 fish per 100 square meters to 14.9 fish. This is a drainage-wide density of juvenile salmon not seen in the East Machias River since 1984. However, what has a lot of people excited are increases in smolts. Salmon hatch from eggs to become alevin, grow to parr, and metamorphose to smolt, who then head out to sea where they become adults. The potential grows for more returning adults as the number of smolts increases. As of 2018, smolt populations in the East Machias have more than quadrupled since the start of the project. Increases in smolt numbers should translate to an increase in naturally spawning East Machias Atlantic salmon. However, for now, the river is dependent on us to put them there.

Zach told me that US Fish and Wildlife and the Downeast Salmon Federation placed gravid adults who hadn't been stripped of their eggs and milt into the East Machias just upstream of the hatchery, so I went to see these fish. They were easy to spot from the surface. Their pale bodies stood out against the dark bottom. I slid quietly into the water from a sandbar and instantly had the gaze of twenty-five Atlantic salmon upon me. I froze and tried to blend into the background. I didn't want to disturb them as they adapted to being free in a stream and pursued the innate urge to spawn. It didn't take long for these fish to disregard my presence. It was apparent these fish were hatchery-raised. They were all paler than they should be, some more than others, and each one had worn fins and lips that come from years of rubbing against light blue tanks. However, that didn't matter. Even though these 2-to-3-foot long fish were raised in a hatchery since they were 2-to-3-inch long parr, they give an idea of what the East Machias should look like in fall: packed with big fish with big bellies, with a singleness of purpose, which is to make the next generation. Moreover, they *were* ready to make that next generation. The females hadn't started to beat redds into the bottom yet, but they were about to. They hadn't been freed from their tanks for more than a few hours, and the ancient ritual had already started. Tails slapped through the surface as fish shot upstream, chasing each other in wide circles. Salmon foreplay.

I started to explore Chase Mill Stream. Water tumbled down a stair-step series of pools. Splashed water froze on overhanging twigs to make pear-shaped, bulbous ice sculptures. Underwater was loud confusion, and entrained bubble screens were blinding and disorienting. Round patches of clean, brilliant, emerald-green sponge clung to the dark rock. Sparkling golden silver fallfish, with precise crisscross lines on their sides formed by their scales, schooled between the salmon and me and glowed in the sun. Juvenile white suckers grubbed up the bottom with their proboscis sucker-disc mouths. Yellow perch shot for cover when the big dome lens port on my camera pointed in their direction.

A female salmon came in close and looked me in the eye. Did she understand the responsibility she held for carrying her species forward and ensuring its survival? Or was she just acting on autopilot, reproducing because her hormones, the chemical control of biological entities, told her to? I'm not sure if these fish can sense the distinct lack of their compatriots, if they understand that, they should be much more abundant than they are and can sense that so many individuals are missing. There was an executive function in that eye that studied me, so I would be surprised if this fish didn't understand how rare her species is.

The loss of Atlantic salmon goes beyond just eliminating a species, which is morally egregious. That loss has ripple effects. When Atlantic salmon became too rare to fish, an entire culture centered on fishing for, preparing, and consuming the fish was lost with them. Moreover, the upriver ecosystem lost an enormous source of energy and nutrition, from the dead adults, to the millions of eggs and alevin that are food for so many other river inhabitants. Their loss caused societal and ecological shifts that reach far beyond the banks of the stream.

I returned to Chase Mills 2 days later. A handful of the sixty-four fish released still remained. The others scattered either up- or downstream. There weren't any signs of redds, but still, I am hopeful that these sixty-four gravid adults, plus the 120,000 parr released by the Downeast Salmon Federation this year, will reverse the extinction trajectory of wild Atlantic salmon.

The salmon in this pool were initially leery of my presence and kept to the far side of the creek. My feet anchored me to the bottom upstream, and my body trailed downstream, waggling side to side in the current. The salmon

First day of freedom for hatchery-raised, adult Atlantic salmon in Chase Mill Stream.

CHASE MILL STREAM

Description: Chase Mill Stream is formed at the outflow of Gardner Lake in East Machias, Maine, and flows a short distance before it empties into the East Machias River. The stream is only a little over a mile long, but in that short span, it encompasses a diversity of habitats from still, gravel-bottomed eddies to cobble-bottomed riffles and bedrock-formed chutes and plunge pools. The diversity of habitats translates to a diversity of fish. A public picnic ground is adjacent to much of the stream, so access to these diverse habitats is easy. Though the stream is small in size, it carries a heavy flow. Use caution in the stair-step pools as strainers are possible, and water force here is great.

Access: GPS Address: 142 Chase Mill Road, East Machias, Maine. There are a gravel parking area and picnic ground on the south side of Chase Mills Road. Walk west 100 yards to the stream located in the patch of woods on the edge of the picnic area.

Above: Chase Mill Stream.

soon accepted me as part of the stream and came close. They swam tight and parallel to each other, and I hoped I would see redd construction. The fish retreated to the far corner of the pool every time I made a slight adjustment to keep from getting swept downstream, and trust had to be built again, though it took much less time than the first scare. They would approach again, close and parallel to each other, and I again hoped for rapid tails beating at the bottom. Some of the males chased others away from females.

While I was fixated by the half dozen dinosaur-looking fish left in this pool and was intrigued by their nuanced movements, how they responded to me and each other, there were other fish who demand as much attention as the salmon. I turned my camera from the salmon, wished them well, and let them be, as I focused on the other equally intriguing but lesser-known fish that were here as well: fallfish, white suckers, perch, and shiners. Lamprey would be here if it were spring, when they migrate, rather than fall. I planned to return.

These beings are all interrelated. It's not a matter of conserving one or another, but rather all of them. The recovery of one species is often hitched to the health of another. Nez Perce tribal elder Elmer Crow thought one of the reasons coho salmon failed to recover in the Salmon River in Idaho is because there are no efforts to restore Pacific lamprey, once so abundant they must have been an important food of salmon. And I wonder if the same applies here in the East. I wonder what pieces of these riverine ecosystems I am missing because they were gone before I knew they existed. I wonder if one of those missing parts is an important link to salmon recovery. Maybe something subtle such as a shift in energy content of the prey of a fish salmon eat. Our systems on Earth are that finely tuned. I left Chase Mills encouraged by the work of the Downeast Salmon Federation and the experience of snorkeling with Atlantic salmon, ready to explore more of those subtle links.

CHAPTER 3

Lamprey

I stood on a trail carved into the side of one of the sand and gravel walls of Cougar Canyon, high above the South Fork of the Salmon River, which snaked its way through the valley deep below. The wind puffed down the slope and rustled the dry grass. The landscape was lunar as all of the trees, the fir and spruce, were charred, dead-gray blowdowns, burned in the Tepee Springs Fire that consumed nearly 100,000 acres in 2015. Some young, foot-tall pines were starting to grow in, but it was still like being on another planet. It made the scene all the more intense and spiritual. I was alone in the 30-degree October sunshine with the wind, with the Salmon River, and whatever might be in its waters.

This is where Elmer Crow thought he saw the last eel. This is where the Pacific lamprey conservation movement was born. And so, this place is sacred to me, for the power of the landscape and for the significance of that day in 1974 when Elmer saw what he thought was the last Pacific lamprey swimming upstream to spawn. Pacific lamprey, or eels, as the Nez Perce people call them, had been in serious decline. They are migratory and spend their adult lives at sea. They swim into freshwater rivers, like the South Fork of the Salmon, to spawn. Dams placed on the Columbia River, starting with Bonneville, cut off lamprey migration routes so they couldn't get to their home country to spawn, which also happens to be Nez Perce home country. Lamprey were also intentionally poisoned when fisheries biologists were only worried about fish that generate revenue from tag or license sales such as salmon. Anything perceived to interfere with that revenue stream was eliminated. The Pacific lamprey populations from entire rivers, such as the Umatilla, were extirpated with poison. Elmer was puzzled as to why the Creator showed him this one fish swimming over a sand flat, and he worried that he might have seen the last one. Then it dawned on him. It was up to Elmer to do something about the lamprey decline. Therefore, he dedicated himself to preserving Pacific lamprey.

I never met Elmer. The only thing I know about him is what I learned from the Freshwaters Illustrated film *Lost Fish*, a story about the connection native people have with these fish and their efforts to protect and restore Pacific lamprey. *Lost Fish* is a story about passion for our natural world. Elmer wasn't scripted but genuine. He spoke with integrity, from the heart, and I could just sense that he believed every word he said and that he didn't say words without thought.

His well-stated life philosophy—"We are the circle. That's what life is about. So when one of us is in trouble, that's when the rest of us need to step in."—is also mine. Except I could never state it so clearly, purposefully, and eloquently.

Elmer Crow was a Nez Perce elder and worked tirelessly to keep Pacific lamprey from going extinct, and I wish I could have had the opportunity to meet him in person. Elmer drowned in the Snake River in 2013 rescuing his young grandson after a passing boat wake knocked the grandson off a sandbar into deep water. I contacted Elmer's family when I learned of his death. I wanted them to know that I too felt loss.

I kept in touch with Elmer's family periodically over the next 5 years. I used Elmer's image and "meaning of life" quote in numerous presentations I gave about freshwater biodiversity loss, and I wanted to let his family know that he was still impacting people years after his death. I had always wanted to travel to the South Fork of the Salmon at Cougar Canyon and to meet Elmer's family. I got the opportunity in 2018 to make such a trip.

I made plans to meet with Elmer's oldest son, Jarrod, who has the distinction as being the youngest person ever charged with a felony for illegal fishing—the result of a dispute between the Nez Perce tribe and the Oregon Department of Fish and Wildlife, when he was fishing with his dad in the Salmon River at the age of 12. Jarrod works for the Nez Perce Tribe Fisheries Department and was going to tour me through the lamprey holding facility that is part of the Nez Perce Tribal Hatchery complex in Lenore, Idaho. I got a last-minute text from Jarrod. He had a medical issue that landed him in the emergency department and lined up his mom and sister to meet with me instead. That showed me a lot about this man's character. He suffered a medical emergency and still took the time to make arrangements to keep our tour rather than just cancel, which would have been perfectly acceptable. I was in awe.

I met Elmer Crow's wife, Lynda, and their daughter, Jamie. Lynda is a librarian in the tiny town of Culdesac in Idaho. We sat at a wooden library table where she showed me photos of Elmer and their grandkids on her iPad as she proudly told me about him.

"Elmer was raised by Nez Perce elders who fought in the Nez Perce war," Lynda started. The Nez Perce war was an armed conflict between the Nez Perce and their allies against the US Army. The Nez Perce were peaceful and welcomed white settlers. When some of the Nez Perce realized what was happening, they refused to be confined to reservations, and the Nez Perce war started. It was one of the saddest moments in the Indian Wars and shameful in US history. The battle at Big Hole Basin, Montana, resulted in the US Army killing eighty-nine Nez Perce, mostly women and children. The elders taught Elmer the native ways, things such as how to make big-horn sheep bows and nets to collect lamprey. They told him they taught him because he would remember all of these things." Lynda shared some of those ways with me. "Eel changes the taste of huckleberry, so the elders would give kids dried eel before picking huckleberry. It makes the huckleberries not taste good, so more berries go in the buckets," Lynda chuckled.

"Elmer was taught the Nez Perce language and was held back in elementary school because he couldn't speak English well enough. He always stuck up for the underdog. Maybe that's why he took to the lamprey so much. Elmer did presentations all over telling people about eels. He was driven to do these things," Lynda shared. "He used to say 'I'm in a position to do something, so it's up to me,'" Lynda added.

Her excitement grew as we talked. I think she and Elmer shared the same passion for preserving lamprey. All four of Elmer's kids work in fisheries, most of them for the Columbia River Inter-Tribal Fish Commission. They carry on his legacy by doing presentations about Pacific lamprey to educate people about this amazing fish, his "brother" eel. Elmer's grandkids are continuing the work, too.

"The grandkids are involved in eel translocation releases," Lynda proudly told me as she shared photos of Elmer, his kids, and grandkids releasing lamprey.

"'I've done my part. Now it's up to you.' He would say every time he released lamprey. And he did his part. Those kids are doing it." Lynda beamed.

"He had such a way with the eels. They would come to him. Elmer thought that eels were part of the answer as to why salmon aren't recovering. They were a large food source for the rivers and filter feeders that helped keep the rivers clean."

The conversation slowed. Lynda's countenance changed from happy and driven to serene. "It was traumatic watching him drown, but I have my grandson. He died in a place he loved with family he loved." The pain 5 years later was palpable, and I couldn't imagine living through such a terrifying experience. Lynda needed to get back to work, and I needed to meet their youngest daughter, Jamie. I thanked her for her time and for sharing both the good and painful memories with me.

Jamie and I chatted as we drove to the hatchery. She told me how she was grateful for growing up in a stable, unbroken family when so many of her friends didn't have that. Family was as important to Elmer as the lamprey. We arrived at the lamprey building at the hatchery. It is a simple pole barn with a dozen lamprey holding tanks inside. When *Lost Fish* was shot in 2012, the lamprey holding tanks were outside. At least now they are under a roof, but it is still an unfunded program.

A photo of Elmer holding a lamprey was taped to the wall, and one of his quotes—"My brother eel is just plain cool."—was written underneath. There was also a historic photo of lamprey covering Willamette Falls so that water wasn't visible. Just a writhing mass of eel all working their way up the falls to continue their upstream journey. I can't fathom that abundance. They must have had a huge effect on the rivers here. They had a huge effect on Nez Perce culture. Lamprey sustained the Nez Perce, and so they were revered. Elder Wilson Wiwa in *Lost Fish* summarizes the relationship as follows: "They gave themselves up so that we may live." Because they were essential to Nez Perce survival, they were critical elements of Nez Perce ceremony. The loss of lamprey is leading to a loss of Nez Perce culture.

Jamie explained this was a translocation project. Lamprey migrate upriver from the sea in the fall, but they can't get past the Columbia River dams. They are collected at Bonneville, the first in a series of fourteen main-stem dams, and are held here in these tanks over the winter. They are released into streams where they spawn in the spring. The young live as filter-feeding ammocoetes in soft sediments for 5 to 7 years. They migrate out to sea and metamorphose into an adult lamprey where they parasitize fish. They return to spawn after 18 to 40 months at sea. "This is translocation, not restoration," Jamie emphasized. "We're really not restoring lamprey. We are just giving them a way around the dams so they can spawn the way they are supposed to," she explained as she fished a few out of one of the holding tanks.

I looked at the circular pattern of orange-yellow, spiky, rasping teeth set in a disc on the end of a gray tube of muscle. The lamprey's bottomless black eye looked back at me, tried to figure me out as I tried to figure out this ancient being. Lamprey first appear in the fossil record 450 million years ago. They are one of the most primeval vertebrates on the planet and predate sharks. They are so primitive, jaws in fish evolved after lamprey, so lamprey are called jawless fish. Instead, they have a sucker disc lined with sharp, raspy teeth, which allows them to latch on to the sides of larger fish and suck body fluids to the point of death.

I could feel the power and strength of this animal as it started to wriggle out of my hands for the water. Interestingly, they drop their teeth over the winter and stop feeding. Their reproductive journey ends in death. I put the fish back, and Jamie and I talked about the lamprey and the translocation project as we watched them agilely navigate the tank, frontward and backward. And we talked more about Elmer.

"He drowned saving my son," Jamie shared. My heart sank again. I didn't know what to say, and a comfortable silence took over. "This was good for my soul," Jamie finally said after a few minutes. It was good for mine too.

And so this place, the South Fork of the Salmon River at Cougar Canyon, is sacred to me. Even more so after meeting Elmer's family. The spot where Elmer Crow thought he saw the last eel. The spot that launched the effort to protect and restore Pacific lamprey started here with one man, "a poor, uneducated Indian," as Elmer described himself. I hoped to see lamprey but knew it was doubtful. They are rare.

Four hundred thousand Pacific lamprey were counted at Bonneville 60 years ago. Current counts yield only 20,000. We started monitoring lamprey at Lower Granite Lake Dam, the last of the lower Columbia River dams in 1995, when 1,122 were counted. Forty-eight returned in 2011 after a low of twelve in 2009. There still isn't passage for these animals through the fourteen main-stem

Columbia River dams. Poisoned rivers such as the Umatilla still haven't recovered. However, there are signs of hope. Umatilla saw a record return in 2018, with 2,600 lamprey swimming upstream to spawn in this eastern Oregon River.

I squeezed into my drysuit in silence on the grassed bank. I was alone with the cold October wind in the wilderness. The first snows of the season had already fallen just a few hundred feet higher in elevation. This side of the Salmon was a wide floodplain covered in grasses and occasional spruce and fir that escaped being burned in the Tepee Springs Fire. The other bank was steep-sided canyon that dropped directly into the river. The river here was a deep, fast-moving pool that tailed out into a gravel flat before a large, rock-studded riffle. The water ran clear.

I waded out into the middle of the riffle and laid down in a few-foot-deep eddy behind one of the large rocks. The water was painfully cold. Knives of freezing water stabbed my exposed cheeks instantly and slowly worked their way into my hands as my neoprene gloves flooded. The Salmon was excruciating and beautiful.

An iridescent blue-green sheen glistened on a convoluted, folded, dark olive growth that covered every rock. It looked similar to a shimmering green brain and felt rubbery. This was nostoc, a blue-green alga in an unusual, mutualistic relationship with fly larvae. Female chironomid flies lay eggs on the surface of developing nostoc algae colonies in early summer. The fly larvae bores into the alga colony after hatching, and the colony changes from a globose to erect growth form, which increases the surface area and, thus, the photosynthetic rates

Nostoc covers a rock in the South Fork of the Salmon River.

South Fork of the Salmon River.

SOUTH FORK SALMON RIVER

Description: The South Fork of the Salmon River is 86 miles long that starts in the Salmon Mountains and flows north to its confluence with the main stem of the Salmon. It runs clear and cold, and this spot near the South Fork Campground contains a variety of habitats, but it is mostly deep, rocky pools and riffles.

Access: GPS Address: South Fork Salmon River Campground, Boise National Forest, Idaho. From McCall, take 55 south to Cascade. Turn left onto NF 22, Warm Lake Road. Drive 27 miles. The campground will be on your right. There is a wide shoulder at the intersection of NF-22 and forest road 428 for parking. The South Fork of the Salmon is easily accessed upstream and downstream of the NF 22 bridge over the river.

of the nostoc. The larvae gets a protected place where it can develop with a readily available, high-nitrogen food source. The nostoc gets more photosynthetic production.

A well-decayed dead salmon was tangled in a submerged branch just upstream of me, so rotted I wouldn't have recognized it if it weren't for the exposed lower jaw. Three others were strewn about this section of river, hung up on various underwater obstacles. They were the lucky, or most fit, few who were able to navigate through the eleven dams between the ocean and here.

I thought about Elmer's claim that salmon are failing to recover because of the loss of lamprey as my hands became numb with cold while I explored pool to pool and the gravel tail-outs on each, hoping for lamprey or maybe even their larval ammocoete form. Elmer was suggesting a tight relationship here, a symbiosis of sorts. The salmon get nutrition from the lamprey, and the lamprey get nutrition from the salmon. I remembered the photo of Willamette Falls covered in lamprey that was taped to the hatchery wall and imagined each sand flat I snorkeled over today loaded with ammocoetes produced by those lamprey. I could easily see how these could be food for salmon parr and smolts. Food that was now a missing, critical link.

I normally look up claims like this, try to find some credible data to back it up. But not this time. Elmer knew lamprey and these rivers better than science ever will, and this time, I needed to learn to trust traditional ecological knowledge. I got out when my body started to shiver. I needed to get warm.

I felt drawn to Elmer and his home territory the minute I saw him in *Lost Fish*. I felt I had to experience the South Fork of the Salmon River at the spot where Elmer thought he saw the last eel in 1975. And I was extremely grateful to snorkel in this place. Maybe it was fitting that I didn't see any lamprey. That's not what the Creator had planned for me that day. Elmer's words echoed on the wind as I warmed in the sun.

"Shame on us. The whole lot of us for letting something that's 450 to 500 million years old go extinct." There was an intensity, frustration, and some anger behind those words that I know well.

I didn't see any Pacific lamprey in Elmer's home territory, but I have had the fortune of swimming with other species of lamprey in very different geography. The first time I saw a sea lamprey, it was in the Octoraro Creek, a tributary to the Susquehanna River below the Conowingo Dam.

I'd been lucky enough to take more than one hundred kids snorkeling on lower Susquehanna and upper Chesapeake rivers in northeast Maryland on 3 of the last 7 days in late May. It was fun work but exhausting. I enjoyed the sunny morning and the clear water of our last trip. It was the last group of 25, and we had just found about a dozen elvers making their way back upstream to find a clean, cobble-bar home where they would mature for the next 25 years or so. It is so rewarding to see kids observe this amazing feat, to watch them become connected to our rivers right before my eyes. The school's principal was also out with this fifth-grade class, and she gave an approving nod. We were reaching curricular outcomes. Kids were learning while they connected with their river.

I rolled onto my back and enjoyed the rush of water, the sun, the laughter of students. Life was good, and I was satisfied. A commotion downstream changed all that. A half dozen students gathered around a section of riffle and yelled, "Eel!" I rolled over and snorkeled to them to find a large, 3-foot-long, orange-colored lamprey firmly attached to a rock.

I had never seen a lamprey in the wild before. Just as I thought the day couldn't get any better, I saw a life-list fish. Some people collect bird life lists. I collect fish, and this was quite the find. I had been hoping to see a lamprey for 10 years. I had been intently searching for 5 years.

Sea lamprey have a reputation for being an invasive parasite killing off the Great Lakes' fish populations, which they are, but in Maryland, they are native and possibly declining in number. They really haven't been all that well studied, and historical population data is scarce.

They spend their lives at sea and migrate into our rivers and streams to spawn. There are few surveys of lamprey where I live, and we don't have a good assessment of lamprey population trends. It is likely they are experiencing the same difficulties and declines as other freshwater migrants similar to shad, eels, and sturgeon.

That day with the students, I watched the lamprey in the water for as long as I could without losing the class. The caramel-brown fish clung to a rock with its sucker-disc mouth. Its eyes were set back on its head and watched me as I watched it. There was a consciousness in that eye, a kind of ancient wisdom. Its spiracles, precursors to gills on more evolutionarily modern fish, pumped water. Its nose was beaten and white due to its travels from the sea to this stream.

Maybe it was the look of the fish and its prehistoric place in the evolutionary ladder. Maybe it was its calm demeanor. Even though it was surrounded by twenty-five students, it just held on to that one rock. Maybe it was the knowledge that its life was almost over after its incredible reproductive journey. Or maybe it was the feeling that I might have been looking at the last one in the Octoraro, just as Elmer experienced in the South Fork in 1974. Maybe it was all of those

Adult sea lamprey.

OCTORARO CREEK

Description: The Octoraro Creek flows through a suburbanizing, agricultural landscape, so water clarity is often an issue. Still, this tributary to the lower Susquehanna is a fun place to snorkel and usually contains a variety of life.

Access: GPS Address: 130 Moore Road, Conowingo, Maryland. There are multiple access points on the lower Octoraro. From I-95 take the Perryville exit. Follow 222 North to Moore Road. Make a Right onto Moore Road. There is a pull-off at an old railroad trestle on the right at around 130 Moore Road, Conowingo, Maryland. If you continue on Moore Road, you will find a second access at the intersection of Dr Jack and McCauley Road. From Moore Road, make a right on Dr Jack. There is a small parking lot on the north side of Dr Jack Road right after crossing the Octorato Creek. Park here, cross McCauley Road, and follow a short trail to the creek, where Basin Run and the Octorato meet.

Above: Octoraro Creek.

things, but whatever it was, something instantly bonded me to that lamprey. Like Elmer, I felt a connection to that one fish.

We took lots of pictures and some video and showed the fish to all the kids. In that instant, the students became strongly attached to their river and that fish. The lamprey was the galvanizing agent.

Nine months later, I cut a trail through a foot of freshly fallen snow to get to the banks of Basin Run, a tributary to the Octoraro not far from where we found the sea lamprey in May. It was a dark and frigid February night, and the creek was partially covered in foot-thick ice. There were black holes where the ice couldn't form over moving water. I sat on the edge of one of these holes and let my legs dangle into the cold water. The drysuit provided some protection, but the cold still crept through the underlying dry fleece layer. I weighed the potential severity of this trip. It was pitch dark, freezing cold, and, most importantly, thick ice covered the creek downstream from where I sat. If the current peeled me from the bottom and pushed me under the ice, I likely wouldn't be able to break through and would possibly drown. The key was not to let the current take me. I eased into the dark, cold water. My light made the whole ice sheet glow from beneath. As soon as I entered the water, adjusted to weightlessness, and got oriented, a juvenile sea lamprey swam out from under the thick ice and into the cone of light from my underwater lamp. It was recently metamorphosed from an ammocoete. Its oral hood, essentially a toothless funnel used to filter algae and plankton from the water, was replaced with a toothy sucker disc. While the mature lamprey I encountered 9 months earlier was worn and beaten and rapidly approaching death, this fish was new and unscathed and just starting its journey. Recently transformed lamprey only spend a few months in fresh water before heading out to sea. This one would be moving downstream shortly. Perhaps hitching a ride on a striper or shad. The juvenile lamprey didn't stick around for long. Once it entered the light, it froze for a moment, turned, and let the current carry it downstream back under the thick ice sheet. Even though my encounter with this youngster had lasted only a few minutes, I felt privileged to have experienced the end of one lamprey's journey and the beginning of another's.

As amazing as these two lamprey were, they seem to be forgotten in the East. They are listed as species of least concern by the International Union for the Conservation of Nature; however, there isn't sufficient data to adequately determine their status. I hope we can learn how East Coast lamprey are faring and take action to protect these primitive marvels. I try to tell people about these wondrous, ancient fish, as well as the other aquatic migrants that are fading away, every chance I get. However, most importantly, I try to share a little of Elmer's passion in the hopes that it will inspire others.

Elmer stood for underrepresented fish, for fish labeled as unimportant. One of those underrepresented fish is the brook lamprey. There are twenty-three species of lamprey in North America. Twenty-one are native. Not all are parasitic. Brook lamprey are small, between 4 and 6 inches, and are cryptic. They spend most of their lives, 3 to 7 years, as wormlike ammocoetes living in loose sediments in slower pools of small first-order streams where they feed on microscopic plants and animals and decaying matter. They metamorphose into adults and lose their gastrointestinal tract entirely. Their only purpose in their short adult lives is to reproduce. They swim upstream in small first-order streams and use their sucker mouths to rearrange gravel entirely too big for their size. It is easy for them to go unnoticed. There is a risk to that. If people don't even know you exist, you won't be missed when you're gone. American brook and least brook lamprey are listed as species of concern in many of the states where they occur throughout their Atlantic slope and Great Lakes range.

You need to be intentional if you want to see them during their spawn and start watching small streams for the slightest sign that they are there, which is usually in early spring. It takes time since they are so well camouflaged, so the search really entails looking for motion in tiny pools in small streams. A friend of mine worked at the Jug Bay National Estuarine Reserve. She sent me an email in early April saying the lamprey were in a small creek on the Glendenning tract at Jug Bay wetland off the Patuxent River, Maryland.

The leaves were just barely peeking out of their buds so that a green blush tinged the forest. The small gravel parking area was full with a dozen cars. I met Coreen, who led me down a trail to the first tiny stream it crossed. We knelt in the soft, damp moss that covered the sandbanks of this first-order creek, barely large enough to be called one. It cut into the sand and gravel geology as it gently and slowly spilled over small branches that were big enough to form logjams. These streams are not well protected. They are often defined as ephemeral or temporary, which changes the level of care that must be taken to protect them from development. Sometimes, they don't even exist on development plans and so can pretty easily be bulldozed unless a planning and zoning officer takes the time to inspect every development site. I found a paper published in the 1970s that surveyed the Delmarva Peninsula for American brook and least brook lamprey. They were found in an impressive number of streams. I contacted the authors to learn those locations so I could repeat the study to see if anything had changed over the last 45 years.

"Most of the places we sampled probably don't exist anymore, all bulldozed," The report author wrote back to my inquiry. "You would probably be wasting your time trying to find them. I couldn't tell you where to start."

I worked as an educator on Clagett Farm, a demonstration farm run by the Chesapeake Bay Foundation located on the western shore of the Chesapeake Bay in Prince George's County, Maryland. A small stream flowed through the property. We took students to this stream to do an investigation of its health and looked for changes in water chemistry, clarity, and the life that called it home. When I started at the program, brook lamprey were abundant. Every net came up with at least one in the bag. A new development was constructed upstream of the farm, and the lamprey started to decline because of increased sedimentation caused by increased runoff coming from the new houses.

I have witnessed the decline of these animals firsthand in my adult lifetime in the mid-Atlantic streams I know, and as Coreen and I stared into the almost stagnant water, I worried that maybe they were gone from this stream too.

"So what?" some may ask. They are just little, pale, worm-looking creatures, insignificant in the grand scheme of things. Some might even call them repulsive. However, I think they are beautiful. Part of that beauty is their perfectly designed body for where and how they live. Part of their beauty lies in their direct connection to ancient vertebrate lineages. Part of it lies in their complex life history involving significant metamorphoses, and when I think through all that is involved biochemically with those metamorphoses, I am awestruck. They are filter feeders and help keep streams clear. They are food for other fish. They are a rivet in the plane called Earth on which we are flying through space. Each species is a rivet holding said plane together. As we lose species, and as each rivet pops out, the plane becomes less stable and more likely to crash. They have value because they add to the biodiversity that stabilizes ecosystems. Beyond the ecosystem services they provide, they are important because they are. Simply because they *are* life. We don't have the right to eliminate other species from this planet, whether we perceive them to be important or not. We have a moral obligation to preserve all life.

However, the part of their beauty that drew me here today is their singleness of purpose as an adult, so purposeful they lose their gastrointestinal tract so they can't eat. All of their focus is on producing the next generation. And all of Coreen's and my focus was on witnessing this.

The water barely trickled through the pools of the creek, and a stagnant scum gathered on the surface. I saw some movement, and there they were. A half dozen least brook lamprey squiggled upstream over and through some twigs that

Spawning brook lamprey.

were entrained in the loose sands and gravel bottom into a slightly deeper pool with slower water. One latched his sucker disc on to a pebble bigger than he was and twisted it out of the way by writhing his body and twirling the large gravel with him. He latched on to another pebble and spun it out of the way. This male was forming a nest for the sticky eggs he would fertilize. A female latched on to the pebble next to the male and their tails twirled together like egg beaters. The female released her eggs while the male fertilized them as they fell into the soft sand bed created by the adults. They will hatch into embryos and remain in the nest for a month before they mature into ammocoetes and seek soft bottoms in slow-moving water where they will burrow and begin filter feeding for the next 3 to 7 years. Their work done, these adult lamprey would die soon and leave it up to the fertilized eggs they left behind to carry the species forward.

Lamprey seem to emerge in the most unlikely of places often when I least expect them. This certainly holds true for my first encounter with Ohio Lamprey. I stopped off at the New River outside of Blacksburg, Virginia, on my way to Cherokee National Forest. I was heading to the Tellico River to try to swim with hellbenders and to meet Jeremy Monroe, director of Freshwaters Illustrated. The drive was just a little too long to make in one shot, so I picked out a campsite right on the New River, at New River Junction, to stop for the night, and to get a quick snorkel in the next morning.

The New River isn't that new. It may be one of the oldest rivers in North America, but we can't make an accurate determination. It has sliced its course down through the Appalachians during its 360-million-year lifetime, depending on the age estimate used. Forested slopes meet the river as the New snakes through the gap it formed in the mountains at New River Junction, a tubing rental operation and campground. I woke up early, crawled out of my tent, squeezed into my wetsuit, and slid into the New. Red and orange rounded cobbles covered the bottom and metallic red-, green-, and yellow-shelled snails coated them. It was an absolutely beautiful scene. As I was enjoying the unexpected brilliant colors of the background, a smallmouth bass emerged from nowhere and hung out with me for a while. It curiously circled me and kept a constant and perceived safe distance. I noticed a white streak hanging from the base of its dorsal fin. It was a few inches long, and from a distance, the bass kept between us, it looked featureless. It trailed along the side of the bass like a handlebar streamer on a bike. As the bass got used to my presence in the river, it circled closer, and I could at least make a pretty certain guess that an Ohio lamprey was attached to the side of this fish.

Ohio lamprey are small—about the same size of American and least brook lamprey. The big difference is they are parasitic whereas American and least brook lamprey are filter feeders.

Ohio lamprey are found in the Ohio River system, including the Allegheny and upper Tennessee rivers, from southwest New York to eastern Illinois

NEW RIVER

Description: The New River is a legendary river noted for its white water and smallmouth bass fishery. The river at New River Junction is beautiful, surrounded by forested mountains that slope to the river's edge. The river here is big and pushy, so use caution. Access is through New River Junction, which is a tubing rental operation and campground. Day access is permitted; however, there is an entrance fee.

Access: GPS address: 2591 Big Falls Road, Blacksburg, Virginia, and New River Junction comes up in Google Maps. From I-81, take exit 118B onto 460 West (towards Virginia Tech/Blacksburg). Follow 460 West approximately 10 miles. Exit onto the Prices Fork Road Exit (not Downtown/VT). Go approximately 3 miles. The road narrows to two lanes, and you will be getting close when you pass Prices Fork Elementary School on your left. Turn right onto McCoy Road, just beyond the Sunoco/Marathon gas stations. There are signs saying Long Shop/McCoy/Virginia Tech Kentland Farm. Follow McCoy Road to the end, approximately 7 miles. Turn right onto Big Falls Road. After approximately a half mile, the road turns down toward the river and over the railroad tracks. The entrance to New River Junction is on your left immediately after crossing the tracks.

Above: New River.

and south to Tennessee. They are considered rare throughout most of their range, so I felt privileged to see this one. Ohio lamprey migrate between smaller, slower-moving streams and backwaters during their filter-feeding ammocoete life stage and medium to large rivers, like the New River, during their adult parasitic life stage. They have been extirpated from parts of their range, and sedimentation, pollution, and river damming affect their ability to survive and spawn.

The bass tired of the novelty I provided and swam off, lamprey attached. Ohio lamprey parasitize fish during their immature adult stage, after they metamorphose from ammocoetes but before they reach sexual maturity. This parasitic stage lasts about a year. Once they mature, they stop eating and migrate upstream into small streams where they make redds and spawn.

The label "vampire fish" and the overexaggeration of its parasitic lifestyle doesn't make this fish endearing. Endearing seems to be requisite to gaining protection in this age of focusing conservation efforts on charismatic megafauna and often even failing at that. Therefore, I wonder if we will be the end of the lamprey's long successful time on Earth. I certainly hope not. They deserve more attention and protection. I have only experienced a fraction of the native lamprey species of North America. There is so much more to watch and learn about these fascinating windows into our collective past. The only way to know their true character is to spend time with them in rivers. Because "My brother eel is just plain cool."

"How do we let something 450 million years old go extinct?" How do we indeed, Elmer?

CHAPTER 4

Eels

I could hear water rushing, though I couldn't see it yet. My head lamp made my breath steam glow silver and raindrops sparkle. Basin Run is normally a small, second-order stream that tumbles down rocky stair-step pools that are barely big enough to lay in without my feet hanging out. But on this October night, it was swollen to twice its size. I reached the new bank of Basin Run; the usual one was 4 feet underwater. The creek ran fast and full of sediment. It had been raining all day, and Basin Run was cresting. The low likelihood of being able to see anything through the sediment-choked water didn't warrant the risk of getting swept downstream and hung up in a strainer. As badly as I wanted to get in, conditions were just too dangerous. I'd come on a rainy October night to witness a mass nocturnal migration of eels but would have to miss it, at least for tonight.

Eels live for about 25 years in the creeks, rivers, and streams throughout their range that extends from the Mississippi Drainage to the west, east to New England, and south to the Caribbean Islands. For some still unknown reason, a portion of the population stops feeding and reportedly migrate downstream en masse on dark nights with rising water around Halloween, though I have never been a witness to what must be an amazing sight. The migrating eels go through incredible physiologic changes as they move toward the ocean: they don't eat, their eyes grow large, their pigmentation changes, they become sexually mature, and their physiology, used to handling the pressures of living in a shallow freshwater environment, changes to handle the opposite pressures of living in a deep ocean environment.

All of these eels head to the Sargasso Sea, a part of the Atlantic that basically lies under the Bermuda Triangle, to spawn. Young eels emerge, ride ocean currents, and swim back up our rivers and creeks. Eels used to be the most abundant fish in the Chesapeake watershed. Maybe they still are, but their numbers have been declining since the 1980s due to a combination of causes. Eels prefer to live in clean gravel and cobble-bottomed streams. More and more of our stream bottoms are becoming choked with sediments due to farming, construction, and urbanization of their watersheds. Dams impede eel migration, especially the young eels returning to their rivers. One researcher found 10,000 baby eels per day gather at the base of a hundred-foot-tall dam in the Susquehanna River through the summer as they try to make their way back upstream.

I'm connected to these fish. My relatives used to build eel weirs in the Susquehanna to trap them during their migration. An eel weir is a V-shaped dam made from piled rocks that point downstream. It's open at the apex, and the migrating eels swim through that opening into waiting baskets. It's a technology Europeans learned from Native Americans. The remnants of one of my family's weirs can still be seen in the Susquehanna near the Swatara Creek. Swatara is derived from the Susquehannock word *swahadowry*, which means "where we feed on eels."

There's a picture in a family photo album of a two- or three-year-old me holding an eel on the end of my fishing line, and that picture captures one of my first memories fishing. One of the best dives I ever experienced was with my dad and eels in the Delaware River. We entered the river at night between Easton, Pennsylvania, and Phillipsburg, New Jersey, and descended to the bottom of the river 20 feet below in clear water. We landed in a field of eels, who stuck half of their bodies out of their burrows and slowly waved back and forth in unison in the gentle current, the way a hayfield undulates in a breeze. They glowed silver-green in our dive lights against the clear, dark water.

Eels are a fish I regularly see when I snorkel, and one section of Deer Creek seems always to hold a lot. One spring, they were late to emerge, and I was getting worried. I'd been waiting for them. The spring before, I couldn't snorkel Deer Creek without seeing at least three or four on each trip. Eels might be the most abundant fish in the Chesapeake watershed, but they are secretive and largely nocturnal, so they aren't as obvious as the less abundant but more visible fish species.

American eel hunting.

I don't know why they are so abundant in this rapid. It's not the easiest place to swim. The water is fast and turbulent, so a fish hunting there that slithers more than swims was a surprise. However, in years past, there they were, in the middle of the rapid, poking their heads into the nooks and crannies of the boulder bottom, looking for a morsel to eat. They were usually so intent on the hunt I often went unnoticed. As I watched, their use of the rapid started to make sense. Their bodies are perfectly shaped to hug the crags on the bottom largely out of the flow. Their slim shape allows them to probe the depths of each potential fish hiding spot. When they finally recognized me, they slithered along the stream bed, fighting the current, and disappeared. I wondered how many eels lived in the rapid. It's one of the fish I anticipate to see on each visit spring, summer, and fall.

However, this year, I hadn't seen any eels in that rapid yet, and spring was progressing. Their springtime presence was the norm I came to know and expect for this stream, and I worried about their fate. I hoped they were present and that I was just missing them due to their secretive nature. It's a strange thing, knowing that rivers and streams change. Knowing that the life in our rivers and streams changes too, and knowing that most of those changes occur at our hands. When one of the members of the fish community doesn't return the next year, I worry that something happened to eliminate them. I worried that the eels in Deer Creek were gone.

I slid into the rapid and hung on as usual. The water wanted to peel me off the rock I clawed and throw me downstream. I darted into an eddy that gave a little protection from the strong flow and inched upstream to the downstream side of the large boulder responsible for the calmer water.

American eel peering from its hiding spot.

I didn't see anything. This spot usually produced at least one eel each trip, but there was nothing. I took a breath and clung to the bottom 3 feet below as I looked in all the boulder recesses for hiding eels. After multiple dives to the bottom, I still hadn't seen any and was just about exhausted and ready to give up. I took one last breath, sunk to the bottom, and hung on to a large rock. There, staring back at me from the crevice between a boulder and the bottom, was an eel. The fish looked at me straight on, its tiny nares pointed up from its brown-and-indigo-blue body. Its eyes stared at me and looked confused and concerned. I must have been an odd sight for this eel. I made multiple dives back to the bottom to watch this eel, and he seemed to get used to my presence. He was a cute fish, and he reminded me of a puppy dog.

I was glad to find at least one eel here but hoped for more, and I continued to explore the rest of this rapid. It was loud due to the tumbling water and bedlam with entrained air bubbles swirling around whipped-up fronds of riverweed that were attached to the rocks below. I saw some movement on the bottom. An eel probed the crevices between rocks. It didn't even acknowledge my presence. A second eel hunted in the main part of the current. I was relieved to see those fish and watch the precise agility they used to search for prey. All was right with the world. I have a lot of concern about the future health of our rivers and streams. And seeing fish return to their springtime place in the river gives me hope.

I was leading a June trip with high school students in the Big Elk Creek, in Cecil County, Maryland. The creek here is very deceiving. From the surface, it looks like there couldn't possibly be anything of worth or value in it. Certainly nothing worth watching. However, every time I stick my face in the Big Elk, I come away amazed, and this trip was no different. We started on the downstream end of a pool and slowly worked our way upstream to where a cobbly riffle dumped into it. Male common shiners, dressed in their pastel orange, yellow, and red breeding colors, dashed about through the softball-sized rocks. Darters hopped from micro eddy to micro eddy, and small green elvers slithered through the bottom substrate. They were a clean, almost emerald, green, and they were intent on their upstream progress. These were young eels returning to this stream from the ocean where they would live for the next 25 years. We watched two elvers from just downstream as they wriggled against the current and masterfully navigated a strong flow by snaking through the softball-sized cobble and marble-sized gravel. They used tiny vortices in the current formed by the bottom to make their way upstream. And then six more appeared. It was inspiring to see this kind of return of elvers to this perceived throwaway stream.

I've witnessed the summer return of juvenile eels to our streams for a number of years, and it never gets old. It's reassuring knowing that these fish are coming back despite global declines. However, I still haven't seen the reported fall adult downstream mass migration. I want to snorkel with the eels, to get their perspective on at least the beginning of their reproductive journey. I want

Elver in the Big Elk Creek.

to experience this, if the phenomenon exists, while eels are still relatively abundant, given their downward population trend. I have snorkeled streams at night in October pursuing the fall eel journey.

I don't like the dark very much. But I like snorkeling, and looking for migrating eels, more than I dislike the dark, so I decided to take advantage of the first full moon after Halloween to get into the river to look for eels and to experience this alien realm.

Terrestrial systems are different at night. They look different; they feel different. There are different creatures out. Things act differently. I expected the nighttime Octoraro Creek to be completely foreign. The place I have visited underwater hundreds of times would be, I was sure, hard to recognize.

I got to the water's edge and frequently looked over my shoulder. I was thankful for the full moon that lit up the stream valley with a warm, blue hue. However, I wouldn't have called it welcoming. There's a lot of human history there, and I've experienced a lot of tragedy in that area. As a paramedic, I have responded to drownings, overdoses, fatal car accidents, and shootings, all within a mile of this spot on the Octoraro, and their ghosts seemed close. So while the guiding moonlight took the edge off my nervousness, I was still a little jumpy.

I zipped up my drysuit, wriggled into my hood, and slid on my mask. I stepped into the stream, laid down, and was instantly disoriented. The spot I'd visited regularly was entirely different in the dark, where I could only see whatever was illuminated in a small foot-wide circle of light. Familiar boulders, logs, and root landmarks were hidden.

An eel rocketed upstream out of my beam of light. Maybe I caught the migration, finally. But it was just one, not the masses I had hoped for. Maybe the mythical mass migration was just a ghost too; a figment of what once was. I've never seen it, and I'm pretty sure that eel was a young one who was just out hunting. I pulled myself upstream, hoping to encounter a whole bunch of eels heading down.

Algae covered the bottom and waved in the current similar to fine olive hair. Leaves in the drift came into view just before they struck my mask, which made me more nervous. There didn't seem to be any fish, but I thought that either I was looking in the wrong places, or they'd taken off as soon as my light touched them. The bottom was a monotonous expanse of sand and gravel, in a stretch of stream that should have been riffle.

Erosion puts more sand and gravel into streams and smooths the irregularities of a diverse habitat, like rock and cobble, which cuts down on the number of species and individuals present. It looked like a hairy desert at night, and the algal fur that coated everything comes from too much nitrogen that we unintentionally put into the water by driving too much, not maintaining our septics, and overfertilizing our lawns.

Rocks came into view only after I was right upon them, it seemed, even though my beam extended 10 feet upstream. A small school of minnows hung and fed in the eddies. Finally, there was some life besides algae. Even though they were a nondescript, muddy brown, their metallic sides glistened when my flashlight caught them just right. Always, there is hidden beauty. Vision confined to a light beam became normal, and I continued to head upstream into the current. I wanted to observe the nighttime workings of familiar daytime ecology and, of course, look for migrating eels. Just as I got used to the unsettling feeling of leaves striking my mask without warning, and restricted vision, my light quit. I was in the middle of the stream with no light and leaves plastered to my mask by the current. It was time to go. I drifted toward the bank where I'd started and hauled out of the stream.

Moonlight reflected like white paint swirled on a black sea as I peeled off my wetsuit hood and drysuit. I felt more at ease. The only real ghosts there were the ones I'd concocted, and the ones of clean and abundant streams past, and maybe mass fall eel migrations.

I am often surprised by eels. When I am in a river looking for another organism, eels frequently show up. I was snorkeling Rio Mameyes, in El Yunque National Forest, Puerto Rico, specifically looking for Macrobrachiad shrimp.

Macrobrachiad shrimp from Puerto Rico.

These are large shrimp, often reaching a foot long, with enormous pincers. They are nocturnal, so I was in Rio Mameyes, alone after dark in the jungle, looking. I found a Macrobrachiad who waved his long, skinny pincers in the water at me like swords. I was fixated on this beautiful blue, red, and white animal when a nearly 4-foot-long, tennis-ball-thick eel swam between me and my camera. I almost jumped out of the river before I realized this was an eel. I followed her as she probed for food. Just like the eels I have come to know in my local Deer Creek, this large female hunted with intention and precision, checking under and around large boulders for shrimp and smaller fish prey.

The next day, I returned to Rio Mameyes farther upstream and farther into the jungle than where I had watched the large female feed the night before. I slid into the clear water and was surrounded by a school of mountain mullet whose black-and-white checkerboard bodies and yellow fins glowed in the bright sun. I swam upstream toward the head of the 75-yard-long pool. One bank of the river was volcanic bedrock. The other was a steep-sided cone of gravel that dropped to 15 feet. The mullet stayed with me, darting about, and occasionally nipped at my exposed toes. I watched tiny black-and-white banded *Awaous banana* river gobies barely an inch long use the thinnest of cracks in the water-smoothed black bedrock to hold against the relentless current. As I focused on staying put in the stream against the strong flow, to get some decent shots of the gobies, I noticed an eel hunting on the bottom in 5 feet of water. As I have watched in other eels, this fish was focused and intent on its task. It didn't notice me or a second eel that approached from downstream who was also hunting. They arrived on the same bare flat of bedrock before they noticed each other. They charged across the empty bottom and locked in a mutual bite that lasted for a few seconds, released, then swam off in opposite directions and continued the hunt.

The eel is one of our strangest fish, and one of our most fascinating, with an incredible life history. I am awestruck when I think of the physiologic changes these fish endure, going from a shallow, fresh ecosystem to an extremely deep and dark marine environment. They can survive this but may not survive us.

Eels were also one of our most common fish but are becoming less abundant, and some fish biologists are discussing the possibility of listing American eels as threatened. We have the opportunity to reverse this decline by removing dams and controlling sediments, and these actions will ensure the survival of this evolutionary and migratory marvel.

Darters

There were hundreds of darters at Principio Falls in Cecil County, Maryland. They had started gathering a few weeks ago, in the middle of February, and I guessed they were congregating to mate. My hunch was verified now that they started to display breeding behavior. These were tessellated darters, some of the most common we have in the mid-Atlantic. Males were covered in brown hashtags that formed bands against their gold bodies. Their dorsal fins were painted in golden and dark maroon bands, and they flared them tall and proud to entice a female, advertising they were the most fit based on their dorsal fin. I assumed it had to do with the size or color or how they waved it around, but it was apparently very important since they invested so much energy.

Tessellated darters were even in the falls themselves, right at the fall line where the Principio tumbles 30 feet over bedrock. I am always amazed at how a dainty-looking fish such as a darter can hang on in such intense conditions. Individuals wedged themselves into the thinnest of crags, barely wider than the edge of a quarter, and held against the current that I struggled against using fistfuls of bedrock. It was apparent this was their home and not mine. I hopped from waterfall pool to waterfall pool, each one as chaotic as the last, confused by entrained curtains of air bubbles. The constant underwater roar of falls didn't let any other noise in. Darters swirled in the currents as they moved from fissure to rock and back. It seemed they were at the mercy of the powerful flow, but after a little observation, it became apparent they were expertly using the twisting currents to navigate to get them where they wanted to go. For the males, this was near an undercut rock in the proximity of a female so he could flex his dorsal and hopefully entice her to mate.

Most fish have a swim bladder, which is a gas-filled chamber that helps control their buoyancy. Darters don't, and their tails are rounded, which makes them inefficient swimmers. Therefore, they spend most of their time on the bottom and move from place to place in short hops or "darts." Males choose spawning sites under overhanging logs or rocks and guard their spot. When a male sees a gravid female, he initially approaches her aggressively with a threatening display of fins erect. If she doesn't swim away, he tries to lure her into his nest.

Either fish initiates spawning by turning upside down with their stomach against the roof of the den. The other fish follows along, and the eggs are

Male tessellated darter guarding his spawning site.

released, fertilized, and stuck to the roof. Males guard the nest and care for the eggs by swimming upside down over the eggs with their pelvic fins gently brushing over them. There are 140 species of darter, and they are only found in North America. New species are still being discovered. They include some of the most ornately colored fish on the planet.

A few months later, I was snorkeling on the New River in Virginia. Just as I was packing up at New River Junction, Jeremy Monroe, director of Freshwaters Illustrated, called me to finalize our plans for the rest of the week. I was joining Jeremy and the film crew from Freshwaters Illustrated as they worked on *Hidden Rivers*, a movie about the freshwater biodiversity of the Southeastern United States. I develop curriculum to accompany many of Jeremy's movies, and I hoped to do the same for this effort. When Jeremy learned I was camping on the New River, he gave me a tip for a riffle that held candy darters, located in the Jefferson National Forest. I've seen pictures of these fish in field guides and wondered if the artists' renderings were more fiction than fact. I didn't think fish that brightly colored—red, orange, green, and turquoise—were supposed to live in North America.

The riffle didn't look like much from the surface. Not much more than shin deep and my body never fully floated. At least some part—a leg, my stomach— was always beached on a rock. However, as soon as I stuck my face in the water, a candy darter shot off. The fish was just as brightly colored as the field guide illustrations. They weren't artistic exaggerations. The candy darter had orange undersides with orange bands outlined in white against a turquoise background

Candy darter.

on its body. Its aquamarine fins were fringed with orange. It looked like someone had constructed a fish out of colorful Play-Doh and placed it in this stream until it shot off. Another darted from behind a rock, and I was able to slowly trail it upstream and snap multiple shots of the amazingly colored fish.

Many darters have limited ranges, which means they are threatened by extinction if something happens to the habitat or water quality in just a part of the small areas where they occur. It could be something we consider minor. Maybe a clearcut that chokes a small tributary with sediment. Maybe an accident that dumps 250 gallons of diesel from a saddle tank into a tiny unnamed stream. Or it could be something major, like a dam. These are the unknown fish that can easily slip from existence due to what we do on land, without thinking of unintended consequences. Candy darters have a limited range and were just listed as endangered. The world would definitely be a duller place if candy darters were to leave it.

One of the most ornately colored darters that lives in the streams I snorkel regularly is the greenside darter. Greensides are elusive. I have unsuccessfully chased them for weeks in Conowingo Creek just for the chance at a picture. I usually see them as dark green squiggles that quickly disappear somewhere into the bottom. They often look like algae blowing in the current, which is part of the problem.

A dark green smudge darted across the gravel flat of the Little Conestoga at the Lancaster County Conservancy Boyer Preserve. I barely saw it, so a positive identification wasn't possible, but based on the little that I had seen—dark green color, robust but small body, and fast bottom swimming—I was sure it had been a greenside darter. I hoped it was a greenside darter. The males get brilliant, emerald vertical stripes in spring and early summer. I really wanted to see this fish and maybe get a picture of it if I was lucky, so I searched the flat gravel bottom for 30 minutes but didn't see a thing. Not even other fish. Maybe seeing the possible greenside darter had been wishful thinking.

Greenside darters are one of those fish that, when in breeding color, don't look like they belong in this area. They look tropical, like I should see them in the Amazon Basin somewhere, or maybe the Congo. However, they are in the Little Conestoga, and I was determined to find one.

The Little Conestoga doesn't look like much, even under the surface. The water is milky, and stringy bands of dark green algae latch on to twigs and rocks and billow downstream. On a return trip, I didn't see any fish at first. Then I thought I saw some movement, but it must have been the algae. Then I saw it again, and a fish emerged into focus from the background. Finally, I was able to decipher their flowing algae camouflage and recognized a green darter before it disappeared so I could follow the fish and capture a photo of the elusive beauty. The fish looked smug. He held his head up high, snout up, and his mouth edges were downturned in a perpetual haughty pout. Emerald-green bands streaked up and down on his body against a dusky yellow background. He sat stoutly crossways to the current with his jade fins waving in the current until he finally swam off and disappeared into the background, and I floated back downstream in this heavily agriculturally impacted stream, very satisfied that greensides were here, despite the insults we throw at the Little Conestoga.

I came to the Tellico River to look for hellbenders, but the tangerine darters commandeered my attention. The Tellico in Tellico Plains, Tennessee, flows over

Male greenside darter.

TELLICO RIVER

Description: The Tellico is another southeastern river that harbors incredible diversity and has its own charm and personality. I know it as a spot to see tangerine darters set in a riverscape of incredible bedrock spires with canyons in between. Others know it as a place to see hellbenders. Either way, it is a place to see underwater.

Access: GPS Address: Tellico Beach Drive-In, 1801 Cherohala Skyway, Tellico Plains, Tennessee. Tellico Beach Drive-In is a landmark and historical fast-food restaurant that serves great food with an amazing view. And there is access to the Tellico River at their drive-in. You don't have to buy any food or ice cream, but I recommend it.

Tellico River.

a series of bedrock fins that transect the riverbed and break the surface. Between them is sandy, gravelly bottom under 4 to 5 feet of water. I snorkeled across the current and the river in one of the troughs between bedrock fins with a hellbender search image. I saw movement to my right and hoped it was North America's largest salamander, the hellbender. Instead, it was a flash of orange. I was a little disappointed until I looked closer. The orange spark was a male tangerine darter. Tangerines are large by darter standards, 3 to 4 inches, and their name is perfect for their color: brilliant tangerine-orange and black. I was not disappointed but reveled in watching this unbelievably, brilliantly colored fish. I let the current press me into the rockweed-covered downstream fin of bedrock and watched this male hop along the bottom looking for a mate. He held himself high on outstretched pectoral fins, to show off his glowing orange breast. The rest of his body was orange, too, except for the appropriately contrasting black, wavy stripe down his side. However, nothing glowed like the orange on his breast that he held high.

The brilliance of color of darters is an inexhaustible palette of color, though the fish themselves are very exhaustible, and we stand to lose many of them if we don't demand actions that ensure their existence. These fish challenge the perception that only tropical marine species are colorful show-offs. They are here among us, in our temperate streams. Tessellated, green, tangerine, and candy darters are just a small sampling.

An orange-green and aquamarine splotched male Tennessee snubnose darter shepherded a brown female around the stream. The brightly colored male seemed to protect the female as she searched for a suitable spot for her eggs. He hovered above her and mirrored her every move as she swam in overlapping circles looking for just the right spot to set the next generation of Tennessee snubnose darters on their way.

Immediately downstream, a redline darter laid on the bottom of a canyon formed by three boulders that shielded it from the current. I clung on to one of them with one hand and let the rest of my body trail downstream. The redline darter had red-tipped fins, as if they were dipped into brilliant crimson paint, and a dark body, which highlighted the red. They are absolutely striking fish and more proof that there is incredible beauty in the waters of our temperate streams and rarity living among us.

Tangerine darter.

Logperch are a kind of darter. They are larger than most darters—4 to 5 inches—and while darters often put on intense colors, logperch remain a striking, black-tiger stripped on a yellow-gold background. There are a dozen species of logperch in North America. I went to Alabama to run some snorkeling trips for 4-H groups, but a week of rain made river conditions unsafe for kids and reduced visibility. I had driven too far not to get wet, so I decided to take my chances in Hillabee Creek, which was near where I was camping.

The water was up and murky, even though it was a gorgeous, sunny early May day. The deep blue sky framed a line of mountain laurel in pink bloom along the bank, and Cahaba lily beds were just starting to show white blossoms. Mist rose off the fast-moving water. I laid down in an eddy just downstream of a flooded Cahaba lily patch. Their stalks looked similar to bamboo shoots underwater. Visibility was not ideal, only about a foot, and everything had a reddish-gray haze from the clay and mud washed into the river over the last week of rain. I pushed out into the faster-moving water over a sand bottom and dug my toes in to hold on. While I struggled, snails had no trouble crawling along in the stiff current. I just lay there head up into the current and watched the snails, who moved remarkably fast. That is, until a large, tiger-striped tube came into view. A mobile logperch landed on the bottom just beneath me and held its pointy nose up off the bottom on its large outstretched pectoral fins. This fish, like the snails, seemed to have little trouble with the current and I don't think the logperch noticed me or recognized me as foreign to the stream. Its tiger striping was remarkable and totally unexpected. I really didn't expect to see any fish, let alone a lifer. I had

Redline darter.

CITICO CREEK

Description: Citico Creek has a variety of habitats. Parts of it are more lake. Other parts are rushing white water over bedrock monoliths. Still other parts are cobble and gravel riffles. It is located in the Cherokee National Forest and is another stream noted for the aquatic biodiversity it harbors, with sixty-seven species of fish. Please be gentle on this, and all, streams. Minimize walking; just float and be. Don't disrupt spawning fish.

Access: Take I-75 to Loudon, Tennessee exit 72. Turn left onto TN-72, and head east for 15.6 miles to US 411. Turn left onto US 411 toward Vonore, and travel 2.4 miles to TN-360. Turn right onto TN-360 (Citico Road). After 7 miles, the highway turns right and crosses an embayment. Don't turn right; go straight ahead on Citico Road. Follow Citico Road for 12.5 miles to Young Branch Horse Camp. Turn right into the campground. A use fee is required.

Above: Citico Creek.

never seen a mobile logperch before, and even though much of the week was a washout, this scene remains one of my favorites, with the incredible flowered view above and tiger-striped view below, even if the fish was a little blurred by the murk.

While this was my first mobile, it wasn't my first logperch. I stood on the side of the 3-foot-deep pool in a southern Lancaster County, Pennsylvania, stream and shook my head in disgust at the four-wheeler tracks entrenched into the bank on my side of the 10-foot-wide creek and gravel bar on the opposite shore.

HILLABEE CREEK

Description: Hillabee Creek flows south from its origins in the Talladega National Forest through central Alabama forests, clear-cuts, pastures, and tree plantations. It drains into Lake Martin a few miles downstream, which is the dammed Tallapoosa River. The creek is large for a creek, and at this snorkel site, Hillabee Creek is 100 feet wide and mostly shallow with Cahaba lily patches growing on the gravel bars that form in the lee of bedrock outcrops that transverse the river. It is a truly beautiful spot, even though the access pull-off is abused. Bring a trash bag to do your part.

Access: GPS Address: 5958 Alabama Route 22, Alexander City, Alabama. From Alexander City, take Alabama 22 east for 6 miles. Access is a dirt road pull-off on the left just before the bridge.

Above: Hillabee Creek.

They had been using this creek and pool as their racetrack. I wondered if the people driving the four-wheelers knew the damage they were doing, or if they just didn't care. Running a vehicle through a stream totally disrupts and destroys bottom habitat, causes sedimentation, and kills benthic macroinvertebrates who can't escape and likely a bunch of fish who just don't move quite fast enough. Besides the ATV tracks, this creek was perfect. Two streams came together just upstream and tumbled over a bedrock shelf that scoured out this hole. I was sure there would be great fish to see despite the ATV disturbance.

The cold water took my breath away as it soaked between my skin and wetsuit. The warm June air made the water feel that much colder, and I gasped a few times until I got used to the chill and welcomed the relief from the heat. Chubs fed in the current, and rosy-sided dace flashed crimson and silver. I forgot about the ATV tracks as I floated in the pool and swirled among all of this life and color. Then a silvery, golden, tiger-striped logperch hopped along the bottom. Then another and another, and soon, I was in a school of at least a dozen Chesapeake logperch. I watched these fish as they used their cone noses to probe between rocks for insects. They even used their pointed snouts to overturn rocks, looking for benthic macroinvertebrates to eat. Such an ingenious feeding strategy. At the time, I didn't know what I was watching. I didn't know how rare these fish were. They are globally threatened and are being considered for federal endangered status in the United States. They only occur here in a small swath of lower Susquehanna River and its tributaries. I have seen these logperch in other places besides that first experience in the small beautiful stream abused by ATVs. However, every time I see them now, I pause, soak up the experience, and burn it to memory for when they are gone, so I can tell stories of logperch to my grandkids, when there aren't any more logperch to watch flip rocks for dinner. I wonder if the ATV riders knew how rare these fish were, and if they knew that by driving through the creek they were damaging them, they would stop. I like to think so.

Darters are in the perch family, though only the logperch members carry the name. I went to the Russian River in California's famed wine country not expecting anything, just to see what I could see underwater. I came back with a species of perch I had no idea existed.

Chesapeake logperch.

The Russian River is lined with towering redwoods whose trunks form more of a wall than a forest. This seemed promising for good water quality and clarity. However, this part of the Russian is far from good. It is impacted by land use, as is every river, which here means grapes and wine. There is a romantic aura around vineyards and the wine-making process, but it affects water quality. I wonder what the Russian was like before 85 percent of the sequoia were logged and its floodplains converted to vineyards. Water contact warnings due to blue-green algae bloom concerns were hammered into the gravel bar at Johnsons Beach. I made camp on the shores of the Russian, across from Johnsons Beach, and strung my hammock between two redwoods.

The moon cast long shadows that fell across the land and the silvery light made the redwood bark look gray. Stars shone through gaps in the canopy and cloud cover. I didn't know what to expect from the Russian, but after seeing the signs, it wasn't much. I tried to sleep and hoped this wasn't a wasted trip. I fell asleep marveling at the enormity of the redwoods that supported my hammock. These 5-foot-diameter, 80-foot-tall trees were just youngsters, and I couldn't fathom the magnitude of their grandparents.

I woke early and decided to go into the mountains to try to get above the poor water quality in the wine country valley and to get above where we dominate runoff. I headed for the Mendocino National Forest. It had been a bad year for fires in California, the worst on record, in fact. The Mendocino Complex Fire was still burning, though it was listed as 100 percent contained. I hiked out on a rocky bluff high above the Eel River and could smell wet campfire interspersed with faint, fresh smoke on the wind that steadily blew up the cliff. The opposite mountainside was a patchwork of black, green, amber, yellow, orange, and brown. Patches where the fire burned were interspersed among unburnt parts and changing autumn leaves.

I wound my way down to the Eel River that flowed through the valley far below. While I was not in the wilderness, I was alone far from help, should I need it. No one knew where I was, and I had no way of contacting help if there was even help to contact. I only heard wind and rattling kingfisher calls.

I hiked across a broad gravel flat that was lined with tall, thick willows. Water deposited lines of gravel downstream of boulders and grasses plastered to tree branches in a line 10 feet off the current bottom indicated this place experiences big floods. I felt the excitement and nervousness that unfamiliar rugged beauty generates. The water was smoky. Red-brown sticky silt covered the bottom of slower sections. The haze and silt were likely from the fire. Fires impact streams, too. Some kind of trout fed in an eddy formed by a large clump of grass.

The Eel is small but pushy, and a lot of water is conveyed in its thin channel. It started to downpour, and the water got hazier. I became acutely aware of water levels as I had no idea how much rain this creek's watershed was getting up the valley. I also didn't know how much of this creek's watershed was scorched

EEL RIVER

Description: The Eel River is one of the largest rivers in California and runs 196 miles through northwestern California to the sea. The river and its tributaries form the third-largest watershed entirely contained in California. The Eel River at Soda Creek is downstream of Pillsbury Lake, which is the impounded Eel. Water levels and flows here are dependent on dam releases and rainfall. The area can flashflood, so being aware of what the river is doing is critical.

Access: GPS Address: 26018 Elk Mountain Road, Potter Valley, California. Soda Creek enters the Eel River here. Traveling south on Elk Mountain Road, the pull-off is on the right.

Eel River, California.

so the rain it was receiving would immediately run off rather than soak in. It could flash. The rain knocked more things into the river from overhanging branches, so the trout picked up their feeding pace to take advantage of the windfall. I watched them as they plucked just about anything from the water column. Some of those things were food. Others weren't, and the leaves were spit out quickly. The rain caused a mini feeding frenzy. The trout were hitting it first and figuring out if it was edible second. I was still concerned about rising water and noticed that the shallow riffle just downstream got eerily quiet and was now covered. The eel had gone up an inch or two already, so I started across the heavy flow to my gear bag. Just as I got out, thunder rumbled down the valley. A bigger storm was on its way,

RUSSIAN RIVER

Description: The Russian River main stem is 110 miles long and flows through Sonoma and Mendocino Counties in California, the heart of wine country. It is a river of anomalies. It flows through a picturesque country, and much of it is lined with towering redwoods. However, the trees are just a thin veil, and right behind those majestic trees is a hard-worked agricultural landscape geared towards grape production. That results in questionable water quality at times. Understand that if you choose to ignore the posted water contact warnings, you accept the risk of possibly becoming ill. Also take care of your pet. Toxins from blue-green algae can kill dogs within hours of exposure.

Access: GPS Address: Sunset Beach River Park, 11403 River Road, Forestville, California. Follow the trail from the parking lot to the gravel beach.

Russian River, California.

and I dressed out of my drysuit in a downpour, which made wearing a drysuit pointless.

I returned to wine country and landed at Sunset Beach on the Russian River. The same water quality warning signs were hammered into the gravel, which I ignored. Thick willow tangles lined the shore. Behind them, sequoia touched the sky, though these juveniles were dwarfs compared to their giant grandfathers and grandmothers, who would still be standing if we hadn't taken them down. The Russian ponds here, backed up by a large gravel bar and shallow riffle. Fish dimpled the surface and sent concentric rings out from where they nabbed an insect. I was encouraged by the feeding activity that maybe I might see some fish. I slipped into the river as quietly and as stealthily as I could.

Murky water and algae covered a featureless bottom. I crept toward the banks, where the willow tangles dipped into the water, hoping that the structure would hold fish. However, a good current flowed through the willows, so I was cautious about getting hung on a strainer.

I watched what I thought was a new kind of sunfish for me, nesting under the willows. They had the flat oval body shape of a small sunny and were silver with black leopard spots. It looked like they were nesting in the submerged tangle of willow boughs, and I just watched as they darted through the branches with ease. I felt like I was disturbing the fish, so I slowly backed out of the willows, making sure to not let the current mat me to one of the submerged branches. I was able to take a few marginal photos, good enough to make a positive identification. These cute little leopard-spotted fish were tule perch, the only kind of freshwater surf perch. Their range is limited to central California. Because of its limited range, it is at risk, even if it isn't formally assessed as at risk.

I never knew these fish existed. Even if I had known they existed, it is entirely different to know these fish underwater on their terms. How many other freshwater species will I never know before they are gone? There is a timelessness to all this. A feeling that I am among beings and processes that make my life nothing more than a small, insignificant blip. And yet what I do directly impacts these timeless beings and processes. I either disrupt and kill or enhance and heal. That night, I had Dungeness crab cooked on an open fire beneath towering redwoods. I am so small and insignificant compared to these trees, yet I have the power to kill them. I am so small and insignificant compared to the rivers I snorkel, yet I can kill them too.

Tule perch.

CHAPTER 6

Minnows

I dug the toes of my wetsuit boots into the cobbles as I struggled to keep from getting flushed out of this riffle. It was hard to hold the camera with one hand, and every time I let go of the rocky bottom with the other to help stabilize it, the current turned my body sideways and forced me downstream. However, the fish I was working so hard to photograph held their position without much more than a few flicks of their tails. The cool water felt good in the early September heat, and the first fallen leaves of autumn twirled past.

I finally pushed myself upstream, flowed back down headfirst partly through the beginning of the riffle, and wedged myself, feet upstream, between two large rocks. This gave me a great vantage from which to watch the fish dart through the current to pluck whatever morsels of food flowed downstream. My feet took the brunt of the buffeting, which freed my hands to work the camera. I swore I watched something beyond the ordinary. The way those fish dashed through the current with the greatest agility to grab whatever my presence forced into the drift—that component of the creek's food supply, composed largely of insects that floated in the mid-water column. They picked off whatever I rubbed from the bottom and whatever the stronger current forced to the cobbles beneath me scoured from the rocks below.

They must have been built to migrate upstream long distances with such grace, something like a shad, or other migratory fish in the herring family. Their body shape was a little more rotund than the characteristic thin herring body form, but their aquatic dexterity surely put them in the same group as those great upstream athletic migrants.

I was disappointed when a biologist friend confirmed their identity from one of my pictures as common shiners. Nothing more than common shiners. The same fish I've captured in nets and traps from creeks from all over the mid-Atlantic for more than 30 years. I didn't think there was anything particularly special about these common fish. Not until I witnessed their swimming prowess in that riffle. All of my experience with shiners had taken place on my turf, in my dry element, on my terms. This was the first time I'd watched them in theirs, and my perception of them has been forever changed. These aren't the clunky, nondescript, unexciting silvery tubes flopping in the gut of a seine net any-more. They are fascinating, accomplished swimmers. Some of the most intense battles I've witnessed in the fish world were between male shiners defending breeding territory.

Seven months later, I entered the cool water of Deer Creek in late April. Spring showers made the water turbid, and visibility was poor. I was about to get out since I couldn't see more than a foot in front of me, and the current was strong enough to upend 30-pound boulders that I clutched on the bottom to maintain my place in the stream. I traversed a powerful riffle and came upon a gravelly slower section of the river. A school of common shiner in breeding color danced in the current. They were unrecognizable compared to their usual coloration. Their pectoral fins were pastel orange and yellow, and their bodies were iridescent red. The males slammed each other out of the way to claim the prime breeding spot and to attract a female above a pile of clean, white-and-orange rounded pebbles. These fish were rainbows in motion, iridescent spectrums of reflected light that flowed back and forth through the current. The battle seemed ruthless, and I couldn't understand what they were fighting for. The bottom looked all the same to me. However, the males constantly and solidly bumped one another out of what they considered to be prime territory, I assumed. Otherwise, the energy they invested in outing opponents made no sense. I was mesmerized. That is until another fish entered the view. This one was a long cylinder of tan with a black stripe on its side. It deposited a rock from its mouth onto the existing pile and then disappeared. It returned a few minutes later with another.

This was a creek chub. Chubs are another member of the minnow family. They are the architects of the stream. They create mounds of clean gravel for

Spawning male common shiners.

Chub building his mound.

spawning, and other species, such these common shiners, take advantage of it. The males grow hornlike tubercles on their heads in the spring. We really aren't sure of the purpose the tubercles serve. It may be to attract a mate. Maybe the male with the most horns wins the female. Or it might be to spar with other males. I have seen two chubs headbutt each other for the prime spot to construct a nest. Or maybe our poor attempts at defining their role and trying to understand the chubs' world and life through the lens of our reality falls way short of their true purpose. Regardless, watching male chubs build mounds is one of the most amazing feats to witness in our natural world. I once watched a chub construct his mound over 2 days. It started with bare bottom. He picked stones nearby and started to pile them between two large moss- and snail-covered boulders. He swam from his nest, mouthed a few rocks on the bottom until he found the right sized one he was looking for, carted it back to his mound, and spit it out. As his mound grew, he had to travel farther from it to find building materials. I watched this male carry a rock that was half his body length and likely weighed more than he did as his tail vigorously beat the bottom, body tilted at a 45-degree angle toward the surface, to make it back upstream to the mound. After he had a good mound started, a female showed up, and he spawned with her. Their fertilized eggs settled into the crevices formed by the rocky substrate he created. Then he rapidly gathered and placed another layer of gravel on top to prevent these eggs from being eaten by marauding suckers.

Other fish gathered. Tennessee shiners dressed in crimson red darted above the mound to find a mate. Crescent shiners with their iridescent, pastel, yellow-pink and orange bodies also took advantage of the chubs' work. Fierce-looking war paint shiners, dramatically colored with a white head, dark blue ring around their eye, red line above their upper lip, and a red vertical line just behind their eye competed for mates above the colorful masses below. Stonerollers whose chestnut-brown bodies were dotted with a grid of white tubercles dug breeding pits in the chub nest.

In the course of 2 days, this single male chub created a mound 2 feet tall and 4 feet wide and provided breeding habitat for three other species that I could see. Probably more that I didn't. Never think an individual can't make a difference.

All of these fish, all of this amazing diversity of color and shape and behavior are lumped together as shiners. There are 127 species of fish called shiners in North America, and it's often hard to differentiate one species from the next. Most of them are some sort of minnow, which is a real family of fish called "cyprinids." However, the common, nondescript name "shiner" is given to just about any fish that glistens a little and most fish that are used as bait.

They comprise nondescript throwaway individual beings and species. But watching them underwater makes them indispensable. I find this often, aquatic organisms that are written off as common or ordinary and mundane when we view them in air are fascinating in their own wet element, and the world becomes a less beautiful place when I think about it without them in it.

Black-nosed dace are common fish, distributed throughout New England, west through the Great Lakes, and south through Tennessee, northern Georgia, and Alabama. They even occupy the most urban of streams. They are mistakenly

Black-nosed dace.

called shiners by most, though I knew them as stripers when I was catching them as a kid in the suburbanized Pumpkin Patch Creek. They were interesting fish as they flopped in the bottom of my net, their silver side bisected with a distinct, clean black line. And while they were always a special catch and attractive in the air, in water, these fish are vibrant and thoroughly alive. They are fast and agile. Their colors were crisp out of the water in my net, but in the water, their colors are more complex: a silver body with a black stripe out of water becomes metallic gold above and silver below in water.

I nestled into the sandy bottom of the Elbow Branch in mid-May and let the cold-water chill become comfortable. Before me, a group of six black-nosed dace males swam in tight circles around as many females. The males' pectoral fins were brilliant orange and glowed against their gold, black, and silver bodies. A male and female pair swam off as the male flaunted his bright fins and orange-blushed sides. The female usually outswam the male and left him in clouds of silver mica-flecked sand kicked into the water by her fast-beating caudal fin. I watched this progression multiple times with multiple individuals, and I left the stream wondering if anyone spawned with anyone, or if this was just all show to size up the fitness of potential mates. All of these subtleties of color and behavior are lost out of water.

The Conasauga River in Tennessee and Georgia houses one of the most diverse fish communities in the world. Its waters are clear thanks to its forested watershed in Cherokee National Forest. I was there with Casper Cox, a river snorkeling and native freshwater fish advocate and pioneer. I pulled my way up to the end of a rapid section where Casper had placed his feet into the current and just watched the fish play out before him. Casper was great at picking a spot and just watching. I call him the "fish whisperer" because he uses his thorough knowledge of fish behavior to attract fish to him.

"Look here," Casper said. "There are two male Alabama shiners duking it out."

Just downstream from us two shiners fought the current as they head bumped each other out of place in the stream. Their colors were brilliant and unexpected: red tails and sapphire-blue dorsals. Powder blue pectorals and anal fins, steel blue sides that graded to a light indigo dorsal surface. White tubercles extended in a narrow band from their noses to dorsal fins, like short-cropped Mohawks. They twirled in the current, above green-and-purple rockweed-covered bedrock ridges, like brilliantly colored pinwheels in a breeze, and while it looked like colorful play, from the perspective of these two fish, so intensely engaged in battle, it was a gravely important matter. Alabama shiners are crevice spawners, and while all the crevices in the exposed bedrock shelf looked the same to me, to the intelligence of an Alabama shiner, there was something special about the particular crevice below the twirling males.

These two males went at each other repeatedly. First, one bumped the other out of place, followed by the displaced shiner regaining his spot, then the second

CONASAUGA RIVER

Description: The southeastern United States has more freshwater biodiversity than any other temperate region in the world. The Conasauga River is in the center of that region. The Conasauga flows 93 miles through southeastern Tennessee and northwestern Georgia and is home to ninety fish species and twenty-five species of freshwater mussels. The Conasauga snorkel hole is a popular swimming and snorkeling destination. It is located in the Cherokee National Forest. The US Forest Service manages much of the land in the Conasauga watershed, which is one of the reasons for its high quality and diversity. The snorkel hole is a large pool bounded on the upper end by an energetic riffle and the lower end by bedrock ridges. In between are a variety of habitats, including a hole that drops to 10 feet where drum like to hang out. There are also cobbles where darters and shiners like to be and sandy bottom for tadpoles and suckers, though each of these fish can be found anywhere in the snorkeling hole. This is one of those places at risk of being loved to death, so if you notice it full or overused, look for another spot. There is good parking and a pit toilet here.

Access: GPS Address: Conasauga Snorkeling Hole, Ocoee, Tennessee. From Cleveland, Tennessee, take 64 east for 8 miles. Turn right onto 411 south. Go 6.7 miles. Turn left onto 313 E/Ladd Spring Road. Continue onto Sheeds Creek Road for 5 miles. The entrance to the snorkel hole is the parking area for the Conasauga River Trailhead (#61). It will be on your right.

Above: Conasauga River snorkel hole.

bumped back. I watched this intense battle until Casper spotted a few tricolor shiner males doing the same thing. Casper engaged one male with the end of a pointer stick that he wiggled just in front of the fish to get the male to throw up his dorsal fin like an orange, black, and white banded flag. Tricolors' dorsal fins are orange, sky blue, and black with white rays radiating out from where the front of the dorsal joins the body. The coloration must be significant for communication the way this male threw his dorsal up against the finless stick. Their orange caudal fins, with electric-blue tips flashed and their translucent pectoral and anal fins, looked like orange cellophane. The iridescent powder blue tubercles on the Alabama shiner, as well as the orange, black, and white dorsal fins on the tricolor shiners, are examples of how male minnows experience some of the most drastic color changes in the animal kingdom during their breeding season. Species that are drab the rest of the year turn painted in order to attract mates.

Fishing Creek ambles through the farm fields of Lancaster County, Pennsylvania. It has problems associated with agricultural land use: sediments that smother its naturally rocky bottom and excess nutrient loads that fuel an overabundance of algae. However, it is still an amazing special place, and the Lancaster Conservancy has preserved a chunk of land around the lower section of this creek, where it cascades through a hemlock-shrouded, steep-sided valley, on its journey to join the Susquehanna. I set out to explore this place.

Water spills out from a 5-foot-deep, sand-bottomed pool into a series of bedrock outcrops that pierce the stream bed to form a gentle riffle that tumbles through sharp-edged rock peaks. I draped my wetsuit-clad body over one of

Male tricolor shiner.

Rosyside dace.

those spires to peer into the 2-foot-deep space between them. A brilliance of color burst in my mask as soon as I submerged. From the surface, the creek was drab tan. But below, a cloud of squirming, vibrant, aquamarine blue, red, and silver grabbed my attention. They looked like neon tetras with glowing blue and red sides. There was nothing drab about this creek. I watched this school spawn above a crevice in the bedrock finger, where a small chub tried to maintain a small pile of clean pebbles, but he looked a bit exasperated and finally just gave up his nest to the dace. I watched mesmerized for as long as I could until the cold water finally robbed enough body heat to cause shivering. I left the action over the bedrock outcrops and snorkeled my way toward the bank. I peered around the side of a large, midstream boulder into the shadow formed between the boulder and undercut bottom and saw clean red-and-silver fish fluttering in the current.

Both schools were rosyside dace, spawning. Rosysides are common, and I see them in just about every mid-Atlantic stream I snorkel. They are always spectacular, whether they are in breeding color or not. They occur from the Delaware to the north, south to the Savannah River, and west to the Ohio. While they are considered globally secure, pollution has resulted in the disappearance of many rosyside dace populations. Just because something is abundant doesn't mean it is safe. These are unknown fish, as common as they are. People don't know they exist. They aren't economically important. They aren't listed as threatened or endangered. Therefore, they are overlooked. But as I watched the neon blue-and-red rosysides spawn over the bedrock crevice and as I watched the clean red-and-silver lines of the school of rosysides holding in the shadows of the boulder, I worried that if the rosyside population extirpation trend continues, we might lose this color to watch in our streams, and the world felt a bit bland at the prospect of these fish being gone.

North Creek is a small headwaters tributary to the James River that flows through Richmond, Virginia, 275 river miles away. The watershed of North Creek is forested, covered mostly by Thomas Jefferson National Forest. It flows down the steep valley over short falls and around large boulders. It is one of my favorite streams to snorkel due to the clear water and abundant, diverse underwater community. I camped along North Creek in the middle of April. I planned on snorkeling the creek every 2 hours over a 24-hour period, just to see how it changed in the course of a full day. The wind howled as I tried to set up my tent, and it almost snatched it away before I could get it staked down. Trees bent and swayed, and the less-flexible ones snapped. A 50-foot white pine crashed to the forest floor 75 yards away. Snow squalls threw flakes sideways that stung like tiny darts and made the stream corridor blur to gray in the distance. I started to question the sanity of this. The weather was fierce.

However, a nice 6-foot-deep pool was right behind my tent, where the creek flowed down a short 3-foot falls. The upstream part was a straight-walled bedrock chute that extended half the length of the 50-foot-long pool. The downstream half was covered in large cobble and small boulders. I eased into the water where it tailed out to shallows, behind a Volkswagen-Beetle–sized boulder and pushed upstream against the stiff current. The smooth bedrock walls of the chute didn't leave much to grab, but I was able to use narrow fingerholds to pry myself into the current. It felt like aquatic rock climbing. I picked my head out of the water. The banks were greening with spring: ferns were unfurling, and violets, bloodroot, and Dutchman's breeches wildflowers were pushing out of the forest floor. Trees were starting to bud, and red maple blossoms added a frothy, pink cloud to the swirling white-gray snow. Above, the atmosphere was loud and chaotic. The wind still tore at trees, and I wondered if the ones lining the stream might come down on me. Snow was pushed in sideways sheets. Beneath, the stream was calm. A constant hum of water flowing over rock replaced the unnerving wind gusts.

I flowed downstream with the current, relaxed with the weightlessness, and forgot about the storm raging above for a minute. I tucked back in behind the large boulder where I had started an hour earlier. A churn of red, yellow, and black grabbed me. Swirling masses of mountain redbelly dace replaced the driving snow squalls.

These are some of the most dramatically colored fish I know. The side of their body is bisected by a thick, black line that is interrupted by a parallel gold streak so that the black line breaks into two parts, with a gold sloping mark dividing them. Above these competing black-and-gold lines, black leopard spots cover the daces' gold bodies. Their dorsals are brilliant yellow. Below, their bodies

NORTH CREEK

Description: North Creek is a small stream that flows out of an entirely forested watershed within the George Washington and Jefferson National Forest in western Virginia. It tumbles through boulder-filled riffles and pools. North Creek is a beautiful, special place, and these clear waters form the headwaters of the James River. Creek-side camping is available at the Forest Service North Creek Campground.

Access: GPS Address: North Creek Campground, 2252 North Creek Road, Buchanan, Virginia. From I-81, take exit 168 Buchanan. Turn left onto 614. Take 614 to North Creek Road. Turn left on North Creek Road and follow up the valley. There are numerous opportunities to snorkel pools at pull-offs along the way.

North Creek.

are crimson with yellow pectoral, anal, and caudal fins.

A school of twenty of these painted gems gathered in the lee of the large boulder. The creek here was dimly lit due to the ongoing snow squall above and the overcast shadow of the boulder below. The dace rapidly twirled around each other as bursts of color in this dark place, looking for the right mate. Some of the females were rotund; they were ripe with eggs. The dace were frenzied to spawn. Two chestnut-brown stonerollers, whose bodies were covered in white spike tubercles, added to the agitation by piercing through the ball of dace to suck up recently released eggs from the bottom. It was reminiscent of oceanic bait balls and the predators they attract. I watched the dace until my shivering became uncontrollable. The air was only 40 degrees, and I had no great way of getting warm outside of peeling from my drysuit as fast as possible, putting on layers, and trying to build a fire in the wind and snow, which I was able to do successfully though my cold fingers didn't want to work through most of the process. I warmed by the fire and cooked dinner and tried mentally to prepare for my next snorkel just an hour away. The wind still screamed down the valley, and the large pine it brought down so close to my camp was still an unnerving reminder of my vulnerability. Then I remembered that life is ephemeral anyway and questioned what exactly security was. However, mostly I thought about the dace, their brilliant colors, and the complex behavior that I didn't understand and mostly how privileged I was to be a witness to it all.

Sometimes it's the color that amazes; sometimes it's the volume of fish. Banded killifish are some of the most common and abundant fish in the upper Chesapeake Bay. While banded killis are in a different family (Fundulidae) than minnows (Cyprinidae), they are lumped into the generic group "minnows" by most people. They are food for a variety of predatory fish, which explains why banded killis are also used as bait, and they can be found in bait shop aquaria right next to the common shiners. I slid into Principio Creek on Thanksgiving Day, where it tumbles down the fall line of exposed granite and turns into a coastal plain stream. From the surface, it looked normal. However, as soon as I submerged, I was in the middle of a surreal view. I was surrounded by a school of banded killis that I estimated to contain about 3,000 fish. Individually, they were striking, with thin, black vertical bands on their sides against a pale blue-yellow body with metallic

Large schools of banded killifish gather in small Chesapeake tributaries on Thanksgiving.

FISHING CREEK YORK

Description: Fishing Creek is a small tributary to the lower Susquehanna River Riverlands region. It flows through York County farm fields and forms a steep-sided gorge in the lower sections. Despite its agricultural roots, it is a beautiful stream in the lower reaches where it flows through hemlocks and large hardwoods. The streambed is made of smoothed exposed bedrock, large square blocks, and rounded cobble and boulders.

Access: GPS Address: 2150 Fishing Creek Road, Wrightsville, Pennsylvania. From Wrightsville, take 624 south for 5 miles. Continue onto the long, level road for a quarter mile and straight onto Fishing Creek Road for a half mile. Park at the bridge, and hike in about a quarter mile to where the flowing stream meets the ponded water off Lake Clarke.

Above: Fishing Creek, York County, Pennsylvania.

aquamarine flecks near their head and on their opercula gill coverings. Collectively, they take my breath away. Individuals moved slowly so that the entire mass shifted in unison out of my way as I floated downstream, like swimming through a cloud of fish. And just like clouds darken the sun, this school of banded killis turned the stream dim and made the sun appear as an amber glow as it shone through thousands of translucent yellow-banded killi bodies.

I have returned to Principio on Thanksgiving Day ever since discovering this phenomenon, and each year the banded killis are gathered thick. They hide in the rich underwater vegetation of the upper Chesapeake during the growing season for protection. I think they seek out the shallow waters of these tributaries as temporary protection from large predators when the underwater grasses die back in the fall. They likely hang out here until the water cools and the predators go inactive, because I only see them en masse in our small bay tributaries for a few weeks right around Thanksgiving.

I have seen this large gathering behavior in other species. I once encountered a huge school of spottail shiner where Fishing Creek empties into Lake Clarke, which is the Susquehanna River backed up behind the Safe Harbor Dam.

I hiked in along the Mason-Dixon Trail from the parking area, through a magical hemlock forest, the day after Thanksgiving. Thin skim ice had formed on the margins of the stream the night before and was completely invisible, except that it made the surface of the stream perfectly flat, and wavelets dimpled the ice-free parts. I suited up on a bedrock slab and felt guilty for breaking the perfectly pure skim ice to get in the water.

I was struck by the late fall colors. The ice cast a blue hue underwater, and the creek flowed over large, flat, thick wafers of metallic, slate-blue schist, which added to the blueness of the stream. Green from the hemlocks flickered through the reflective surface. The water looked blurry downstream of where the flowing water met the impounded, and I assumed this was due to significant differences in water temperatures that create thermal waves and make everything look blurry. However, as I slowly drifted downstream in the cold water, I realized I was looking at a huge school of spottail shiners, at least a thousand fish strong.

These are common fish and nondescript. They don't have elaborate fins or brilliant colors. They are easily overlooked and mundane. Their only distinguishing characteristic is a dark spot on their tail, thus the name spottail shiner. However, collectively, the school added yellow to the blue-and-green underwater palette. Waves on the surface made the sunlight strobe and caused the school to flash.

Watching thousands of the fish shoaled up was wondrous. Why were they all there? Were they congregating to spawn? Or were they taking advantage of food flowing into Lake Clarke from Fishing Creek?

Spottails are considered unimportant. No one catches them, and only a handful of people realize they even exist. However, swimming with these fish was like moving through a school of fish holding on the Great Barrier Reef; they were that abundant and moved in choreographed unison.

Just because they aren't economically important or noticed doesn't make them less valuable. All fish serve important roles in the ecology of our rivers and streams. Watching them live in their element highlights that importance. There's nothing common about the common.

CHAPTER 7

Tomcod

The idea was ridiculous. Wake up at 5 a.m. on New Year's Day 2019, drive 12 hours to Machias, Maine, and jump into a frozen river after dark to look for a fish that probably wouldn't be there because I probably missed its small spawning window.

"Sure, yeah, I'll meet you there," I agreed to meet a stranger at a place I didn't know. As the temperature dropped and the snow deepened the farther north I drove, I wondered if this was a wise decision.

I was going to meet Brett Ciccotelli, a biologist with the Downeast Salmon Federation. He told me to look for a silver pickup with a cap on it parked on the side of a dark road covered in patches of ice. That describes just about every pickup in this part of Maine. However, he was right where he said he would be and came booming out of his truck. I was road-weary from driving 13 hours.

"I think we will start here, then go to Hog Bay. I didn't see any last night, but they may be there now."

My fatigued brain had a hard time keeping up. Brett was intense. This was all on his own time, and I was grateful. I would never be able to find these fish on my own. He led me to a small dirt track that was covered in ice.

"It's all frozen, so you shouldn't get stuck in mud," he said as he jumped back into his truck. I followed him onto an ice-covered dirt road in the complete darkness of a Downeast Maine night.

The first stop was a small tidal creek where the Downeast Salmon Federation had removed a dam. Brett had a tomcod trap set there. I struggled to keep up with him physically, too. He walked fast and assuredly on sheets of ice that had formed throughout the fresh tidal marsh, while I gingerly penguin walked and tried to look like I knew what I was doing. The trap was empty, and we headed to the next stop, Hog Bay.

We know tomcod biology, but there are still, and I hope always will be, mysteries. Their reproductive timing is one of them. They are fickle spawners and swim into the mouths of freshwater rivers at the head of the tide to reproduce right around the winter solstice. That's how they got one of their common names: frost perch. There doesn't seem to be any rhyme or reason as to where or when they will be in a given stream. At least, it was no pattern that makes sense to us, but to tomcod, it is all probably entirely logical.

Their reproductive routine makes it even more difficult for us to assess their presence. They spawn at night on a high tide that reaches up into the fresh tributary, so the fish can get into the rocky parts to procreate. How do they know how to do that?

"They aren't strong swimmers," Brett remarked. "So the tide helps get them to the rocky habitat they need to spawn."

I may have missed my small window to watch these fish in fresh water this year. The run on the East Machias ended 2 days ago, Brett didn't see any here at Hog Bay last night, when he left a New Year's Eve party to check, and the tomcod traps the mostly volunteer tomcod assessment team of the Downeast Salmon Federation sets to monitor the fish have been empty the last two nights.

Dwayne Shaw, the executive director of Downeast Salmon Federation, met Brett and I at Hog Bay. I couldn't see much of the water since it was a coal-black night. We waited for the tide to just about crest before I suited up into my fleece undersuit and drysuit. I watched the heavens as we hiked through the woods to Card Mill Stream. I forget how abundant stars are in a sky not polluted with light but was reminded of that vast universe we are a part of, and participants in, as I looked up through the balsam firs at an infinite number of lights. It felt remote, like I was in the middle of the Maine wilderness. But Hog Bay Road was just 100 yards downstream. I could only hear the water rushing over the boulders and the occasional crunch of ice.

I had to break skim ice to get into the freezing dark river after being up for 17 hours. I could very well end up being awake for 24 hours straight, all for what I thought was likely a wasted effort. I was probably too late by a day or two to see the spawn and these fish this year. I really doubted my decision as the freezing water stung my lips and penetrated my neoprene gloves. Dwayne and Brett tried to spot tomcod from the shore and to direct me if they saw any.

The lights attached to my camera housing frame barely illuminated the tannin-stained waters, and even then, there was a gray haze in the light. I scanned the bottom back and forth for a fish I thought wasn't here. I felt like I was putting on a show of effort more for Dwayne and Brett than for actually seeing tomcod. They invested time in being here with me. I didn't want them to think it was a waste when I didn't find any tomcod. I wanted them to think I made a valiant attempt and the fish just didn't cooperate. I wondered if I was willing my own failure to see these fish and started to genuinely search after I noticed some kind of motion in the periphery of the light cone. Maybe the tomcod really were here. Maybe I would actually see one. These were tough conditions because of the cold, dark, tannin water and current, and so even if I were fortunate enough to see a tomcod, I doubted my skill as an underwater photographer to capture an image.

I clung to the bottom to keep from getting pushed out into the estuary, though my self-rescue plan was simply swimming for shore once the current tailed out.

I didn't want to have to try that strategy. I passed a bodiless tomcod head as I clawed upstream, evidence that these fish were definitely here.

I looked at a piece of wood that was wedged between two rocks. Something wasn't quite right about it, which led me to study it until the piece of wood swam off. It was a tomcod. They were here! My search for these fish became intense. I had a limited amount of time before my hands wouldn't function due to the cold, and I wouldn't be able to hold my camera. I had already wasted too many minutes establishing their presence. I needed to find these fish. I swam farther upstream into the blackness through a boulder section of bottom. I shone my hand held light into the crevices and saw a few tails. They had a mottled greenish-purple pattern. I was on to tomcod! I watched six or so slither between, under, and around basketball-sized rocks. They moved similar to eels or lamprey through a boulder field, perfectly fit for this habitat and the habitat perfectly fit for them.

A heavy current made me hold on to one of the rocks with one of my hands, which meant that that hand couldn't hold the spotlight to find the tomcod hiding in the shadows. I finally figured out how to prop myself in the current by bracing my feet against a downstream rock, which freed up both hands to manage the camera and hand light that I needed to penetrate the shadows between the large cobbles. The fish tried to elude my light. I shot photo after photo hoping to catch just one usable image, but these fish are skittish and hid in the shadows in the jumble of the boulder field. Often, all I would see was a tail hanging out with the fish's head buried in a gap under a boulder. I kept using my light to try to flush these fish into the open so I could get a photo, and they consistently outsmarted me by presenting

A male tomcod wriggles between boulders.

only their tails. I think the tomcod I watched in this boulder patch were all male, because they were smaller and greenish rather than purple-brown and large. Finally, my diligence paid off, and I was able to coax one out by shining my light behind it. I pulled the camera housing trigger as fast as I could work my frozen finger and hoped at least one shot came out. They are cute fish with barbels that hang from their lower lips. They have a gentle aspect about them, and they just kind of slink among the boulders. I just wanted to spend time with these fish and not worry about framing them in the camera viewfinder, but capturing their image was important to telling their story. They are forgotten and invisible.

"But they used to be known," Sarah Madronal said as I met with her the next morning to learn more about tomcod and develop a plan on where I might see tomcod in other Downeast streams. Sarah is the tomcod project manager for Downeast Salmon Federation, and she and her mostly volunteer team survey forty locations for tomcod.

"Lots of people used to fish for them. There is high local knowledge in the older generation," Sarah added. "But most people don't know about them anymore."

Tomcod were commercially harvested from the 1920s and 1930s through the 1950s. They were called London fish and were considered a delicacy, with sweet, delicate white flesh. Tomcod caught in bold coast rivers were shipped to Boston. Spearing was the typical capture method, and the Downeast Salmon Federation still hears stories of people who had a Christmas Eve tradition of going out to the head of the tide on creeks to spear tomcod for their Christmas stews.

They were important before they were commercially fished. Archaeologists expected to find herring bones when a Downeast Native American site was excavated. Instead, they found tomcod.

The tomcod population dropped due to pollution and overfishing, so people don't fish for them anymore. "Except for a few old-timers," Sarah qualified. "They are a forgotten fish."

Institutional knowledge is even gapped. The Maine Department of Fish and Wildlife didn't know if there were regulations governing the take of tomcod when Sarah was applying for the permits she would need to do her survey.

The first tomcod survey done by the Downeast Salmon Federation was completed in 2017. Before that, 1987 was the last report anyone had done on tomcod populations.

"Downeast Maine is a black hole for data. I'm just trying to get basic information," Sarah said. "We don't know what their population is or changes in their distribution. They arrive around the solstice, but we don't understand why or how or where they come up to spawn. This year to last, we are seeing them in different places."

Sarah and her team of twenty volunteers surveyed forty locations for tomcod this year. Some of those were trapped. Others were assessed based on the presence or absence of fish-eating birds. Tomcod or signs of tomcod were at 50

HOG BAY

Description: Hog Bay is a finger of ocean that pokes inland around Mount Desert Island to form the Mount Desert Narrows. It ends where Card Mill Stream flows into it at Hog Bay Road. The stream is covered in thick Maine forest, mostly balsam firs, and creates a picturesque scene. There is a 12-foot difference between high and low tide, so this place changes dramatically. Consider tide as part of your trip planning unless you intend to hike above the head of the tide. Use caution if snorkeling on an outgoing tide as tidal currents here can be very strong.

Access: GPS Address: 226 Hog Bay Road, Franklin, Maine. This will put you in the vicinity of the bridge that crosses Card Mill Stream. There is a pull-off on the north side of the bridge, on your right if you are driving north on Hog Bay Road. It is a short hike to the creek.

Above: Card Mill Stream flows into Hog Bay.

percent of the locations surveyed. However, this is a presence/absence survey and provides little information on population size or trend.

"I know places that have larger populations but don't know about population numbers," Sarah said. "We found them in places where they aren't listed as present in the most recent study."

When asked what threats there are to tomcod, Sarah paused. "Well, it's not overfishing since they really aren't fished, and they don't seem to be sensitive to pollution." Tomcod are famous for having adapted to heavy PCB contamination in the Hudson River, with no apparent ill effect.

"Their biggest threat is not knowing they exist," Sarah declared. "And a lack of data to make decisions so we can be proactive rather than reactive."

I decided to return to Hog Bay to catch an incoming tide that was forecasted to crest 2 hours after sunrise. I arrived an hour before dawn. The deepwater river I had snorkeled the night before had become a shallow, rocky riffle. I'm not used to 12-foot tides. I got in anyway, hoping that maybe some frost perch might be riding the rising waters through the cobble to the head of the tide, the spot where the high tide ends and flowing river water begins. The morning sky was a little lighter than the night before, but I still needed my head lamp, hand light, and camera lights to see. I scraped my way upstream over bottom that I had easily floated past two nights ago.

The boulders where I watched the tomcod were mostly out of the water. I probed around their bases, hoping I might watch some fish, but the only thing I saw was a headless tomcod body. I found another as I drifted back downstream. I was disappointed that I didn't see live tomcod. However, finding the bodiless heads, while macabre underwater, was significant. These fish play an important role in providing nutrients upstream, and a whole system of predators depend on this fish at a time of year when food can be scarce. Diving, fish-eating ducks feast on frost perch, and my guess is these remains were either eaten by ducks or otters.

It started to snow when I got out of the river, and 6 inches had fallen by the next morning. White covered everything as I drove to the Pleasant River at Columbia Falls where the Downeast Salmon Federation office is located. This is another converted powerhouse, like their Peter Gray salmon hatchery. There is a series of falls here, where the Pleasant rushes over bedrock ledges in its last run as a river before it turns to estuary. A concrete wall was added to direct the force of the Pleasant River through turbines that were located in the basement of the Downeast office. A small hatchery is where the turbines used to be. Most of the dam has been removed, but a few patches of concrete are still visible. The biggest waterfall, immediately downstream of the old dam site, drops 10 feet at low tide and disappear when they are covered by the high. It was a long shot to see tomcod, since it was daytime. But the tide would be high, and there was a possibility. No one ever snorkeled the waterfall hole for tomcod before.

The river here braids through bedrock outcrops. Snow covered everything: trees, bedrock islands, and the ice formed on the slower-moving channels. Everything was slick. I carefully followed Brett out to the river.

"You might want to move away from the edge," Brett advised as we started across the first channel and I inched a little too close to a crag that used to be dam crest.

"There is nothing slicker than snow on ice, and it would be embarrassing to fall over that," Brett pointed to the ledge a foot away that led to rocks 15 feet below.

The tide was in, so the falls were submerged by 10 feet of tannin-stained, dark-tea-colored water. Shelf ice grew out into the river as a ring that mirrored the contour of the bedrock monolith and was under a foot of water, so that it looked orange through the tannins. Brett climbed over the 15-foot-tall rock as I gingerly stepped onto the shelf ice to inch my way around its point. I wasn't sure if I would break through and land in 10 feet of water, and while I was already in my drysuit, we hadn't scouted this site to look for currents that might push me downstream.

"There is a big eddy here," Brett called down. The eddy was upstream circulating water, which was my second safety plan. My first was to stay in contact with the edge, one hand on the shelf ice, to keep from getting swept downstream, which was covered in thick ice. All of the volume and force of the Pleasant River flowed beneath this ice. I wouldn't have much of a chance if the current were to suck me under. Plan C was Brett, an accomplished whitewater paddler, who stood by with a throw bag. My last-ditch strategy was to swim at the edge of the ice and vault onto it like a seal. This is much more difficult than it sounds, as it would be easy for my legs to get caught in the current and pull the rest of my body with them. I had my plan, and let Brett know. I put my neoprene hood, gloves, and mask on, sat on the ice shelf, slid into the water, and hoped I could touch bottom. That would be more assurance that I could stop an uncontrolled downstream run. My feet touched, finally, in chest-deep water. I let go of the ice with one hand, hung on with the other, let my feet come off the bottom, and floated. I tested the current. The bulk of the force was in the middle, so it was easy for me to navigate. I relaxed and let the river come into view.

It was frenzied and Martian. While the 10-foot falls was submerged on this tide, shorter drops just upstream made the underwater realm loud. Entrained fine bubbles made it hazy, and the tannins turned it all red. Dark green rockweed was mashed flat to its orange bedrock anchor and looked similar to black, thin fingers that quivered in the current. Slush accumulated on the bottom 5 feet below. Bands of it filled in some of the gaps on the bottom out in the main flow and grew toward the surface. It looked like coagulated fat and made everything blurry.

This is a phenomenon called anchor ice that forms during periods of extreme cold. Water dips below the freezing point, but ice can't grow on the surface due to the moving water. Ice platelets develop in the water column and gather on the bottom. Sometimes, anchor ice creates a thick blanket and can cause rivers to flood. Flocculent bits of ice smacked my face and stung.

I crept around the bedrock point, still nervous about the downstream ice sheet. Brett watched overhead, ready to throw a line should I need it. The river here was less loud, which decreased the chaos, and I relaxed after getting a feel for the current and my ability to stay put. A salmon parr lazily drifted in the lee of ice peninsulas that jutted into the current. The fish was entirely unexpected, and its yellow-and-red spots and gray vertical bars were accentuated by the white-orange ice tannin water background.

The bottom dropped away to nothing on the downstream side of the bedrock island, and I was floating on a wall of ice that plunged out of sight in the red

Ice covers parts of the Pleasant River at Columbia Falls, Maine.

distance. Brett thought he saw a stickleback on the ice shelf here, so I spent some time looking but didn't see any. It was unnerving to float over water that dropped to an abyss. While reason told me the bottom was 15 feet below, it could have just as well been 1,000.

I didn't see tomcod but got to experience a river from a very different perspective and learned a little bit more about how these systems operate. I am grateful that I had the opportunity to see how life is in these streams have adapted to survive cold coast rivers in winter.

What started as a crazy idea—snorkel Maine rivers in freezing conditions near the winter solstice to look for a forgotten fish—turned into one of the most extraordinary snorkeling experiences I have ever had. Whenever and wherever I look underwater, I am enthralled with the beauty and intricately tuned biology, no matter the season.

CHAPTER 8

Sculpin

There wasn't much going on in Deer Creek concerning fish during an early spring snorkel. The water was still frigid, nothing was moving, and I didn't see anything between the cobbles besides a few caddisflies. The water was fast and hazy due to recent rains, and I was just about to get out. I traversed the hard current across a set of riffles just to enjoy the rush of water and the feeling of flying one more time when two large, green eyes peered back at me from between two rocks on the bottom. The sight startled me. I wasn't sure what animal they belonged to. Once I realized they weren't moving but just watching me, I crept in for a closer look. I saw a huge downturned mouth on a large head, attached to a small tail in comparison. This was a sculpin. They look similar to tadpoles with a big head relative to their skinnier tail, kind of like a giant comma.

Sculpins live on the bottom and are ambush predators. They are amazingly camouflaged to blend in with their surroundings and patiently wait for insects or other fish to wander by. Their face is dominated by a huge mouth that they whip open to suck in unsuspecting prey. Smaller sculpin eat mayflies while larger ones eat caddisflies, crayfish, and worms. Smaller sculpins are often eaten by larger ones. A common belief among trout fishermen is that sculpins eat trout eggs, but the converse is true: trout eat sculpins, which explains why sculpin fly patterns are popular with fly fishers.

This unexpected encounter motivated me to check out a small tributary to Deer Creek, Big Branch. I know this creek well since I snorkel it regularly. It is one of the most dynamic streams I know, and as familiar as I am with it, it usually changes between trips. This time, newly cobbled riffles had formed beneath a large beaver-controlled pool, due to a rearrangement of the beaver dam, which redirected water flow and scoured the finer particles from the larger rock. I wasn't there for more than a minute before a northern hog sucker sped downstream and disappeared into a collection of leaves and beaver chews hung up on the bank. I looked for the fish in the tangle and noticed a sculpin looking back at me from the gravel bottom.

I knew sculpins should be there but have never seen any, and for as many times as I have been in Big Branch, I was starting to wonder if maybe the bottom was just too sandy to support sculpins. However, I realized it was likely their camouflage that made it seem that Big Branch was sculpin free. The orange band on a dorsal fin attached to a tan and white mottled body barely stood out from the amber white and tan gravel background. Once I was able to discern one from the background, they all seemed to pop out, and I realized juvenile sculpin were dominant in this gravelly stretch. They dissolved into the background as soon as I took my eye off them. These juvenile sculpin stand a good chance of being eaten by a trout or another sculpin.

A male sculpin staked out a cavity under a rock and swam short distances to entice an egg-laden female into his abode, where they turned upside down, pressed their abdomens to the ceiling of the male's newly constructed home, and stuck fertilized eggs to the roof of the void. The female swam away shortly after and escaped being eaten since males eat smaller females. The male stayed with the eggs to fan them, which would keep them silt free. Sculpin eggs don't do well in sediment.

A year later, I snuck out of a conference in western Pennsylvania in the early spring and slipped into a mountain stream that must have been choked by sediment a century ago, during the heyday of the Pennsylvania lumber boom when forests were clear-cut and soils flowed into our creeks. This visit was much different, and what was likely a silted-in stretch of creek one hundred years ago was now a clear pool lined in clean granite rock.

A sculpin emerged from the background, which closely matched the fish's patterned coloration. Gray, white, and tan spots speckled the sculpin's body. Huge, rayed pectoral fins helped keep the fish on the bottom, and starred eyes stared back at me. The river had been restored, but that didn't mean there weren't

Mottled sculpin.

LINN RUN

Description: Linn Run is a small trout stream in southwestern Pennsylvania. It bounces and bubbles around granite boulders and over bedrock shelves. Its valley is covered in hemlock, hardwoods, and laurel. Linn Run State Park protects 612 acres of it.

Access: GPS Address: 770 Linn Run Road, Rector, Pennsylvania. Linn Run Road runs along the stream. There is a parking area for the state park on the left, with easy access to the stream.

Linn Run, western Pennsylvania.

any threats. While sculpin are common right now, nothing is guaranteed forever. A new threat could emerge and wipe them out. I never take anything for granted in our streams, no matter how common a species is, so I spend the afternoon watching, admiring, and appreciating the fish that are all mouths with tails hop from nook to cranny as they hunt for food in a currently clean stream.

Mottled sculpin seem to be more abundant in winter and early spring in mid-Atlantic streams. At least I see them most in this transition between painfully freezing water and almost bearably cold. Maybe it's because there aren't many other fish out this time of year, so they get my attention despite their cryptic coloration. Or maybe they are actually more abundant in this cold biological doldrums of a season because the fish that would normally eat them are hunkered down for a winter twilight slumber. Sculpins are specially adapted for cold water with specialized antifreeze glycoproteins in their blood, and maybe that keeps them more active through late winter into early spring.

Stoney Creek is a nondescript suburbanizing stream, located in the geographic no-person's-land, between piedmont and coastal plain in northeastern Maryland. It has the typical features you would expect to see where houses are taking over woods. The stream is far from pristine, and while it's not filled with trash, it isn't clean. White and blue plastic grocery bags occasionally hang from branches arching over the stream, where they were plastered during the last flood. Stream corridors make convenient routes for sanitary sewer mains, and Stoney Creek isn't any different. Manhole monuments of concrete and steel rise 5 feet above the floodplain. Amtrak trains scream through a thin veil of woods that hides them from sight, and the back of a new shopping center perches on a hill overlooking the stream. A homeless encampment of three tents sits in the skinny strip of woods between the creek and shopping center. It's a typical stream, tucked into the folds of suburbia and forgotten.

I slipped beneath the surface, and as usual, a whole new world appeared. Algae covered everything and created an otherworldly scene where flowing golden fur glowed in the sunlight everywhere I looked. It was like swimming through a painting of a make-believe world. While the view was interesting, it was also expected. That much algal growth is a sign of an overfertilized creek, and most of our suburban streams are overfertilized by nutrients that run off from our yards and streets. I figured this trip would be mostly about witnessing incredible stream-scapes and geologic architecture rather than seeing life.

The water was extremely cold, and after just a few minutes, it penetrated my drysuit and insulating layer and chilled through to my skin. Knives of cold

Winter mottled sculpin.

stabbed my exposed face the minute I got in the water, and soon, my thighs started to sting. I saw a lone caddisfly on a rock, and as I watched the caddis graze, a sculpin darted from under a cobble out into the open.

It had large, downturned, puffy lips that defined the edges of a mouth that took up most of the fish's face and a tapered body shape camouflaged in mottled tan and gray. A bright orange band framed the edge of its dorsal fin. It was perfectly constructed to be an ambush predator. This fish was well-hidden and waited for an unsuspecting aquatic insect or tiny fish to wander by, when it would explosively snatch the prey.

Sculpin are pretty common in cleaner water, but I had never seen a sculpin in this area and certainly hadn't expected to see one in this suburbanized, sewer-lined, forgotten stream. Sculpins inspire hope in me, especially sculpins in this impacted stream. They require cold water and relatively sediment-free substrate. When I find them in a creek that has a developed watershed, I wonder if the sculpin are adapting or maybe our sediment control regulations are working. Either way, I celebrate that they are there, and that gives me hope that we can figure things out and preserve freshwater biodiversity.

Stoney Creek might be suburbanized, it may be forgotten, but this fish is a good reason to remember all the experiences I have had in suburbanizing streams. It's a good reason to continue to explore and witness all the incredibly unexpected sights and natural drama and to remember the people who have fostered my love for streams, even ones that some would consider unlovable.

There are thirty-three species of freshwater sculpin in North America. Two of the most widely distributed are the mottled and slimy sculpin. Mottled sculpins occur from the Great Lakes south into the northern part of the Mississippi drainage through Illinois, Ohio, into Pennsylvania and Maryland, and north through eastern Canada. Mottled sculpin also occur in the West, in the upper Columbia River drainage, in Idaho, Montana, and parts of Washington.

Slimy sculpin are native to the United States, Canada, and Russia. In the United States, slimy sculpins are found mainly in the Great Lakes and their tributaries, small cold streams found in southwestern Wisconsin, and the upper Mississippi River watershed. They have also been found in other areas of North America such as southeast Minnesota, northeast Iowa, the upper Columbia River, and Alaska. They occur throughout most of Canada. Slimy sculpin occur farther to the north than mottled sculpin, and their ranges potentially overlap where I live in the mid-Atlantic. The mottleds seem to dominate, and I have never seen slimy sculpins, though it's hard to tell them apart in the field. I headed north to the Great Lakes in the hopes of seeing slimy sculpin.

Lake Huron is the second largest of the Great Lakes, behind Superior, and it is huge compared to the water I'm used to. I awkwardly ambled over a shoreline of large cobble to the lake's edge and felt dwarfed by the massive expanse of clear water when I got in. It was unnerving. This used to be a port for massive ships

ROCKPORT RECREATION AREA

Description: This is an old rock quarry turned state recreation area and Great Lake access. Piles of glacially smoothed and deposited rock lay mined but unloaded and give the place a Martian feel. This is a very interesting spot for the geology and big clear water alone, plus the intriguing life. It is big water, so use extra caution, and the rocks are slick. Watch for boat traffic in the summer.

Access: GPS Address: Rockport State Recreation Area, Alpena, Michigan. The access is a set of stairs to the left side of the large parking area to the left of the boat ramp, which leads down to the lake over a steep shore of boulders. You can also hike north along the rocky shoreline and access the lake there. Stay away from the boat ramps.

Above: Lake Huron at Rockport.

where they were loaded with rock from a nearby quarry. I could see to 50 feet easily, maybe even 100. It was so foreign being in such huge, clear water.

A line of eroded, submerged pilings led to deeper water where boulders on the bottom looked similar to softball-sized stones from my floating perspective 50 feet above. A sick fish, either a trout or salmon, slowly wove through the pilings as it listed from side to side and added to the ghostly, haunted feel of the place. I swore I was being watched.

These lakes are sick. Fifty years ago, they were eutrophic, or overfed. They served as the sewers for the northern part of the country and received the waste products of the industrializing upper Midwest. They were so polluted, their tributaries caught fire, and images of the burning Cuyahoga River probably helped pass the Clean Water Act. We need to remember those images as the Clean Water Act is currently attacked and weakened. Those conditions can return. The passage of the Clean Water Act helped clean the Great Lakes, but they remained impaired due to too much nitrogen and phosphorus coming from our sewage, lawns, and cars. Until the zebra mussel arrived. Zebra mussels are native to the Baltic Sea, a brackish inland sea in Scandinavia. It is suspected they arrived at the Great Lakes via ballast water. When ships run empty, they are tippy, so they take on ballast water to weigh them down and keep them stabilized. Once they reach the port where they will pick up cargo, the ballast water is pumped out along with all the creatures contained in that water. It is suspected that zebra mussel veligers, planktonic juveniles, were in the ballast water of ships originating in the Baltic, and colonized the Great Lakes. Zebra mussels are filter feeders and remove planktonic algae from the water. The algae feed on all the excess nutrients we put in water. The nitrogen and phosphorous we put into the water that made the algae grow created a smorgasbord for the zebra mussels. The result is the other end of the spectrum: an oligotrophic, or underfed, system. The excess nutrients are still there. The algae that feed on the excess nutrients are still there. The zebras just suck them out of the water so fast it results in a nutrient-poor system so that there isn't any food to support it. A hollow ecosystem results. And that was what I felt as I snorkeled through the clear water of Lake Huron. I felt like I was snorkeling through a ghost. The Great Lakes fisheries have been on the brink of collapse due to not enough food for years.

The wind picked up and drove waves that bounced me along the surface. I returned to shallow water and could see lines of dark gray wedged between boulders and cobbles. These were colonies of zebra mussels with their shells partly agape to filter what algae remained from the water. I didn't see any more fish besides the sick steelhead or lake trout I watched barely weave its way between the submerged pilings when I first got in. It was still an interesting snorkel; the underwater landscape was haunted and intriguing. However, as I grabbed on to boulders to pull my way along the shoreline, I saw some movement. There was a fish squiggling among the mussels, and I followed it in and out of the shadows of the boulder bottom. It swam a twisty path, and I wasn't sure if it was leading me closer to shore or out toward deeper water. I worked hard to keep up, kicking and pulling myself along on the tops of boulders to stay with the fish. Finally, it drifted to rest on top of one of the larger rocks, and I got a clean look. It was a sculpin, unmistakable with a big head and large, puffy-lipped, downturned mouth. It was very dusky, almost black, and had an orange band on the top of its dorsal fin. This was likely a male slimy sculpin. Males get dark in the breeding season and advertise their reproductive fitness to females by developing a bright band on their first dorsal fin. This makes them easy targets for predatory species and attractive to females since it communicates they can survive despite being more easily preyed upon. Spawning occurs in late April and May in a protected area such as under rocks or on the undersides of submerged logs, and the male protects the nest until the eggs hatch in 3 to 4 weeks, but there are reports of male slimy sculpins protecting their young after they hatch. They live to be up to 7 years old.

This male was looking to attract a mate, and he waved his orange-fringed dorsal fin in slow undulations on top of this rock, entirely out in the open, with few escape options should a predator approach. No bass, pike, or trout came near, but a possible force in the future reduction of slimy sculpin numbers hopped along the base of the slimy sculpin's rock. A round goby, with an almost comically bulbous head, green and yellow undersides, and a large black dot on its dorsal fin, bounced along the bottom in the crease of the boulder, with an almost arrogant air. The slimy sculpin didn't notice its nemesis and continued to advertise for sex or death.

Slimy sculpins eat benthic insects. Round gobies eat the same things and are more aggressive at acquiring food. But this isn't the reason for the declining sculpin and increasing gobies. Male gobies kick male sculpins off prime nesting sites to claim them for themselves, which puts more reproductive pressure on the sculpin and leads to less reproductive success for the sculpin. Round gobies are native to the Black and Caspian Seas. These, too, were brought to the Great Lakes in ballast water, like the zebra mussels. Even though they have potentially negative effects on native bottom-dwelling fish like sculpins, darters, and logperch, they are still fascinating to watch.

Round goby.

The Thousand Islands are an archipelago of more than 1,800 islands in the St. Lawrence River. They are home to amazing fresh waters and ample snorkeling opportunities. I found a quiet cove in Wellesley Island State Park to explore. The bottom was a patchwork of thick underwater plant growth and exposed, flat, smooth slabs of red-and-gray granite bedrock. The diversity of underwater plants and habitats resulted in a diversity and abundance of fish. Yellow perch gathered in the deeper depressions, and largemouth bass patrolled the perimeter. It was an interwoven complex of recesses and voids, of every shade and hue of green all undulating with the wind-driven waves that pushed the surface up into peaks, as shafts of sunlight illuminated one patch at a time, leaving the rest in shadow.

I drifted back into the shallow fringes of the cove after exploring the clear 30-foot-deep center. While bass and perch dominated the depths, round gobies ruled here. Their movements seemed antagonistic. They flared black-spotted dorsals like large warning flags. They must be communicating something, and I read their body language as aggression and defending territory. Extended pectoral fins picked big heads high off the bottom to stare down opponents. They threw the black dot up into the water at just the right time to inflate their size and make them look ten times larger than actual. At least that was my interpretation of the displays happening beneath me. I don't know if those assumptions are accurate, but I am certain territory was being defended, and body posture was the weapon. As I bounced in the wind-driven waves in the shallows and watched every bit of thirty gobies pushing each other out of the way for the prime territory, I heard a voice from the shore.

"See anything?"

I picked my head out of the water, startled.

"Ummm, yeah," I stammered. "Bass in the deeper parts, perch in depressions in the weeds, and gobies really thick in here." I pointed to the bottom as a wave crested over my shoulders.

"Oh, yes. The gobies. They used to be all over the place until the bass figured out they were food."

It's a story I would hear a few times during my Thousand Islands stay. How the smallmouth were mediocre but then really started to put on weight once they figured out gobies were food, and now the bass are larger and stronger than people have seen in a generation. And how the goby is the principal diet of smallmouth bass. This is a different outcome than the one originally forecast when the gobies first invaded in the 1990s. They are territorial, aggressive, and have huge appetites. Therefore, it was logically predicted that the gobies would reduce the bass population through predation on nests and fry. Maybe a balance has been struck, the way ecology is always so good at balancing between the invader and the native.

I didn't come to McCall, Idaho, for sculpin. I came for Pacific lamprey and maybe a salmon or two. And I didn't get into Upper Payette Lake expecting to

WELLESLEY ISLAND STATE PARK

Description: In some places in the Thousand Islands, the water is more like a lake. In others, it's more like a river with a strong current. The visibility is usually pretty great, and the bottom is an interesting patchwork of different kinds of underwater vegetation and rock outcrops. The water can be big with long fetches that drive the surface into waves. There is a lot of recreational boat traffic. Big water, iffy currents, waves, wakes, and boat traffic mean "use caution." However, there are protected areas that are easy to find. Smooth slabs of granite are good access and egress points as long as you slide along on your butt. They become slick with algae, and walking on them is treacherous.

Access: GPS Address: 44927 Cross Island Road, Fineview, New York 13640. There are a number of coves in the park that offer good snorkeling and protected water, but access might be a little difficult depending on topography and slick rocks. An easy place to start is at the swimming beach, outside of the lined swimming area.

Above: St. Lawrence River at Wellesley Island State Park.

see lamprey but rather so I could experience a montane lake environment. Fish jumped from the middle of the lake into the air en masse. They weren't feeding. There were too many of them leaping at the same time, and it was too cold for a hatch of insects. Something was chasing them. I didn't know how deep the Upper Payette Lake was, but it dropped off quickly. I slid into the water, reluctant and leery. The bottom abruptly sloped away to nothing in the distance, and

I wasn't sure what was out here hunting, but I didn't want it to hunt me. I stuck to the shallows. The wind howled down off one of the peaks that overlooked the lake and screamed across the surface to me, where it pushed waves into my face and tried to drive me to shore. I swam around a point and got out of the wind. The bottom transitioned from cobble to silt, and I was careful not to kick the fine mud into the water and blow my marginal visibility. I followed a submerged log out into the middle of the cove and found a sculpin nestled where the log met bottom. Sculpins are hard to differentiate, and this one was no different. The only thing distinctive were two forward-slanted bands under its second dorsal. The unknown sculpin didn't like my company and scooted off, easily losing me in the bottom. I was cold and still leery about what was hunting large fish in the middle. Sharlie, a sea monster seen in Payette Lake 9 miles to the south, Idaho's version of the Loch Ness Monster, could be here, feeding. I got out, cold and paranoid.

I drove back to the cabin I was renting as my hands painfully thawed and happened to run into Cassie, one of the owners of the cabin. I told her I was snorkeling in Upper Payette. Her eyes got big and excited. "I free dove there," she said and ran into her near-by rancher to retrieve a video. "This was one of the freakiest experience I have had free-diving these lakes around here," she said as she excitedly started a video captured on a GoPro of a school of large, toothy tiger muskie watching her ascend from a 60-foot free-dive. That explained the jumping fish.

The next day, I returned to the Payette River, where it empties into Payette Lake after draining Upper Payette Lake. Again, I was hoping for lamprey but didn't expect any.

The bottom quickly dropped off to 40 feet. The lake just downstream is 400 feet deep. Big fish and unknown creatures, like Sharlie, can exist here, and I irrationally felt uneasy as I skittered across the 40-foot-deep section into the shallows on the opposite shore of what I thought would be more river than lake. I was grateful to land on a shallow gravel flat that extended downstream for as far as I could see, with the 40-foot-deep channel running right alongside. A black and light gray, almost white squiggle caught my eye and attention.

Idaho has ten species of sculpin. Many of these are endemic and have very small ranges limited to one specific drainage. While my motive for going to Idaho was Pacific lamprey and not sculpin, I was entertained with the displays of this black-and-white torrent sculpin. We did a little dance around a 5-foot section of submerged log. As I peered into the cavity formed by the branch on the upstream end, the sculpin scooted downstream, and when I came around to the downstream side, the fish moved upstream. This went on for 10 minutes until the fish finally gave in and settled on the bottom next to a freshwater mussel. They are a species of concern in Montana where their numbers are suspected to be declining and are considered rare but stable in Idaho. However, these are

PAYETTE LAKE

Description: This access is on the upper part of Payette Lake, where the Payette River flows into the lake. The scenery here is fantastic! Ponderosa pine, larch, and firs touch the sky in front of Rocky Mountain peaks, and all of it is reflected by the mirrored surface of the lake. The river twists through soft gravel bars and gets deep in the channel in places. The water clarity is excellent, and the flow isn't too strong.

Access: GPS Address: From McCall, take Warren Wagon Road north for 8 miles. It will turn into East Side Road just before crossing the bridge over the Payette River. Park on the right side after the bridge. A trail leads to the river's edge. Alternatively, the Northwest Passage Campground, which comes up in most GPSes, is a quartermile to the east of the bridge access.

Above: Payette River at the entrance to Payette Lake.

just guesses. We don't even know some of the details of their basic biology. For example, upstream spawning migration between January and April was documented in Washington, but overall torrent sculpin movements are poorly known.

I saw multiple black-and-white, racing-striped torrent sculpins and watched each one for as long as the fish would allow. They mostly watched me back and kept a healthy distance. I lost track of time, distance, and place, so that when I eventually pulled my head from the river, I didn't know where I was and couldn't see my access. These fish thoroughly captured my attention, along with the scale of the river. From the surface, it seems like a pretty standard small stream, but

Torrent sculpin in the Payette River.

underwater, it is huge. Typical for everything out West, I am learning. The scale here is just large.

I wished the sculpin well as I shivered my way out of the river. Their future, like the futures of other sculpin species, is uncertain. These bottom dwellers are fascinating to watch. Sculpin are beautiful fish that display complex and nuanced interactions like undulating orange fringed dorsal fins as an advertisement for sex and aggressive territorial disputes. The fact that we know little about the basic biology and behavior of many of these species makes it difficult to determine how they will respond to changing habitats. It is also an exciting opportunity to spend time with sculpins and discover something we didn't know, something that illuminates the complex lives of these captivating fish, and something that may help us ensure their survival into the future.

CHAPTER 9

Herring, Quillback, and Shad

I'd been checking Principio Creek daily since late February 2012, anxiously waiting for the return of the herring. The Department of Natural Resources sign nailed to a tree was not a good omen, but I thought it was more preventive in nature. Possession of any herring, unless you had a receipt to prove you bought it last year, was now illegal due to a 93 percent reduction in herring numbers on the Atlantic Coast over the last 25 years. But I really didn't think that 93 percent reduction applied to the Principio. The 2011 run, just last year, had been incredibly abundant, so abundant that it had been easy to think it would continue.

Herring are migratory. They spend the majority of their lives at sea and migrate to our freshwater rivers and streams to spawn each spring. The same time the previous year, in 2011, I'd shared the base of Principio Falls with three fishermen who were trying to snag the migrants for bait. I watched thousands of fish push up through short falls and chutes, and I watched thousands of fish lay and fertilize eggs. This is the fall line, where piedmont meets coastal plain. The Principio spills down a 20-foot falls into a stair-step series of pools and cascades all carved in red-gray gneiss bedrock. The bottoms of pools are covered in varying shades of orange and white quartz gravel. Sand settles into the slower-moving parts. Herring can make it up the shorter chutes, but the base of the 20-foot falls is the limit of their upstream migration. This place is normally chaos due to the flow and turbulence. Water sheets into downstream pools from foot-tall falls and creates curtains of disorienting, silver air bubbles. The noise of crashing water is constant. The herring bring bedlam and disorder that makes the Principio's chaotic baseline feel like a calm pond. They totally disregarded my presence as they shot upstream and down in waves chasing each other. Fish repeatedly ran into me, bounced off, and went around. Unlike other fish who pair off to spawn, herring are communal spawners and work themselves into a frenzy before releasing eggs and milt into

Spawning river herring at Principio Creek.

the water column. There were so many eggs in the water they impaired visibility and settled onto the bedrock and gravel bottom like sand.

I left Principio in 2011 confident in the future of the herring run and looked forward to the opportunity to witness one of the most amazing events in our rivers and streams every spring. They were so abundant and frantic to mate, there was no way they could ever be depleted. However, the fish never came back in 2012, and every day I checked through April, I came away wondering if I was early or they were late, but I figured they would be back. They had to be. There were so many of them last year. It was a seasonal rite of passage I was confident I could hand down to my kids, maybe even my grandkids. It was something in nature I could count on returning. Until that moment. The first week of May arrived without sighting any herring, and I had to accept that they weren't coming back that year.

It seemed like such a limitless resource, and while I'm not a proponent of overfishing, I didn't think the fishermen last year had been doing any harm. There were just so many fish in the creek, how could the couple dozen they removed have an effect? Nature would make more. Maybe that's why we are where we are, because of that very flawed thinking that our resources are so abundant we can never deplete them.

The lack of a run in the Principio was concerning, especially in the context of a 93 percent reduction in mid-Atlantic seaboard herring. Maybe the Principio run was gone for good and all that remains are the pictures I had taken the year before the 2011 run. Or maybe the warm and dry weather we had reduced all

River herring migrating upstream.

the runs. It sure seemed like the Deer Creek shad run fizzled after a robust start. I hoped it was the weather.

One year later, in mid-April 2013, I stood on the bedrock that overlooked Principio Falls and hoped for herring. I wanted to capture the fish in photos, not on stringers. I started counting days to their arrival long before the end of winter. I hoped their absence the previous year had been just an aberration and not indicative of the precipitous decline in their numbers. I hoped the Principio still had a herring run, and I had to wait an entire year for the chance to get into the water and see if the fish had returned.

I scanned the stair-step waterfall pools for any sign of herring and found none. If they were there, they weren't as abundant as in 2011. I suited up and slid into the water. There weren't any fish. Not even darters, which had been abundant in almost every snorkel exploration here. I crawled upstream against a strong current, slid up a short falls, and dropped into the first pool. Initially, I just saw water clouded by algae fragments and fine, entrained air bubbles, but then the first silver shape came just barely into view, and then another. There were about six herring in the pool, where at least fifty held the last time I'd snorkeled with them. But six was better than the zero I'd seen in 2012. I floated and watched for a while, absorbing the sight. They pointed upstream like arrows. Their tails and bodies glowed deep yellow in the setting sun, and for as hard as their tails beat the water, their bodies stayed straight and unwavering. I had a hard time holding on in the same rapid these fish navigated with ease. I watched these six fish act out on ancient instinct to get upstream to clean freshwater gravel beds to spawn, to

River herring masterfully navigating strong current.

start the next generation of herring that would return to the river to start the next generation and so on. There was something immortal about the whole thing. I clumsily followed them through a turbulent riffle that they masterfully navigated.

I ascended a 3-foot bedrock ledge, slipped into the next highest pool, and found more herring acting with the same singleness of purpose to get up the short falls to their spawning grounds. These were clean-looking fish, with a navy blue stripe down their backs and purple wash over silver scales on their sides that graded to gold then white silver on their undersides. I floated in the pool at the base of the falls, an interesting spot as it is a 4-foot-deep, 1-foot-wide crevice into the bedrock that flattens to a foot-deep shelf on the downstream side before the Principio spills into the next crevice pool downstream. A large eddy recirculates upstream and collects detritus and sand in its center on the bottom, thick white foam on the surface. Herring twirled in the eddy, just starting the mating dance. I felt better seeing this other dozen or so fish. Maybe the Principio herring run was intact. Maybe I would be able to share this incredible feat with my grandkids. Maybe I could pass that legacy on. There is something immortal about that too. I snapped photos as fast as the camera would allow.

I returned in the last week of April, hoping the run would be in full swing. An older gentleman stood by a pool a hundred yards downstream. He had a full gray beard that almost reached the belt buckle buried under his overhanging stomach. He wore a dirty T-shirt, jeans, and a tattered baseball hat. He sipped on a beer while he looked into the water. I searched the pools closer to the falls. We were both looking for herring.

PRINCIPIO CREEK

Description: Principio Creek is the highest-quality stream in Cecil County, located in the northeastern corner of Maryland. Principio is about 9 miles long. Its watershed is predominantly agricultural, sand and gravel pit, and forested. More suburban land use is appearing in the watershed. Principio empties directly into a finger of the upper Chesapeake Bay called Furnace Bay. Principio is named after the Principio Furnace, one of the first blast furnaces in North America. The furnace was located on this site in the early 1700s since it had the ability to turn a waterwheel, which powered the bellows, forests for charcoal, and a local abundance of iron ore. It was the most technologically advanced furnace of its time and produced weapons for the Revolutionary War and the War of 1812. It was destroyed twice by British troops.

The short stair-step falls at Principio Furnace is the fall line, where the hilly piedmont meets the flat coastal plain. This is the uppermost limit of shad and herring migration in Principio Creek. The stream has amazing diversity, despite its gravel-mined, agricultural and suburbanizing watershed, and the stretch just below the falls, downstream of Route 7, never disappoints. Use extra caution here due to slick rocks and forceful water.

Access: GPS Address: 1800 Philadelphia Road, Perryville, Maryland, should get you in the vicinity of the Route 7 bridge that crosses the Principio. Pull off on the westbound shoulder of Route 7 at the Principio Bridge. There is enough room for two to three cars. Watch for traffic, and please respect private property.

Above: Principio Creek.

"See any?" I called over the roar of the river.

"Nope."

Silence fell between us as we watched the water.

"I remember when they were so thick, their backs broke the water; they was stacked on top of each other. But then this creek took a beating since then. Too much mud in the water," he said.

He went on to tell me the seasonal nuances of the shad and herring runs and the movements of other migrants in the creek, such as eels. I could tell that he cared for this river very much, just like me, but he knew it much better.

We watched the water in silence, both of us wanting to see the splash of a tail or the flash of a side. Any sign that the fish were running upstream. There was nothing. I felt disappointed and very concerned. There had been more fish here this year than in the last, but that isn't saying much. And once again I had to wait a year to see if the run would return.

"It ain't nothin' o' what it used to be," my new friend said.

"No, it's not," I replied. "But hopefully they'll come back."

"I hear they're running thick in the Northeast," he hollered over the water.

So I went there, to a pool at the base of the falls near the Amtrak bridge on the Northeast Creek. The last time I'd been in the Northeast, I'd admired the alien stream-scape of a significantly degraded creek just upstream of the falls. The bottom was a flat sand, mud, and gravel plain covered in tan and olive algae. Oxygen bubbles formed on the algae and added quicksilver highlights. Castle spire fronds of algae reached toward the surface where enough bubbles provided lift.

The Northeast is significantly degraded by sedimentation and eutrophication, or overfertilization that makes too much algae grow. Still, this section was interesting, messed up as it was. It was a nice place to visit once, but there were many other streams for me to explore, so I'd never returned. Until now.

A thick, furry growth of algae covered everything. I could see it from the surface, and I wondered if the trip would be similar to my last: a swim over an interesting stream-scape but one that really didn't hold much diversity. Then a few tails slapped the surface as the fish struggled their way up through the rapid. The herring were there.

The bottom was angulated and fractured bedrock and dropped to a 4-foot hole. The first fish I saw was a large logperch, large as far as logperch come. Logperch are bottom-dwelling fish that have large pectoral fins and tiger-striped, green-and-yellow bodies. They are wary, and this one hopped along the bottom to get away from me. A school of some kind of medium-sized minnow swam upstream. A few sunnies held in the corner of the deeper pool. A hefty eel hunted. I couldn't believe the diversity. In just a few minutes, I saw a half dozen species of fish. Then the herring arrived. Schools of the silver fish swarmed around me in an energetic mating frenzy. Many of the shiny torpedoes swam into me. It had been a few years since I snorkeled with so many fish, and I reveled

Iridescent metallic scales make river herring one of our most beautiful fish.

in the melee. Their movements seemed chaotic and random, but maybe that was just my perception, and they planned each move in some kind of pattern I couldn't discern.

The 4-foot hole grew dense with herring and a couple of shad and was so thick that I couldn't see the bottom. Watching those fish was reassuring and should give me hope at a time when it seems all the news about the environment is negative. Hope that we can restore what we've degraded, and hope in the knowledge that even in their degraded states, our local rivers and streams are still pretty amazing places.

I returned at the end of May when the run was petering out. A shad lay on the bottom on its side and still passed water over its gills but barely. Its body was a mottled dark purple and blue instead of clean silver. A fine dusting of silt was entrained in a mucus hood over its head. A sad sight, but the shad had run its course. This is the natural order. Shad migrate in the spring, and some of them die in the process, unlike salmon where each migrant swims upstream to its death, many shad return year after year to spawn. However, this shad was part of the group that wouldn't be returning next year.

As I watched this fish work to pump water over its gills, I felt for this animal. It wanted to live. It was struggling to survive even though it was such an obviously futile attempt. At the same time, its presence was a sign of hope. That shad are there at all is a miracle. The Northeast is a fairly impacted stream, and there is a 4-foot-tall dam a half mile upstream just tall enough to stop shad from making their way any farther up the river.

However, the fish was there, which I assumed meant it made its way as far upstream as it could, laid its eggs or fertilized some, and set the process in motion for future runs of shad. This fish lived the life it was supposed to live, and it was now done. There shouldn't be anything sad about that; rather, there should be joy and hope that we should all be so lucky.

I continued on over thick growths of stringy algae. But the sunnies didn't mind, and as I floated into a large eddy on the side of a short riffle, I was greeted by curious small bluegill and large defensive male pumpkinseeds in full red coloration. I stayed for as long as the cold water allowed, watching the bluegill get closer and the pumpkinseeds take aggressive postures then swim off in a tight circle only to return nose to nose with me. A lot of these fish are not native to the Northeast. Many species of sunfish were introduced there, and they have become part of the natural aquatic backdrop. The algae doesn't belong there either, at least not in these quantities. But even in impacted streams, there is something of worth and value to see. For the Northeast, that's ancient migrations hanging on and, in some cases, making a comeback, as well as nonnative fish putting on incredible displays of color and territoriality.

I returned to the Principio in the spring of 2014. Blueback herring were holed up in pools of the Principio Falls, spawning and oblivious of me, the intruder.

Herring can spawn multiple times, but a few die each year in the process.

Thick migration of river herring.

Masses of metallic blue and silver shot past upstream and swirled back down-stream in pulsating eddies of fish. Their numbers had returned.

A dead half-eaten herring lay on a bed of eggs that concealed part of the carcass. The entire bottom was covered in eggs, and they occasionally swirled up past my face mask when an eddy whirled them back into the water column. Nothing goes to waste, and I was sure the rest of the herring would be eaten by something in the next few hours, giving sustenance to a heron, or otter, crayfish, or catfish. Just as I was sure most of the millions of eggs would become something else's dinner rather than develop into new blueback herring. It's hard to tell whose eggs are whose and who fertilized which ones. It's just one procreative soup, and each fish contributes with the hope and expectation that their young will make it, assuming that they achieved a form of immortality by passing their genetic information to the next generation.

The remains of the dead herring were a reminder that I would be there as well someday, and the eggs were a reminder that my kids would be there to carry on. The amazing annual feat of migration, of life and death, models the brevity of our journey and the spiraling cycle of life.

SHAD

The bottom of the pools looked gray from the bridge in the early spring sunlight. But the gray patches moved. I knew they were full of shad. I walked fast like a kid on a pool deck, down off the bridge, and down the embankment to the shore of Deer Creek. I suited up quickly. I was so fast that I almost forgot to zip my drysuit closed. I waded into the river, and when I got close to the first hole, I laid down in the 2-foot-deep water.

Before I thought I should be, I was surrounded by foot-long fish, all moving in unison. I found a large rock, planted my feet on the upstream side, and stretched out into the current. The shad were jittery, and each time I cleared water from my snorkel, each time a car drove over the bridge above me, or each time I got too sideways to the current and was thrown off the rock that kept me propped against the current, they scattered with panicked, jerky movements. But soon, they returned to their upstream quest and rhythmic, almost mesmerizing, undulations. Dappled sunlight turned fin edges neon blue, and large eyes stared back at me.

The school, a few hundred fish strong, was made up of hickory and American shad and smaller river herring, and it looked like each pool held about the same number. They all swam together and presented their sides to me to form a wall of fish.

Swimming with this many fish is always a thrill. However, the fact that this school was made up of American and hickory shad, both at historically low numbers, made the experience that much more special. To think that I was surrounded by possibly hundreds of a kind of animal that is at risk of dying off gave me hope that the fish would make it. I also felt honored to be witness to their

Mixed school of shad and herring.

incredible run, to possibly be one of the last humans to see such a sight. I have hope for the shad, but it is a guarded optimism.

Shad are in the herring family and are anadromous, meaning that, like salmon, they spend their lives at sea and endure an arduous spring journey as they swim inland to spawn in smaller creeks. All herrings are at risk, and some are endangered. American shad numbers are at an all-time low. Hickory shad are listed as endangered just a few miles up the Susquehanna in Pennsylvania. They were staples of Native American and early European settlers' diets and were called the "savior fish" for feeding the Continental Army during the harsh winter of 1778. Dams, which sever migration routes, and sediments, which cover gravel spawning beds, are the two current reasons for the ongoing lack of recovery. There aren't any dams between this stretch of Deer Creek and the Atlantic, so shad can make the 175-mile journey from the ocean to this riffle unimpeded by concrete walls.

Shad used to be incredibly abundant, and perhaps stories of them swimming so thick you could walk across rivers on their backs without getting your feet wet had some credibility. Each spring in the 1800s, a net was strung across the mouth of the Susquehanna, between Perryville and Havre de Grace, and the entire local economy was seasonally driven by the shad run. Shad couldn't get past Conowingo Dam to get to their spawning grounds, so reproduction declined. Couple decreased reproduction with increased sediment loads due to deforestation and heavy fishing pressure, and their numbers dropped.

The negative effect dams had on migratory shad was recognized early. The state of Pennsylvania has required fish passages on dams since the 1800s. Unfortunately, the passages installed were poorly designed and did little to restore fish migration routes. Even today, many passages are only marginally effective. We are good at destroying but not so good at restoring.

Conowingo Dam, the first in a string of six that block migratory fish from reentering the Susquehanna River, has two fish lifts installed. They are essentially a kind of elevator that carries fish one hundred feet up where they swim under Route 1 into the water behind the dam. It seemed the multimillion-dollar investment reversed the trend of declining American shad populations at Conowingo Dam. Then another unexplained decline occurred in a population that is already at historic lows.

Turns out that the latest threat to the shad may be rockfish. Rockfish eat menhaden. Menhaden are forage fish in the same family as shad. We are learning that rockfish switch to eating shad when menhaden numbers are down. The menhaden fishery has been largely unregulated, and as many fish as possible are sucked from the Bay and converted to cosmetics and fertilizers. At the same time, rockfish made a tremendous comeback after a moratorium on their take was implemented in the 1990s. Of course, this isn't the definite cause of the more recent shad decline, but to me, it seems the most plausible. Either that or all the engineering the power companies have invested in, all the fish lifts constructed to get shad above the dams, have been folly, the flawed idea that we can engineer ourselves out of any problem.

As John Muir said, when we look at any one thing in the universe, we find it hitched to everything else, and that certainly applies to the fish world. Our actions matter. As I swam with this wall of fish, I certainly felt that connection.

The next April, I watched Deer Creek from the Shuresville Road Bridge on Easter weekend. The water just upstream sporadically erupted as the early evening darkened. *Must be shad*, I thought, and after a few minutes of looking, I confirmed my suspicion: the shad had arrived to spawn, and their tails rapidly beat the shallow riffle into a boil. I needed to get into the water to witness this timeless rite from the perspective of these fish. The fish returned, driven by the primal urge to ensure their immortality by passing their genes on to the next generation. I wanted to witness this incredible act.

I slipped into the water downstream of the shad and fought a heavy current. I didn't see any fish as I crawled my way against the flow. Spring rains had the creek flow up and visibility down, and I could only see about 5 feet before the gloom of turbidity took over. A fisherman from shore directed me to where the fish were spawning—a little farther upstream and a little farther out in the current. Ghostly blurs appeared on my periphery as shad shot past, then I felt a slap on my shoulder. I was right in the middle of the spawning school. I could barely hang on to the bottom against the current while shad darted by with effortless but strong tail strokes. It was obvious their compressed bodies and powerful, deeply forked tails make them perfectly designed for the reproductive task at hand.

Silver tails flashed just upstream as females released eggs and males released sperm, while fish continued to rush ahead. From above, their olive backs made them invisible against the bottom. From beneath the surface, their silver bodies were obvious through the early spring's hazy water.

This was the first school of the year, maybe one hundred fish strong, which had made it to the swimming hole in Susquehanna State Park. There were a few yellow perch there, too. Yellow perch, also recently reduced in number, seemed to have made a comeback, and their population is growing.

I celebrated these ecological victories as I floated in the pool above my favorite rapid and watched each individual struggle against the current to reach its clean gravel spawning ground. People recognized that shad were declining and decided to take action to stop the loss. While the future existence of shad is uncertain, they are still here. Their existence is a testament to what we can accomplish when we put our will behind action. It's a demonstration of the tenacity and resilience of ecological systems. There are definite limits, and we can easily exceed them. At the same time, there is elasticity, and if we recognize those limits early enough and act, the system can recover. All is not lost. Not yet. But we need to act.

Shad have been making treks such as this for 120 million years or so. And yet we might make them extinct in my lifetime. I feel fortunate to have experienced the timelessness of this event, at least timeless in relation to my fleeting human life span. Knowing these fish are there and spawning makes me believe more will follow, and that maybe the great mythic shad runs I've heard of that occurred before I was born may once again fill our streams.

It's fitting that shad returned on Easter weekend. It's a time of promise, resurrection, and rebirth, and their presence in the creek signals the continuation of their species, the optimism that more will return next year. More proof that maybe their species has been resurrected. It's one of the most hopeful events we can experience in our streams.

Seeing these first migrants makes me optimistic that we will recognize the limits we are fast approaching, drop the rhetoric, and get busy. Seeing these fish renews my commitment to show people the incredible life just beneath the surface of our local streams.

QUILLBACK

The shad and herring had been running for a few weeks, and I was still in awe of their migration after being in the water with them a dozen times here in Deer Creek. Their spawning is the sign that I look for to tell me that spring is here.

Others had joined the shad since the first day of their journey. I watched carp swim with them, and a large eel bisected a school in an eddy. The shad draw more humans as well, and available parking spaces became rarer as the shad run increased. Room in Deer Creek to snorkel between fishermen got a little tight. Herons and humans, shad and carp, all participate in this rite of seasonal passage.

But the spring migration had reached a crescendo and was trickling away. There were fewer fishermen, more parking spots, and fewer fish. I was a little disappointed to see all the action and excitement of their incredible journey slow until next year. Witnessing the drama of the upstream drive and experiencing a little of it by swimming with the fish on the journey makes me feel alive. A few remaining hickory shad pushed their way upstream to spawn. I hovered on the edge of the current in a large eddy and stretched out into the stream to get as close to the school as possible without interrupting the procession.

My feet stretched into the downstream eddy of a shore-side boulder, and my upper body extended into the strong current at the head of the rapid. My snorkel vibrated and hummed in the flow, and I wasn't sure if the sideways force was going to snatch my mask, but both it and I held. The fish got used to me as long as I didn't move. They were sleek, athletic, strong, and muscular, and they maintained a position in this deeper section of rapid without much effort. That is until I coughed due to an inhaled water drop from my leaky snorkel, then they rapidly darted, most upstream, with a singular flick of their deeply forked tails. A few

Shad push through a rapid pool.

minutes later, more fish filled in. I just hung out with the shad, becoming part of an eons-old ritual of upstream migration, and enjoyed the privilege of witnessing this feat. There was an intensity of purpose with the shad. There wasn't much that was going to keep them from their destination, and I absorbed as much of the view of their journey as I could.

The fish scattered, and the pool became eerily still. There weren't silver tubes struggling upstream in the hazy distance. There weren't the lower jaws with overbites characteristic of hickory shad, wiggling side to side in the current. There was an unexplained quiet in the pool, and I thought I saw a large silhouette pass just barely out of sight. If I were in the ocean, I would have been thinking predator from the way the fish disappeared when a shadow arrived. But this was a freshwater stream, and I figured my imagination was at work. The shad returned, and I went back to enjoying their activity.

It happened again. The shad scattered, the pool became still, and I had a creepy feeling that something big was moving just out of view. Then I saw it—a large, shadowy shape coming up through the middle of the rapid on the bottom. Then another came into hazy view and another. There was a school of them, whatever they were.

As they came farther upstream, closer to me, I could make out some features. The fish were 2 feet long and rotund. They looked too big to be there, in the swift-moving water. Shad are compressed side to side with deeply forked tails that propel them upstream through strong downstream currents, and these fish were much too tubular and less hydrodynamic to make such a journey. However,

Quillback swimming against a strong current.

there they were. I thought they were carp at first, but then saw they didn't have any barbels, which are whisker-like sensory organs near the mouth that help carp search for food in murky water. Their pectoral and pelvic fins were edged in electric blue, and the front edge of their dorsal fin extended into a long thread or quill, which gives them their name: quillback.

Quillback are a type of sucker that are found throughout much of North America. Their range includes the Great Lakes, extends south to Louisiana, as far west as Wyoming, and east to the Hudson River in New York and Vermont. While the International Union for the Conservation of Nature (IUCN) considers quillback to be a species of least concern and populations to be stable overall, they are a species of concern in New York and Vermont, where their numbers are dropping. They are omnivorous bottom-feeders and usually feed in schools.

Quillback are another migrant in our rivers and streams. Whereas shad migrate hundreds if not thousands of miles, quillback cover shorter distances. They spend most of their lives in larger rivers and migrate into smaller streams to spawn. They were looking for the same thing as shad: clean gravel beds where they reproduce once a year. Sedimentation is a possible cause of the decline in New York and Vermont quillback populations.

It was a true thrill to hold on to the bottom in the middle of six of these foot-and-a-half-long fish. They seemed to acknowledge and accept my presence and kept on pumping their caudal fins against the current, right next to me, so that I could feel the pressure waves coming off their tails through my wetsuit. I've been around for more than 50 years and am still learning about our rivers and streams. I never knew quillback traveled upstream in search of gravel beds to spawn. I never really looked for them. Learning like this makes life exciting.

Quillback have become one of the species I look for in spring as part of the migration. I went snorkeling in the Octoraro Creek, near where it empties into the Susquehanna. It was a celebration as hundreds of herring and shad streamed past me. The Octoraro's run had been weak of late, but the run this year looked pretty good. The water was clear, and I enjoyed being in the moment, watching. I drifted over a 6-foot-deep pool and found that the bottom was whipped into a flocculent cloud. Large metallic powder-blue sparks flashed through the clouded haze. It was like watching a lightning storm from above. Bolts of glowing blue shot through the water. I went to the bottom and watched quillback rocket around in circles in this deeper pool, trying to attract mates with pectoral fin flashes. The fish knew I was there but had other more important things on their minds, and they swirled around in haphazard patterns. The pool was a chaos of fish, and I was in the middle of it all. But what appeared to be a mass of disorganized reproductive energy was actually ordered. The spawn I watched wasn't very random

Quillback are beautiful suckers.

at all. Rather, two to three males intentionally and exclusively spawned with a single female. There was a pattern here among the rushing fish and electric blue flashes. It just wasn't visible to me.

A few weeks later, in late May, I walked across the dry riverbed of the Susquehanna just below the Holtwood Dam. The scene looked more like the Serengeti than the Susquehanna. A wide-open area of green water willow grassland was interspersed with an occasional tree that had survived the seasonal torrents. Bacteria and algae formed a biofilm covering over submerged rocks. It's what makes them slick. When water levels drop, the biofilm dries out and turns white. Large expanses of bedrock, whitewashed with dried biofilm, reflected the sun's heat and reminded me of hiking over a salt flat.

I reached the edge of a hundred-yard-long pool that was effectively severed from the main flow of the river. I geared up with my back to the pool and heard a large splash. I turned but didn't see anything. Nothing moved after watching the water for a few minutes. I went back to putting on my wetsuit and heard another one. What was making these splashes?

The pool was dark compared to the brightness of the exposed flat bedrock. Dark green algae covered everything and absorbed much of the light. The bottom was angulated bedrock that dropped into deep narrow ravines. The water

Susquehanna River below Holtwood Dam can look like a savannah in the dry season.

DEER CREEK

Description: Deer Creek is a 52-mile-long stream that starts in south-eastern Pennsylvania, in Southern York County and flows southeast into Maryland as it drains 171 square miles of rolling hills in the lower Susquehanna Valley. It joins the Susquehanna River 5 miles upriver from the Chesapeake Bay. It is designated as a Maryland Wild and Scenic River. There are no dams between Deer Creek and the Atlantic Ocean. The first dam on Deer Creek is at Wilson Mill, 4 miles upstream from the mouth. A fish ladder was placed in this dam in 2000, which restored migratory fish runs to 25 miles of stream above Wilson Mill, until they reach the dam at Eden Mill. The last population of Maryland Darter, a fish presumed to be extinct, was located in Deer Creek.

Access: GPS Address: 942 Craigs Corner Road, Havre de Grace, Maryland. This site is a popular swimming hole in Susquehanna State Park. Park along the side of the road across from the Baltimore City Deer Creek water pumping station.

Above: Deer Creek, Maryland.

was murky with churned-up bottom, a sign that something big was in the pool with me. I came upon two good-sized smallmouth bass showing off for each other, part of the mating dance, and I figured that was what had caused the splashes and churned bottom. But still, I was nervous. The bass just weren't big enough to account for all that noise. Suddenly, a big school of huge quillback burst past me. Some of the fish bumped into me in their eagerness to mate and escape. I felt like I was swimming through the buffalo stampede scene in *Dances with Wolves*. The school felt like it was a hundred strong, but it could have been the same twenty-five fish over and over, blowing by me, running into me, darting to and from every direction. Some of them came so close I could touch them with my nose, and their big scales became apparent. I couldn't track them or predict where the next one was coming from. They each had such a strength about them, such an incredible amount of life, an all-or-nothing attitude. The school swarmed and circled and darted, and as fast as they arrived, they were gone, and the pool sat still and clouded.

Our rivers and streams burst with biologic power in spring and early summer. There is so much energy, excitement, and drama in the quest to produce the next generation. And I got to witness and experience the struggle to ensure the survival of an unexpected migrant species simply by snorkeling my local stream.

CHAPTER 10

Sunnies and Bass

I fished for largemouth bass for their fight and ambush and the challenge of convincing them to take an artificial bait. To figure out where they were lying in wait, and throwing the right fake enticement, offered in just the right way, to elicit an adrenaline-producing strike. I have come to appreciate them for their beauty, intelligence, and predatory prowess even more since snorkeling with them.

I first realized there was more to largemouth than a fight on the end of a hook while snorkeling Alexander Springs. Alexander is one of twenty-seven first-order springs in Florida. It is a timeless place, and it is easy for me to picture Alexander long before Europeans commandeered it from the Timucuans, the native people who called this magical place home. I could see how Ponce de León might think these waters could be fountains of youth.

Live oaks and cypress, dripping with Spanish moss, magnolias, red maples, and sable palms, surround the spring bowl where roughly 113 million gallons of water a day boil out of the spring mouth to instantly form Spring Creek, which flows to the Saint Johns River 10 sinuous miles away. Scrub palmettos fill in the thick forest. Aquamarine blue water over the 30-foot-deep spring boil grades to hues of deep green where the bottom is covered in meadows of underwater vegetation, dominated by wild celery. White sand bottom patches reflected quicksilver on the underside of the surface.

I watched a big largemouth slowly weave between emergent lily stalks that had bulbous yellow flowers on their above-water ends. The 2-foot bass had a big, dark band down his side that divided it into a clean off-white, slightly green belly and mottled olive emerald-green back. The fish wore a confident air and made slow, purposeful movements. His dark penetrating eyes stared at me. I would have been nervous if the fish were a foot larger.

The sunlight glowed green through the floating lily leaves as this individual stalked small bluegill. When he got to the edge of the vegetation patch, he emerged along with four other bass. Were they hunting in unison, cooperatively, or did they just happen to all emerge at once? I watched as they turned and reentered the lily patch. Slowly and methodically, they wove through the thick vegetation equally spaced, herding the bluegill to the far end when they all made a dash through the gathered school of sunnies, trying to snatch a meal. It reminded me of images of sharks carving through a bait ball. This certainly looked like they were hunting together. It looked like cooperation, which requires communication. But it couldn't be. I know these fish as solitary predators. The lone wolves of the fish world. It's part of their persona. These lowly fish aren't supposed to do this; they weren't supposed to cooperate. They shouldn't have the mental or emotional capacity. They are supposed to be bait-snatching automatons, acting on instinct rather than intellect. I watched these fish make a few more passes in the same coordinated manner. I was convinced they were working together to hunt.

Largemouth bass are the biggest members of the sunfish family. They are native to most of the Mississippi drainage, from Virginia to Texas, and north to Canada. Because they are extremely popular fish to catch and support a multibillion-dollar industry, they have been stocked widely in North America and now occur throughout the United States. Part of the attraction of fishing for these fish is the same attraction I have in watching them. They are ambush predators, and they are calculating and cunning. They eat fish, crayfish, frogs, and ducklings, as well as anything else that might fall into the water, including mice. Some largemouth are cannibals, and I watched young bass nervously skitter away from these big boys.

Largemouth bass in Alexander Springs.

ALEXANDER SPRINGS

Description: Alexander Springs is a recreation area within the Ocala National Forest and includes a campground and day use area. The day use area has bathrooms, showers, and a snack bar. The spring has a sand beach area separated from the water by a retaining wall and steps that allow access. A lifeguard is on duty in the summer, when the spring can become crowded.

Access: GPS Address: Alexander Springs Recreation Area, 49525 County Road 445, Altoona, Florida. Alexander Springs is located between Astor and Altoona in Florida, which is 1 hour from Orlando, and Daytona, 2 hours from Tampa. From SR 40 at Astor, take Butler Street to CR 445A, and turn left on CR 445. The recreation area is 5.8 miles south on the right. From Altoona, drive north 5.2 miles on SR 19, and turn right on CR 445. Continue another 5.1 miles to the entrance on the left. There is a $6 per person admission fee. It is well worth it.

Above: Alexander Springs is a magical place.

I saw a bass on a bowl he shaped into the sand bottom, but December was a little early. They spawn in the spring, and the preferred spawning area has direct sunlight and protection from rough water, at a depth between 1 to 6 feet, within 10 feet of shore. The male chooses a site that is easy to defend, near some kind of cover like a sunken log or boulder, with easy access to deep water. In addition, the male will not build a nest within 30 feet of another visible spawning nest. The bigger bass build nests in deeper water and spawn earlier, so maybe this was an early spawner. It was definitely a big fish. Largemouth can live to be 15 years old, but most are under 11 years old.

Smallmouth bass are another fish I used to seek for the thrill of the chase and, ultimately, the bite. I have come to know them differently since snorkeling with them. They are calculating, thinking creatures. My first insight into their cognition and behavior came while I snorkeled the Neversink River at Claryville in the Catskill Mountains, New York. The Neversink has a variety of habitats here, from shallow riffles to deep pools. Beaver were active on the opposite shoreline, and freshly gnawed branches were stacked on the shallow sediment bar that formed on the inside of a gentle bend in the river. The outside of the bend, where I floated, was carved deep to 10 feet and lined with exposed rock along the shore. I just finished watching darters bicker over territory in a shallow run downstream of a riffle and let the gentle current take me over the deep hole.

A smallmouth male watched over his eggs that were laid in a depression he carved into the bottom of the 10-foot-deep hole. When he noticed me overhead, he stopped his slow circular patrol above his future offspring and looked up. After a few minutes of evaluation, he tenuously came toward the surface. His red eyes were inquisitive, trying to figure something out. I imagined he was trying to determine if I was a threat. Or maybe he was debating whether the fingers that I wiggled on the side of the camera housing were food, but this was unlikely since males typically don't eat for the 4 to 6 weeks they spend guarding their nests. I wondered if his actions were instinctual, that he was just responding automatically to environmental stimuli, or if there was thought going on. Perhaps it was some kind of assessment and processing of data the bass gathered through his exploration of me. His approach was slow and deliberate until he got to within a foot of me and stopped. He watched me and regularly glanced to the bottom to make sure his eggs were safe. We floated together for longer than I expected until the novelty of this big, floating thing wore off, and he just as slowly returned to guard his nest on the bottom.

Smallmouth are also members of the sunfish family. A $630 million recreation industry focused on their capture has been established in Chesapeake Bay states alone. Smallmouth are not native to the Chesapeake or the Susquehanna River. They are originally from the Mississippi drainage. They were dumped into the Chesapeake and Ohio canal from a train water tank after they were picked up from the Ohio River in 1854 and were introduced to the Susquehanna in 1869.

While not native to the Susquehanna, they have become part of the ecology and the human and natural history of the river. I know these fish from my home river, the Susquehanna, which supported a world-class recreational smallie fishery just 10 years ago. I first watched them in the Susquehanna near its mouth upstream of the town of Port Deposit. The river here is big, and it is dam-controlled. The flows are dictated by our appetite for electricity. Bedrock gneiss outcrops form a mystical landscape of rocky hoodoos when we turn our AC units

NEVERSINK RIVER

Description: The Neversink is a 55-mile tributary to the Delaware and is considered the birthplace of American fly fishing. It, along with other Catskill Mountain rivers, provides drinking water to New York City, so much of its watershed is protected, in order to protect New York's water. The Neversink River at the Claryville Fishing Access is a beautiful stretch. The shore is covered in tall grasses and wildflowers. The river has a variety of habitats from deep pools to shallow riffles and a soft-to-rocky bottom. As a result, there is a variety of life to see here: trout adult and parr, bass, suckers, darters, dace, and sunnies.

Access: GPS Address: 776 Claryville Road, Claryville, New York. There is a small Sundown Forest Preserve Fishing access here with only enough room for six cars in the parking area. Follow the short trail to the river. There is safe, easy access here.

Above: Neversink River at Claryville, New York.

off, generating gates at Conowingo Dam close, and the water levels drop 10 feet. The place becomes reminiscent of the Mount Roraima plateau, depicted in the animated movie *Up*. When the gates are open, this world is flooded and scoured by rushing water, so I was amazed to find a smallie nest in this extremely variable and dynamic environment, but there they were: a male and female paired off over a bowl carved into the gravel bottom of the mile-wide river. The male softly nudged the female into his nest, and they slowly spiraled in a gentle dance until she was right over the heavy gravel bottom of the bowl. She laid on the bottom and listed to one side as the male fertilized the eggs she expelled. He will guard the eggs until they hatch in 4 to 6 weeks and will stay with the fry for a few weeks more, until they start to wander too far from the nest for him to protect. The oldest recorded smallmouth was 26 years old. Smallmouth have nest-site fidelity, and this nest was probably within 150 yards of where he nested last year.

In 2005, fishermen began reporting thousands of dead and dying young bass. Fish with sores and melanistic spots became common. What had once been a world-class fishery was at risk of total collapse. This was all in the span of only 13 years. Potential causes included fertilizers and pesticides used in farming, endocrine-disrupting pharmaceuticals such as estrogen in birth control, invasive green algae blooms that are caused by high phosphorus loads, and flame retardants that wash from clothes. All of these don't come from the end of a single pipe but rather are nonpoint pollutants. They come from multiple places, from all of us, and are much more difficult to control than point source pollutants that can be regulated at a single point of entry into our waters. Recently researchers at Michigan State found that largemouth bass virus may be the cause. It is not lethal in smallmouth but does open the door for other pathogens, especially when combined with poor water quality conditions. Bass weakened by largemouth virus develop lesions and sores that allow bacteria and fungus to set up shop, which usually proves fatal. Concerns remain, but the fishing is improving, and large fish can be found in the lower Susquehanna again in numbers reminiscent of the late 1990s. It is possible that the smallmouth have established some immunity to largemouth virus. Other unrelated issues affecting Susquehanna smallmouth are intersex bass—male smallies with both male and female gonads—likely due to endocrine-disrupting chemicals, such as herbicides, pesticides, and pharmaceuticals, which mess with biologic hormone systems.

Despite the recent identification of the Susquehanna smallmouth bass decline and their apparent rebound, I am still concerned about the future of smallies on the Susquehanna. We haven't made any progress at eliminating a significant part of the cause of largemouth virus: poor water quality. And so while these bass seem to be secure for now, I still hoped I wasn't watching one of the last smallmouth courtships on the Susquehanna. I hope that we have the fortitude required to take the necessary steps to restore and protect water quality and lessen the chances of another outbreak.

There are concerns that largemouth virus is spreading into the Delaware, though I hadn't seen any signs of that when I snorkeled on a warm summer day in Narrowsburg, New York. Rather, I got to witness an amazing interaction between myself, a very healthy smallmouth, and a rock bass.

I am always careful to not snorkel on a fish nest or redd. I don't want to dislodge or crush the eggs that lay in the depressions carved into the river bottom, so I always look before I wade into the stream on my way to floating. I entered the Delaware at the Pennsylvania Fish and Boat Commission Narrowsburg Access with the same caution. I didn't see any evidence of fish nests immediately near me, though there was plenty of smallmouth and sunfish nesting activity in the area. I laid down in the warm, 2-foot shallow water and was instantly accosted by a smallmouth. The fish came at me with an intensity and ferocity I had never experienced. It even struck me as I tried to take its picture. I must have been on or close to its nest, and I didn't see it before getting into the river. Male smallies can become very aggressive just before their eggs hatch, and I assumed this was the case. Maybe I wasn't on this smallmouth's nest but was close enough to it that the fish decided to attack to defend his young. My focus was on the smallmouth as he came after me with repeated strikes. Apparently, the smallmouth's attention was solely on me as well, because we were both equally surprised when the smallmouth was attacked by a rock bass neither one of us noticed, guarding his nest under an undercut rock. Both males were able to lunge with amazing bursts of speed. The smallmouth at me, and the rock bass at the smallie. It took me a while to understand what was happening, but finally, I felt incredibly privileged to watch such a display of aggression, defense, and territoriality. The two fish continually came at what they perceived to be a danger with incredible speed and force and precision. I was ten times the size of the smallie, and the smallie was twice the size of the rock bass. Size didn't matter to either one. Fighting off the threat, perceived or real, did. The pectoral and caudal fins on both of these fish twitched rapidly. Their body language showed they were agitated by the presence of an intruder. In the case of the smallie, it was me; in the case of the rock bass, it was the smallmouth. Their commotion stirred flocculent from the bottom into the water so that it looked like snow.

The sides of the rock bass were a black-and-golden checkerboard that highlighted his red eye. He glowed gold in the light. His movements were lightning

Smallmouth bass.

DELAWARE RIVER AT NARROWSBURG

Description: Narrowsburg is on the upper Delaware River. The Delaware is notoriously deceiving. It looks like it has a lazy, gentle current, but it is hauling. Also, the river is shallow near the access but gets deeper about 15 feet offshore, so use extreme caution, and always be aware of your surroundings, what the river is doing, and what you are doing in the river. The bottom is rocky and covered in fine sediment. Bass, sunnies, crayfish, snails, darters, and freshwater mussels are abundant here.

Access: GPS Address: PA Fish and Boat Narrowsburg Access Parking Lot, Hansdale and Delaware Turnpike, Beach Lake, PA. The access is actually just across the river from Narrowsburg, New York, in Beach Lake, Pennsylvania, just downstream of the Bridge Street Bridge across the Delaware. From Narrowsburg, cross the river on the Bridge Street Bridge and take 652 south. The access will be on your left.

Above: Delaware River at Narrowsburg.

fast, precise, and calculated. Their native range includes the Saint Lawrence River and the river basins of the Great Lakes, Hudson Bay, and the Northeastern Mississippi River, from Quebec to Saskatchewan in the north, and south to the Savannah River drainage in northern Georgia and northern Alabama. They have been introduced throughout the eastern seaboard and the Great Plains states. Rock bass compete with smallmouth for food, which includes perch, minnows, insects, and crustaceans, as well as occasionally young of their own species.

They are preyed upon by largemouth, pike, muskie, and walleye. They can live to be 10 years old, and they are another member of the sunfish family.

One of the most ubiquitously abundant group of fish we have in North America are sunnies or sunfish, and while smallmouth, largemouth, and rock bass are part of the sunfish family, they usually aren't recognized by most people as belonging to that group. Maybe because their names are bass. Sunnies are what most people think of when talking about this family, and they are colorfully diverse, widely distributed, abundant, and fun to watch.

The Brandywine River at the Stroud Preserve has a diversity of habitats: slow-moving areas with sandy/silty bottoms, underwater vegetation beds, cobble flats where the river picks up speed, woody material near the shoreline, shallow riffles, and scour holes. The diversity of habitats should provide a diversity of fish, and I expected to see a ton as I slid into the river near the downstream riffle. The reflection on the smooth surface rippled as I pushed off the shore.

I dug my fingers into the soft bottom to claw my way upstream. While the river was calm, it was still moving. I drifted past thick beds of dark green hydrilla, a kind of nonnative underwater vegetation. The hydrilla was interspersed with sand and gravel flats that should provide decent habitat for fish, but I didn't see any. I slid over cobble piles and saw no fish. The river bottom dropped off into deeper holes and still no fish. I started to doubt whether I would see anything on the trip. That's how it goes sometimes. Sometimes river snorkeling is more about enjoying the underwater riverscape, enjoying the river from a very different perspective. I continued upstream and looked for sunnies.

Male rock bass.

I can always count on sunnies just about anywhere I snorkel in spring, summer, and fall. They are everywhere, and while they are a common fish, their behavior is always interesting and enjoyable to watch. I headed for the overhanging branches near the shoreline and coasted under the bridge. There, blending in really well to the backdrop of sticks and silt, was a school of a half dozen sunnies intently watching my every move.

Sunny is a generic term applied to members of the sunfish family that includes twenty-eight species. A few of the sunnies in the Brandywine were pumpkinseeds. They are the fish familiar to most kids who go fishing.

These fish were beautiful with deep yellow-orange undersides, metallic sky-blue lines that ran through a reddish-orange flecked field on their heads and gill covers, red eyes, and black, white, orange, and yellow flecked sides. Pumpkinseeds are generalists and eat an assortment of insects, snails, crustaceans, and fish. They feed at all levels in the water column and are effective predators of mosquito larvae. They have fine gill rakers that look like small combs on the gills that enable them to filter small food particles from the water. All predators eat juvenile pumpkinseeds, including the adults of their own species.

The bottom of that stretch of river was dotted with bowl-shaped nests the males had constructed, and they got right in my face mask to defend their territory. Others darted after males who wandered into their turf. I settled into watching a large male who held his ground against me, an organism hundreds of times larger; it was a demonstration of their tenacity. I moved my head to the left, and he stayed nose to nose. I moved to the right; he moved to the right. It looked like his breast turned redder the longer I stayed, and his motions grew more aggressive toward me.

Males swam out from their nests to entice a female in. The males who were able to convince a female into his nest swam in a tight circle side by side with the female as she laid over on one side. The female released her eggs as the male released his milt or sperm, and the fertilized eggs fell into the bowl of the nest. The males will continue to defend the nest even after the eggs hatch, and they have been known to scoop up wandering fry in their mouths to return them to the bowl. Pumpkinseeds have a strong homing ability as well. Pumpkinseeds that were relocated to other parts of lakes were able to return to where they were originally captured.

A smallmouth bass patrolled around me, careful to keep me in sight as I drifted with the current. A juvenile bass darted for the opposite shore. I could see the ghostly outlines of large river chubs in the bottom of a deeper hole. Common shiners fed on the morsels I inadvertently kicked off the bottom and darters lay among the gravel, ready to pounce. Even if I hadn't seen the other fish that represent the diversity I'd first expected, it still would have been an amazing trip. Sunnies always entertain. Sometimes in shocking ways.

Stony Creek is a suburbanizing stream in northeastern Maryland. It is on my commute home, so I often stop off for an after-work snorkel, especially

BRANDYWINE RIVER

Description: The Brandywine is a Pennsylvania Wild and Scenic River that flows through the cradle of American Revolutionary freedom in southeastern Pennsylvania. The East Branch, which flows through the Stroud Preserve, originates on Welsh Mountain and flows 20 miles until it joins the West Branch. The main stem of the Brandywine flows another 20 miles to join the Christina River in downtown Wilmington, Delaware. The Brandywine winds through a wide floodplain that contains numerous wetlands. Its watershed is largely agrarian and idyllic: rolling hills, large family farms, and old stone farmhouses and barns, many of them equestrian. The Stroud Preserve is a former farm, still used in agriculture, but managed and forever protected as open space by Natural Lands, one of the nation's leading land preservation organizations.

Access: GPS Address: 454 North Creek Road, West Chester, Pennsylvania. Follow the trail from the parking lot downstream to where a piece of the Brandywine braids off the main stem. The bank here is not steep and is easy to navigate. Or walk from the parking lot across the bridge and get in on the upstream side of the bridge. The shore here is large rocks that make it pretty easy to walk down to the water, but use caution.

Above: Brandywine River at Natural Lands Trust Stroud Preserve.

in summer. There is a deep hole beneath an Amtrak bridge that usually holds a diversity of fish, including bluegills, another kind of sunfish. Bluegill are native to the Mississippi drainage but have been widely introduced and currently occupy just about all of the United States. Spawning begins in early summer and goes through August. The males first arrive on the breeding site and make a spawning bed in shallow water. It is possible to see multiple bowls carved into the sandy bottom right next to the other with males actively guarding the edges of their nests. As a female approaches his nest, a male will try to entice her with grunting sounds while circling her. The females are attracted to the larger males. Maybe louder grunting is also part of the mate selection process. Males in breeding season sometimes develop deep, bright red-orange breasts, and I wonder if that is part of the attraction, too. Bluegills can live to be 5 to 8 years old.

Bluegill are so common I sometimes don't notice them but rather focus on other less abundant species. One particular trip to Stony Creek, I was focused on a big largemouth bass. The bass owned the pool and moved slowly with reassured confidence. I watched the 2-foot bass slowly patrol and didn't pay any attention to the bluegill. That is until they started to bite my nipples. Maybe they thought they were worms. Maybe they were defending territory. Either way, the nips came as a surprise, and my attention quickly shifted to the swarm of twenty little bluegills that surrounded me.

These were smaller bluegill, maybe second-year fish. They were a pale, drab yellow, with a dark spot on their second dorsal, and faint vertical stripes on their sides. Once I noticed them, they stopped their nipping but stayed close. A few individuals came right up to my mask and camera lens, and I wondered if it was their reflection in the glass that drew them close, or if they were genuinely curious about the big thing behind the lens.

Bluegills show a lot of geographic variability in their coloration, and the first time I saw them at Alexander Springs, I had a hard time identifying them even though I had seen them a hundred times before in my local rivers. While the bluegill at home tend to be interesting but drab as far as sunfish go, the bluegill at Alexander are some of the most flamboyant fish in the spring. Maybe it's because of the iridescent purple fringe they sport on their dark maroon fins, plus the obvious black vertical bands on their sides that make them look like sergeant majors, a tropical reef fish. Or maybe it's because of their gregarious character, though the ones I'm used to are just as sociable. The swatch of reddish-brown color on their faces explains another common term for bluegill: coppernose.

There are a number of other sunfish species who call Florida springs home, and they, along with the bluegills, were sprites of color dancing through the clear turquoise waters. Many sunfish species interbreed and hybridize, so getting a positive identification can sometimes be tricky. But that didn't matter as I floated in Alexander and enjoyed their rainbow dance. I really didn't care about the exact identity of the species in front of me. Rather, I enjoyed watching their beauty and behavior: how they responded to me, the river, and the other sunnies. Each species seems to have a unique demeanor.

Coppernose, or bluegill, in Alexander Springs.

Bluegill are the most brazen and get right up to my lens and mask. This seems to apply everywhere I have seen these little buggers. Redbreast sunnies are some of the most striking fish. As their name implies, they have a brilliant reddish-orange breast that almost glows and grades to an orange-brown back with iridescent blue highlights. They rival pumpkinseeds in coloration and beauty. They, like the pumpkinseeds, are like artists' palettes. Redbreast are curious but leery and only let me get so close before they swim off. Spotted sunfish have orange-red or pink spots on a cream-white background. Parts of their iris are turquoise. These are the most skittish of the bunch and rarely let me creep in for a close look.

Lucky for us, these fish are not in trouble. They are all wide-ranging and have been introduced into waters that aren't native to them, expanding their territory even more. We should be able to enjoy their beauty, antics, and sentience for decades without concern for their demise.

However, I noticed a large black saddle on a large spotted sunfish during my last visit to Alexander. Melanistic spots may be indicators of illness. Or they may just be dark spots on fish that shouldn't have them. The Susquehanna smallmouth bass illness was characterized by melanistic spots occurring on bass, so this sight was a bit frightening. Just like the Susquehanna, Alexander Springs and all Florida springs are facing water quality and quantity issues due to how we as humans treat land and water.

Many Florida springs are sick, evidenced by black, stringy algae that covers everything. This is a sign of a spring and ecosystem out of balance. We presumed that increases in nitrogen and phosphorus were driving the increase in

Spotted sunfish.

black, stringy algae growth. The algae covers submerged vegetation and kills it by stealing its sunlight, and the springs experience more bare sandy bottom, or bottom covered in stringy algae rather than native, healthy, vibrant vegetation. Alexander has a 57-square-mile spring shed, so it would make sense that land uses in Alexander's 57-mile spring shed, like septic tanks and forests converted to agriculture, would cause increases in nitrogen and phosphorous and be the underlying cause for the increased algae.

Maybe nitrogen and phosphorus are driving that change in some springs, but not in Alexander. Data shows little increase in nitrogen and phosphorous. A few unexpected and slight changes in a finely tuned system might be setting it out of whack. Slight changes in chloride and dissolved oxygen, because of our water withdrawals from the underground aquifer, might be affecting the snails who live here. This may result in uncontrolled growth of algae, since the grazers are reduced. Even a slight change in flow velocity might be a cause. The physical force of a robust water flow kept the algae from colonizing the native underwater grasses. As we punch wells into the aquifer to keep our expanding development watered, we decrease the flow velocity coming from the springs and increase the opportunity for algae to stick and grow.

Just because things are common doesn't mean they are safe. Abundance doesn't mean immune from decline. The passenger pigeon should have taught us that. The shad story reinforces it, and the Susquehanna River smallmouth bass fishery provides another example. But for now, I enjoy watching members of the sunfish family, whether they are called a bass or a sunny, almost everywhere I snorkel. And I take nothing for granted.

Toads, Frogs, Turtles, Snakes, Gators, and Benders

TOADS

I stood on the bank of the Big Elk in Maryland and listened to the high trills of American toads as the sun set. First, one called to my right, then another answered to my left. A third called from across the stream. April felt early for American toads to be calling for mates, but here they were, trilling away. I scared one couple, in amplexus, into the water. Amplexus is how toads mate. The smaller male climbs on top of the larger female and tightly grasps her, not letting go until she deposits her eggs, and he fertilizes them as they are expelled.

American toads are an urban success story. They have figured out how to prosper in the most densely populated areas, even though we aren't sure how. They are killed by dogs, chopped by lawnmowers, and squished by cars; yet, still, they thrive. Toads are amphibians, which means they spend part of their lives in water and part on land. They move into water to breed, and in urban areas, toad-accessible water can be scarce. The eggs hatch in 3 to 12 days into tadpoles, which look like tiny black squiggles. The tadpoles sprout legs, absorb their tails, and become toadlets in 50 days when they hop out of the water.

I wanted to capture images of the toads in amplexus because it is such a sign of hope and an incredible story of amazing nature accessible to everyone. There were only 10 minutes of daylight left. It would be dark by the time I got into my drysuit, so I decided to come back in 2 days, when my schedule wasn't as tight. I figured the toads would still be there trilling and in amplexus.

I returned as planned, but the toads were done; their eggs were laid. I should have gotten in the water with the toads when I had the chance. Things change fast in a stream. I suited up anyway to explore what is a very impacted creek.

Strands of toad eggs.

The Big Elk is a heavily urbanized stream. The bottom is completely embedded in deposited silt so that it's now one continuous sand flat, with no cobble and, therefore, little habitat. Overfertilized water results in long, stringy, mustardy tan algae that covers everything.

The stream was featureless except for a half-submerged tree trunk and a tire filled with sand. I was snorkeling over a barren lunar landscape. But then—life! A white sucker swam from a deeper hole and got used to my presence so that I could watch it without it hustling for cover. Tessellated darters sent up fine puffs of sediment as they shot away. A small school of small sunnies held under the sunken tree. I turned to see if anything was trailing me and saw a large school of common shiners. I had stirred a lot of the string algae off the bottom into a flocculent cloud, and the shiners fed in it. I got a face full of the olive, chunky haze as I turned upstream and really hoped I didn't get any in my snorkel. I tried not to gag, as I thought about the possibility.

I continued to crawl upstream over the plain sand bottom. Then I saw lines of black dots in thin jelly tubes. They looked like small black pearls encased in clear plastic sheaths. Some of the strands were curled around upon themselves, and others trailed straight in the downstream current. They were the eggs that would hatch into tadpoles in a few days. These were the descendants of amphibious urban survivors. I might have missed the opportunity to capture toads mating, but I captured images of the next toad generation. There is nothing more hopeful in ecology than reproducing populations, and I felt grateful to be able to witness the process. At times, it feels like nature and humans are incompatible.

That wherever we go, we push out all that is natural. It is easy to think that nature doesn't exist among us but rather is relegated to the truly great spaces like Yellowstone or Shenandoah. But watching these toads in this urban stream showed me that nature is here too, and it is just as inspiring.

FROGS

Just a few degrees make a huge difference, so when temperatures climbed into the 40-degree range, it looked, felt, and smelled like spring. It was a prime opportunity to get into one of my favorite creeks to see if things underwater were changing as fast as they seemed to be on land. I was specifically trying to learn the timing of a large darter gathering at a local waterfall. I'd watched them congregate there for the last 2 years and wondered if it was just a fluke, or if the meeting was intentional and specifically timed with the season.

The air might have been warm, but the water still stung as I climbed in. I'm used to it now, and soon, the cold didn't register. There were no darters still, and I started to get a little concerned. There had been darters there at the same time the previous year. In fact, they had been there 2 weeks earlier the previous year, and I'd hoped they'd return. The water temperature was 3 degrees colder than the year before, and maybe that slight difference explained their absence.

I inched my way down a shallow riffle and saw movement out of the corner of my eye. I couldn't make out what splashed into the deeper, faster-moving water, but I assumed it was some kind of fish. I slid over algae-covered rocks and sailed into a pool with a strong recirculating current.

Cold-stunned frog.

A frog twirled in the eddy and did slow turns between the surface and sand-bar bottom. I thought it was dead and thought, *What a waste.* I wondered what killed it as I circulated with its motionless body through the river. It looked so clean. Its legs were a creamy white and brilliant yellow. Its abdomen looked strong and its body intact as we twirled together in a kind of a postmortem dance. It lifelessly flew through the water. I reached out, grabbed it, and felt one of its hind legs push slowly but firmly against my hand. The frog wasn't dead. It was cold. Frogs, like other amphibians, are ectotherms, which is a more accurate descriptor for animals typically called coldblooded. Their blood isn't necessarily cold. Rather, their body temperature generally matches the temperature of the surrounding environment. So, when it is cold out, ectotherms, including frogs, are less active, and many hibernate for the winter. When it warms, they get active.

Some frogs must have taken advantage of the warmer day and emerged. The movement I'd seen earlier that I'd assumed to be fish wriggling for deeper water I now thought had been frogs, right on the cusp of the breeding season, wanting to be the first ones out to increase their chances of attracting a mate. The males inflate sacs under their throats to produce calls that attract females. Each species of frog has a distinctive call. This cold frog was probably one of the eager ones.

I placed the frog in a calm, shallow pool near the shore, and it assumed the usual frog position, legs under body, poised to jump. Soon, this river would be full of darters and trilling frogs, hopefully migrating herring, too. The pent up biological energy was almost palpable. We were right on the cusp of spring, and the frogs were flying.

Oddly, I've had more encounters with frogs during winter than I have in warmer weather. They are too fast in summer, I guess. However, one winter night, I came across an interesting find. My head lamp and dive light illumined the bottom. Stubbly riverweed, remnants from a warmer time, clung to the orange bedrock. The lights threw odd-angled shadows, and I felt like I was diving a freshwater sea on Mars, if Mars had freshwater seas. I was just about to get out of the freezing water but decided to make one more pass down a short rapid. There, on the bottom, wedged nose-first under the upstream lip of a cobble, was a frog. Her banded hind legs were drawn up tight under her sides. For a minute, I thought she might be dead. What was a frog doing out in barely above-freezing water? Had she been overwintering here? Seemed like a pretty forceful flow for a frog to overwinter. Maybe the trade-off was the oxygen-rich water.

The frog's nictitating membranes covered her eyes so that they glowed zombie white, and I wasn't convinced she was dead. I really didn't want to disturb the frog, but my curiosity won, and I gently poked her hindquarters. She tucked tighter into the rock. The frog was definitely alive and had chosen to spend at least this part of winter here, huddled on the bottom of this rapid. I watched the frog for a while and tried to get a good photo without disturbing the amphibian any more than I already had. I could see my breath float across the moon as I got out of the water into the cold, dark night, exhilarated.

Amphibians are in trouble. Habitat loss, climate-change–related disease, and insecticide-induced mutations are taking their toll. Therefore, I'm always appreciative of what I get to watch in our rivers. It's even more profound when what I watch is something as unexpected as frogs in winter.

TURTLES

I don't usually snorkel with the intention to observe turtles, but I often find them. One trip to a preserve in suburban southeastern Pennsylvania, a 55-acre green oasis, resulted in a really important turtle find. A creek skirts along the edge of the property. The water looked churned up and a little milky.

There wasn't much life there, at least not at first, so I admired the unique asteroid texture of the clay and gravel stream bed. I grappled my way upstream and surveyed the bottom. It was winter, and life had wriggled into the substrate and moved to deeper spots, which made it hard to find.

The river carved a 3-foot hole out of the clay and cobble under a tree root mass. It was dark in the back of this hollow, and I almost ignored it. I took a breath, clung to the bottom, and inched my way in. As soon as my eyes adjusted to the low light, I saw a large turtle wedged into the bottom. I came up for an excited breath and eased back down to try to get a positive identification and a few pictures. I didn't want to disturb the reptile since I was fairly certain it was hunkered down there for the winter.

The prominent vertical red stripes on its shell confirmed my suspicion that it was a northern red-bellied cooter. This was a first for me. I have seen these beautiful animals on the surface, but I've never snorkeled with one. I watched from a distance to make sure I didn't interrupt its hibernation. Seeing firsthand where and how a turtle hibernates was incredible. The fact that red-bellied cooters are threatened in Pennsylvania, and federally endangered, made this find even sweeter. Red-bellied numbers have declined due to the loss of habitat to suburban development. It was no coincidence that this red-bellied cooter was there on a preserve.

I left the stream feeling energized and excited for my next exploration of a stream secured by protected land. How we treat land matters. The critically important work of land preserving organizations protects not only essential terrestrial habitats but aquatic ones too, and I couldn't wait to see what discoveries await in other preserve creeks.

A few months later, in late spring, I was in Big Branch, a stream that runs through a preserve in northeastern Maryland. Large male sunfish took me on as I approached their nests. They flashed neon turquoise stripes, and one even turned red. A big school of large fallfish swirled in a hole beneath some big woody material. A smallmouth bass challenged me just like the sunnies, charging at my mask. Swarms of young darters hopped along the sand flats. Mixed schools of rosy-sided dace, black-nosed dace, and common shiner swam past me against the current in lock step order and looked like a group of leaves in the wind as they flowed back downstream in disarray. This was the typical Big Branch. Full of tons of life that display extraordinary behaviors.

I reached a big upstream pool and started the slow float back down and decided to go a little past my usual takeout to explore an oak that had recently fallen into the river. As I approached, I thought I saw the shell of a turtle, but it could have been a rock sticking out of the mud and sand bottom. Then I saw the head. Sure enough, it was a snapper. I've never seen this animal in the water. All of my encounters with snappers have been on land where they are slow and clunky, except for their strike. But in the water, this animal is agile and graceful. And just like on land, this animal didn't want anything to do with me. It started to back away as soon as it saw me approach. I kept my distance not out of fear but rather respect. I'm not afraid of snappers. I don't ascribe to the commonly held belief that these turtles can shear a broomstick in half. I've trapped turtles for 5 years as part of a mark and recapture program to determine population size and migration patterns, and I found them not to be the finger-removing monsters they are made out to be. Rather, they respond like any other animal when threatened and cornered.

Once, while checking traps for the mark recapture study, I found that one of the nets contained two large snappers in addition to a dozen painted turtles. I took all of the painted turtles out of the trap and worked to free the first snapper. The turtle was surprisingly strong, and I had difficulty holding on to its hind legs as I untangled the net from its long, dark claws. The turtle unleashed its coiled neck with a lightning-fast strike at the air that made its entire 20-pound body leap off the deck. It wasn't even aiming for me; it was a defensive jab and jump at the air. As I focused on freeing this first turtle, I lost track of the second and felt a strong punch on my right hand. The second turtle was there and lashed its head at me, mouth closed. I gave this turtle the opportunity to inflict injury, but it didn't take it. I've been hit by the head of a closed-mouthed snapping turtle many times since. It's as if they use their head as a warning shot rather than immediately striking with a snapping mouth.

The turtle I watched in the water was more agile than the ones I'd encountered on land. It was in its aquatic element and started to back up as I approached. Its shell was covered in green shag algae fur, and its starred eyes remained fixed on me. I tried not to get too close or make abrupt moves because I didn't want to disturb the turtle. But the current had other ideas, and I wound up floating too close for the snapper's comfort. It left me alone in the creek with a few graceful flicks of its hind feet.

Turtles don't just inhabit pristine environments. I've seen them in highly altered streams. Jordan Creek runs through Allentown, Pennsylvania. The creek's banks are walls of concrete, and the river is forced into a thin sheet of water over a low head dam. I crept into the plunge pool from the downstream side. I am always uneasy in plunge pools formed by dams. They are unnatural features and can contain dangerous and confusing trapping currents. They also often contain dangerous trash that can hang a snorkeler up: shopping carts, rebar, whole trees. And they are full of the roar of falling water and blurred with veils of entrained air bubbles, which makes it hard to see if any hazards are present. This plunge hole was relatively tame but still loud and chaotic. I peered through the air bubble curtains thrown into the pool by falling water and saw two eyes on a striped neck looking back at me. I couldn't discern what it was at first, but then the entire shell came into focus through the bubbles. This was a red-eared slider laying on the bottom of a quiet part of the plunge pool below the dam craning its neck toward the surface to watch me watch it. Red-eareds are native to the Midwest and are common pet store turtles. This reptile could be a pet that gained its freedom when its keeper got tired of caring for it. Or it could be part of the introduced eastern Pennsylvania population that is now reproducing.

The Susquehanna River around Harrisburg is pretty heavily exploited. The land surrounding this part of the river is developed, and numerous dams and power plants use the river to generate power. I got into the river south of Harrisburg to explore, to experience adventure in a built-up setting, and to understand that even urban rivers are wild. The bottom was angled bedrock that slanted at 45 degrees and was covered in olive algae. There were lots of nooks and crannies for life to hide, and I saw smallmouth bass and very abundant crayfish. I drifted

Map turtles in the Susquehanna River.

over an eddy where leaves, twigs, and the shells of dead Asian clams and crayfish had accumulated.

A small turtle looked back. Its saucer-sized body was clean and green with thin yellow lines squiggled over its skin. The lines extended onto its shell but were less distinct. They looked like the lines on a contour map, which gives this turtle its name: map turtle. I initially got very excited, because I thought it might be a northern map turtle. Northern map turtle populations are shrinking due to poor water quality, and they are endangered in Maryland, just 40 miles south. It turned out that it was a common map turtle rather than the less abundant and declining northern map, but that didn't diminish the excitement I felt when I saw that beautiful creature. I usually see turtles when I'm not looking for them.

I slid down the 5-foot, slick bank onto the sandy bottom of Emuckfaw Creek near Horseshoe Bend Historical Park, Alabama. I wasn't sure I was allowed to be here, and I wasn't exactly sure how I would get back out, but I would figure that out later. I laid down in the 3-foot-deep creek and watched. Some kind of shiner I didn't know congregated in an eddy behind a large rock embedded in the sand bottom. The fish flashed their peach sides as they danced on the current until some motion on the bottom grabbed my attention. A flattened musk turtle crept along the sand and hunkered behind a rock, keenly aware of my presence. His orange-yellow neck was striped with black, and it snaked around at a 45-degree angle to his body to watch me. His starred eyes looked at me with an intent and aware stare, and he evaluated my every move. His shell was a flattened orange-brown dome. I grabbed on to a rock to stop from moving closer to the flattened

Flattened musk turtle.

EMUCKFAW CREEK

Description: Emuckfaw Creek is a small stream that empties into the Tallapoosa River about a mile downstream. It winds through a bottomland hardwood forest and has a sandy bottom interspersed with bedrock outcrops. This is a party spot, so watch for broken glass and bring a trash bag to pick up after other people.

Access: GPS Address: 12578 Alabama Highway 49 (Hamlet Mill Road), Daviston, Alabama. From Horseshoe Bend Military Park, drive 1.25 miles northeast on Alabama 49. The pull-off is on the left. Drive down below the bridge. Access to the creek is a little difficult due to a steep bank.

Emuckfaw Creek.

musk turtle. I didn't want to disturb this turtle any more than I already had. He stayed frozen while deciding his next move.

I have seen this go/no-go decision-making in other turtles in other places. There is a healthy population of river cooters living in Alexander Springs, and I watch a number of them each time I snorkel there. River cooters are large turtles by freshwater standards, often 1 to 2 feet long, with high-domed shells. I see them out feeding in the open in the morning before many people show up to swim in the clear, turquoise spring water.

I quietly stepped onto the soft sand between cypress knees, brown cones of roots that grow up out of the water, as mist rose and sparkled silver in the early morning sunlight, and laid down in the clear water. The chill took my breath and made me gasp, but soon, the water trapped by my wetsuit warmed, and I settled into a comfortable, relaxing, slow-paced, silent exploration. I watched four dark mounds spread across the bottom 50 yards away grub for food through stringy green algae. I drifted toward the turtles, trying to keep my motions slow and subtle. They continued to feed on underwater vegetation without noticing my approach. The turtles sent puffs of sand into the water as they grazed. I crept closer using small flicks of my feet and a subtle doggy paddle with my hands to sneak in closer without alarming the turtles. One finally saw me, froze in mid-bite, and took off for the far side of the spring, its hind legs paddling in a furious scurry to escape. Another cooter grazed just on the edge of an emergent lily patch, spotted me, and looked up still chewing. This turtle watched me for a while. The food was good here, apparently, and it seemed that the turtle was debating whether he should scamper away, like his comrade, or stay close to the relative protection of the lilies and keep feeding while keeping an eye on me, which is exactly what this turtle did. He took a bite of lily, extended his yellow-striped neck toward the surface and me 4 feet above, and chewed. He was a striking animal. The yellow stripes on his neck were clean and almost glowed against the black background. He took another bite and watched me while he chewed, until a female turtle swam into view. Courting her became more important than me or food, and the cooter swam off to impress her.

Once while watching river cooters in another Florida spring, I noticed something large moving in the background. Whatever it was slowly undulated along the edge of the spring bowl, where the water met the forest. Then, I saw its large

Florida cooter.

American alligator.

tail. It was an alligator! I swam as fast as I could towards the gator. I was so excited to witness such an ancient being, an animal that was endangered that then made a thriving comeback to the point of nuisance from our perspective as they end up in our ponds and pools. And they are potentially at risk again as the sex of alligators, similar to turtles, is determined by nest temperature. As the climate warms, more male alligators are being hatched, which doesn't give a great outlook for the future of this species. I stopped kicking and drifted. I wanted to get close, but I didn't want to disturb it.

This looked like a relatively young alligator, maybe 4 or 5 feet long. It slowly moved along the margin of the spring until it saw me. Then it froze. Its tail dragged on the bottom, and its toed hind feet also touched. The alligator looked crisp. I could see the indentations and folds in its thick skin, and I very slowly drifted closer. I hoped the gator would confuse me with a log and stay put so I could get some photos. However, I was also listening and looking for signs of aggression. I have had alligators growl at me, which sounds like a low rumble, when I got too close. The problem was I couldn't see those gators on the shore, I could only hear, and feel, their guttural warning. The gators that will get you are the ones you don't see. But this one was in plain view, and it was apparent it didn't want anything to do with me. I drifted in too close, and in a flick of its tail and push of its feet, it disappeared into the thick vegetation that lined this spring. Alligators are misunderstood animals, as evidenced by this encounter. They are not aggressive, and the fear surrounding them is largely unwarranted. They have the potential to be dangerous, but they just want to be left alone to hunt and feed and reproduce.

SNAKES

There are other things in our rivers and streams that generate unnecessary fear and that really just want to be left alone to feed and reproduce. Snakes head that list.

A family rushed past me away from the stream on the trail that leads to Deer Creek. "There's a water moccasin down there in the creek bed. I wouldn't go down there," the father says, hurriedly.

"Thanks for the heads-up," I said and continued to the stream as people surged out of a favorite swimming hole, leaving better visibility and more room for me. I knew I wouldn't find a moccasin. It would be a northern water snake.

I don't like snakes. I like to watch them, but I'm not big on handling them. I've been bitten before—always my fault. I've learned that when you grab one, they tend to grab back. Water snakes are common in our rivers and streams in summer, and every time I see one in the water, I try to swim with it but usually can't keep up. They really don't want anything to do with us and quickly disappear into the distance. However, once in a while, I get lucky and see the snake before it sees me and swims away. I watched a water snake hunt on the bottom of the Delaware in 6 feet of water. The bright red, brown, and gray diamond pattern on its body looked like a moving, intricate mosaic. The snake methodically probed for fish under and around rocks. I surface dove to the bottom to get a better look and clung to a boulder while I watched the snake hunt. It saw me, startled when it did, and quickly swam away. I was able to keep up for a few feet but was no match for the aquatic agility of the reptile, and it easily escaped my sight.

The force of the water matted vegetation beds to the cobbles. The bottom faded into the haze of deeper water that gave the river an infinite feel. Large web-spinner caddisfly nets folded and billowed in the current. Another water snake appeared in mid-water before me, bobbed to the surface, and dove when it realized I was there. It wedged between the bottom and a rock and almost blended in, and I ended up losing it to the background when it moved to a better hiding spot. They are such misunderstood and victimized animals, often confused with venomous snakes and usually stoned to death. And so normally, I see them as they are being killed.

I witnessed a family stoning a northern water snake to death on Deer Creek. The father hoisted a basketball-sized cobble above his head and smashed it on the snake's head just as I walked to the river. His kids tossed baseball-sized rocks at the dead snake's body for good measure.

"What did you do that for?' I asked, trying to contain my anger.

"That was a moccasin!" the man said with a cigarette hanging from the corner of his mouth.

"No, it was a water snake, completely harmless."

"No, it ain't. I'm from here, and I know a moccasin when I see one!"

Northern water snake hunting.

Ignorant ass. I really questioned the value of time spent doing environmental education in rivers and streams. That family spent time on a creek and obviously didn't care about the life that's there. That experience made me question a tenet that has underpinned the last 30 years of my life: that as we get people to the stream to experience it, they will connect with the life there, and that is foundational to behavior change.

A few weeks later, I was snorkeling a shallow rocky section of the Susquehanna while being interviewed for a story about Susquehanna River snorkeling.

"Snake!" the reporter shouted.

Northern water snake on the surface.

CODORUS CREEK

Description: The Codorus is a 42-mile-long tributary to the lower Susquehanna. It is pretty heavily impacted by raw sewage overflows, urban runoff, agricultural runoff, and flood control practices as it flows through downtown York, Pennsylvania, about 20 miles upstream. The Codorus has mostly healed itself by the time it makes its way to the Codorus Furnace, a mile above its confluence with the Susquehanna. The furnace here made cannons and cannonballs and played an important role in rearming Washington's troops at Valley Forge. It is on the National Register of Historic Places.

Access: GPS Address: Codorus Furnace, 4161 Furnace Road, Mount Wolf, Pennsylvania. Park at the Furnace and cross Furnace Road. There is a trail that leads to the creek through the tree line. Use caution parking, pulling out, and crossing. Traffic moves fast on Furnace Road, and there are blind curves around the furnace.

Above: Codorus Creek.

"Where?" I shouted back, about to jump out of the water. I knew better, knew that water snakes are non-aggressive, but memories of getting grabbed back after grabbing them were still fresh.

"Over there. Its head is just behind that rock."

There was a slab of bedrock that separated me from the snake, so I couldn't see it. The reporter guided me in.

"He's right over there, just on the other side of the rock."

I inched around, really hoping it would be long gone as part of me didn't want to come face-to-face with a water snake. But I had to prove to this writer that water snakes really were non-aggressive, so I pressed on.

I cautiously peeked around the rock. Nothing but crayfish.

"He took off. It's way over there." The reporter pointed across the riverbed, proving my point about the snake being non-aggressive.

The next summer, I saw what looked like a stick poking out of the surface while snorkeling on the Codorus Creek. I quietly slid into the water and slowly crept closer with the water line in the middle of my mask so I could see above and below the surface on the hunch that it was a water snake. I was right. At about 20 feet, I could make out the reptile's round eyes set against a reddish-brown head. The snake wasn't sure what to make of me, and its tongue started to flick more frequently when I got to within 10 feet. Snakes sense their environments with their tongues, and this response let me know the snake knew I was close. I stopped moving toward him and just watched. He was stunning, and I still can't comprehend how anyone could kill these animals out of pure ignorance. They are incredibly beautiful animals, graceful and adept in the water and fast on land.

Unfortunately, their reputation as venomous and aggressive often leads to their death. Water snakes aren't venomous and won't come after people. Their diet is almost entirely fish, and it's really amazing to watch them hunt and successfully snag a fish that is often surprisingly large for the snake's body size.

But still, they are regularly the target of rocks thrown by people who just don't understand how harmless they are or how important they are to the stream system. Maybe they just can't see past their unfounded fear to notice the beauty and agility of these extraordinary creatures.

HELLBENDERS

I got a text from Jeremy Monroe, director of Freshwaters Illustrated, a nonprofit dedicated to bringing the underwater world of our rivers and streams to light through video, saying that the Tellico River just behind the cabin I was staying in held hellbenders. Southeastern US rivers are home to some of the most diverse freshwater biology in the world. Freshwaters Illustrated was there to document that diversity. I was there as part of my efforts to develop a curriculum to accompany Freshwaters Illustrated films. Seeing a hellbender on this trip would be phenomenal. Hellbenders are foot-long salamanders, giants in salamander terms. They need cold, clean water to survive, so their numbers are declining, and their range is shrinking since cold, clear streams are becoming rare. I had never seen one, even though I had been searching for the last 5 years, looking for them any time I was in their range.

Hellbenders are important to me because they represent wild rivers. They are a species that was present where I live, that are now thought to be gone because of increased sediments that come from the things we do on land, and because some fishermen killed the ones they caught. Even today they are found dead wrapped in fishing line on rivers in the southern Appalachians. I would like to think that there are still hellbenders in the lower Susquehanna. The large slabs of bedrock characteristic of this stretch provide the perfect habitat for them and is part of the reason for my hope that a population is still hiding somewhere in the 9 miles of river below the Conowingo Dam. Even if the lower Susquehanna hellbenders are gone, I believe that maybe they can be restored. I wanted to see one in case they disappear from the wild, but I have hope that we can protect the populations that are left. I wanted to find them in the Tellico River in Tennessee, in case we can't protect those that remain.

Dave Herasimtschuk, a photographer and videographer with Freshwaters Illustrated, saw a half dozen hellbenders out in the open at the same spot a month ago when waters were much colder. The search was on. Jeremy, Dave, Casper Cox, and I slipped into the river and searched for 2 hours before dusk.

The Tellico is interesting. The river is wide and flat. Ridges of bedrock poke through the bottom and wrinkle the surface across the width of the river so that the river goes from ankle-deep on the ridgetops to chest-deep in the valley between, in the matter of a foot. It was easy to snorkel across the width of the river simply by staying in these transverse channels. Moving up- and down-stream was more problematic and required either hauling out on the sharp rock, or searching for a water-carved gap, which often terminated in a dead end. It was like snorkeling through a bedrock maze. Completely disorienting. Fortunately, a luxurious growth of green-and-purple rockweed cushioned the jagged bedrock, and letting the current push me into the downstream rock spine felt like snuggling into a comfortable mattress.

I searched through 4-foot-deep, smooth-walled canyons the water had carved from the otherwise jagged bedrock. I dove to the bottom to peer into the shadows formed under the ledges of larger rocks, which is typical hellbender habitat, and I looked in the small crannies of the fractured bedrock, which isn't. Orange-and-black striped tangerine darters were plentiful, and their colorful displays made not finding any hellbenders OK.

We conjectured why we hadn't seen any hellbenders even though they had been so abundant a month ago. Cold water can hold more oxygen than warm water, so we thought they'd either headed upstream for cooler waters or were active at night since water temps mirror air temperatures and drop after dark. Hellbenders respire through their skin, so water conditions are pretty critical, which is one of the reasons they are at risk. They are very susceptible to low oxygen levels and high sediment loads and can't tolerate either. Therefore, either the hellbenders Dave encountered a month ago headed upstream to cooler waters or had assumed their typical secretive, nocturnal habit. We decided that a night snorkel in the Tellico might help me find one.

It was a few minutes before midnight when I slipped into the dark water. I debated a bit before getting wet but decided I had to make an attempt to find a hellbender. The water feels bigger at night. The deepest spot on that section of the Tellico could have been 3 feet deep, but it seemed like 30 since my sight was limited to a narrow cone of light. I couldn't see more than the reach of the beam, which felt terribly short. I slowly crept upstream through canyons carved through the bedrock, holding on tight to the search image of a dark brown, foot-long salamander with a broad mouth and wrinkly folds of skin.

I found a hog sucker that seemed to be sleeping or was dazed by my light, because it let me get in close for some photos. A few large redhorse suckers startled me as they rocketed out of the dark. I turned to try to get a picture, and one of them hit my thigh hard in the chaos my bright beam of light created in a narrow, deep section that was all silted up from the commotion. I tried to systematically search by traversing across the river, moving upstream a few feet and coming back. The dark, deep canyons were a little unnerving, and at times, I felt like I was floating in space—dark, cold space. I didn't find any hellbenders, and my frustration grew. I started to really question whether I would ever see one in the wild before it was too late.

Two years later, I had an opportunity to snorkel in Pisgah National Forest, North Carolina. National Forest streams are usually excellent places to snorkel due to their forested watersheds, and I looked forward to the trip. I wasn't thinking about looking for hellbender until I heard they were extremely abundant here. Someone who had snorkeled the river had said they saw six hanging out right in the open that summer, right where I was.

But it was the last week of November. The river was clear and loaded with fish, and that wasn't important. I was looking for a flattened, round, well-camouflaged, mottled head of a salamander, and nothing else mattered. I envisioned it barely peeking out from under a flat rock, and I searched for an image to match the one in my head. I started to shiver after 2 hours and got out.

It definitely would have been amazing to see a hellbender. These animals are so secretive and well-camouflaged, and the rivers in Pisgah afford so many places where a hellbender can effectively hide from a snorkeler. I'm sure my search was very incomplete and that I was just at Pisgah at the wrong time of year, and if I returned in their breeding season, I'd see one. Still, every time I search and come up empty, part of me worries that their numbers are dropping to the point where I may miss my chance to observe them in the wild, but I wasn't done looking.

The Hiawassee River is dam-controlled, and so its level downstream of the dam ebbs and rises based on our demand for electricity. I checked the generation schedule at the Hiawassee Dam and saw I had most of the day before water would start to flow through the generators, changing the character and complexion of this relatively placid place. I hurriedly suited up, waded into the shallow water,

HIWASSEE RIVER

Description: The Hiwassee River is 147 miles long. It starts in Georgia and flows into North Carolina and Tennessee where it joins the Tennessee River. It is dammed in four places by the Tennessee Valley Authority. It is another river in the biodiverse-rich southeastern United States. The recreation area is part of Cherokee National Forest and is downstream of the Hiwassee Dam.

The Hiwassee is a beautiful river, and it feels remote at the Hiwassee Recreation Area. It is wide here as it narrows into the Hiwassee Gap and braids around Taylor Island. The bottom is smoothed black slate that has a metallic blue sheen. It is truly a breathtaking river. The river at the Recreation Area is dam-controlled, so check the Hiwassee Dam generation schedule to determine water flows before you snorkel. This is also a party spot, so be sure to bring a trash bag to clean up after other people.

Access: GPS Address: Hiwassee River Recreation Area, 5070 Tennessee Route 30, Delano, Tennessee. If traveling north on 411, make a right onto TN Route 30 at the Hiwassee Food Mart. Drive 2.25 miles. Parking for the recreation area is on the left. Access to the river is obvious.

Above: Hiwassee River.

and laid down. Black, smooth, round cobble lined the bottom of the wide river. Larger smooth, rounded boulders formed transverse lines toward the middle. Everything was covered in a fine mist of green rockweed. The current was stiff but easily managed.

I found a chub constructing a nest, and he kept my attention. He was an ambitious fish and carried rocks that were likely heavier than he was to his mound and heaved them on the pile. I wasn't paying attention to my surroundings, just the chub and the other fish that were drawn to his gravel pile. After watching this fish construct a mound a foot tall and 3 feet wide in the course of a day, I happened to look to my left to see a hellbender watching me! This salamander could have been there the whole time. It looked like a roll of greenish-brown carpet that perfectly blended with the background. After 10 years, I was finally face-to-face with a hellbender! His tiny, pinpoint eyes were set on the sides of his head but still looked forward and carefully watched me. The skin on his legs and sides was folded into long, flowing flaps of wrinkles. His large mouth spanned his entire face. Tiny hand-like feet, with white-tipped toes, gripped the bottom.

I stayed transfixed by this salamander, the largest in North America, and soaked in the experience. The hellbender didn't move; it just watched me. I tried to stay in the moment, but after 10 years of searching, I didn't know when I would see the next one, if ever, and that thought kept interrupting. After watching the hellbender for a half hour, I gently and slowly crept closer. I didn't think the hellbender would notice; it was such a subtle change. But he didn't want anything to do with me and gracefully shot away in a frantic wriggle. I lost him to the background. I knew he was there somewhere. I just couldn't pick him out from the surroundings. I hope they are always there, whether I can see them or not. The knowledge that they exist is enough and makes the world a richer place.

A hellbender, the largest salamander in North America.

CHAPTER 12

Benthic Macroinvertebrates

All of the fish described in this book ride on the backs of benthic macroinvertebrates: organisms that don't have a backbone, live on the bottom of rivers and streams, and are small but large enough to be seen without the aid of magnification. They are often insects and are used to define the quality of rivers and streams. However, none of the fish I have encountered would exist if it weren't for the benthic macros. They have adopted unique ways of living in streams and serve as the links between life and death by converting decaying matter into animal biomass. Some even spin webs.

What seem like small perturbations become world-changing events down at the scale of our stream-dwelling neighbors. I've learned that I can cause those world-changing events just with my presence. Caddisflies, like many aquatic insects, spend the majority of their lives as juveniles underwater. They emerge as adults, often en masse, and their emergence is one of the greatest events in nature. I've been on the Susquehanna River on July nights in the middle of these hatches and could hardly see, the flies were so thick. Once emerged, the adults of many species don't eat. They mate, the females lay eggs, and they die.

Caddisflies, along with other bottom-dwelling insects, such as stone and mayflies, are the building blocks of healthy stream ecosystems and are eaten by just about any creek-dwelling fish. Many caddisfly larvae build intricate homes out of small bits of stone, sticks, or other plant matter. But hydropsyche caddisflies build webs that harvest organic particles from the current. Some species construct great ballooning socks. The open ends face upstream, and the 2-inch-long sack trails behind in the current and catches whatever floats in. The larval caddisfly then eats the edible bits that are trapped.

While floating in a foot and a half of water, amazed at the abundance of webs stretched between cobbles in a section of stream that at first glance appeared lifeless, I noticed one of these larger socks nestled into a shallow crevice between a few rocks, out of the direct hard current that would have probably shredded the net but in just enough flow to keep it inflated and catching for the caddisfly. How hydropsyche caddisflies know where to construct their webs in just the right places with just the right flow conditions is beyond me and indicates a degree of intelligence humans don't possess.

As I floated on the surface, my body changed the hydraulics in that section of stream and forced great flumes of water to the bottom, great for hydropsyche caddisfly webs. While I couldn't feel any difference in water velocity, it was obviously a more significant flow for the web. The intricately constructed sock waved violently in the strong current. It flattened to the bottom and widely expanded and quivered but withstood the force until I could orient my body so that I didn't interfere nearly as much with the movement of water passing through the web. What seemed like such an insignificant change in water flow to me posed a very significant threat to the caddisfly who occupied that particular web. Hydropsyche caddisflies filter streams. The more nutrition a stream receives, the more algae grows, and the more there is to filter. An abundance of hydropsyche caddisfly nets indicates an overfed and sick eutrophic stream. At the same time, they represent life finding a way in difficult conditions and give hope. I've learned that I can count on caddisflies to be present in the streams I snorkel, even the ones that have become overfertilized through suburbanization. Even in the middle of winter. One cold trip, in particular, taught me this.

Ice covered half of the water in Deer Creek, a tributary to the lower Susquehanna, and I wondered if the effort to get into a drysuit was worth it. I doubted I'd see any fish as cold as the winter had been. But Deer Creek was clear, and I'm always grateful for good visibility, so I crept out to the edge of the ice sheet that grew from the bank until the fast water wouldn't let it congeal and slid into

Caddisfly larvae cover a rock in a rapid.

the rapid. Instantly, tiny spikes of cold stabbed any exposed skin on my face. It pierced through my cheeks to my teeth and sent sharp pains into my gums. It was like biting into ice cream without the sweet reward.

At first, there didn't seem to be much life. The usual riverweed covered the boulders but was thinner and drab compared to summer. It looked like the rocks were balding. I didn't see any non-plant life, as the water continued to sting the exposed skin on my face. I swam out into the fast water and clawed upstream into a familiar eddy behind a large familiar rock. This is where I go for short quick snorkels, when I just need to get in a river. Bubbles from the water churning over this desk-sized rock whizzed by as straight-line blurs and made the water appear cloudy.

Smooth cylinders started to emerge on the face of the large boulder that forced the river flow to divide. Humpless caddisflies live in these smooth cylinders that looked like they were made out of sheets of green-and-blue cellophane, but in reality, they were made from pieces of vegetation by the insects that lived inside. They stretched their chestnut legs up into the current, to filter morsels of food from the water as it rushed by. My placement in the river changed the current dramatically for these small insects, and I could see their extended legs tremble in the new faster current I created. Other caddisflies clung to algae threads tethered to the bottom. I was worried I would blow them off their rock or algae strand, so I quickly changed position to change the flow of water to protect the caddis.

I drifted out of the slower eddy and crept into the powerful current where I was whisked downstream. I snagged a rock edge with one hand and let my floating body trail behind. I felt free. I slowly crawled upstream against the strong water and noticed that there were hundreds, possibly thousands, of caddis cases all facing up into the flow, all with black legs stretched into the current, feeding. I became very conscious of my hand and foot placements as I climbed into the rushing current. I didn't want to wipe out hundreds of caddis with an errant foot- or handhold, so I looked for blank spots on the rocks before moving a limb.

This is how I usually see caddis—in their larval, aquatic-cased forms. But once, I was fortunate enough to witness adult caddis laying eggs.

Deer Creek ran relatively clear through the same rapid in late March. As soon as I put my face in the water in this familiar spot, a very foreign stream-scape appeared. For as many times as I've been here, this was new. Algae covered the rock moss carpet in pinks and orange pastels, and silver dots crept down the lee face of the large rock that split the rapid.

The silver dots were caddisflies, and they glowed as they inched down the front of the boulder back into the rapid. I thought they might be recently metamorphosed adults, emerging, and tried to get some close-up photos to document this phenomenon. However, I wasn't sure what these flies were doing—coming or going. Adult caddisflies flitted just above the surface in clumsy flight. But as

Female caddisflies reenter the water to lay eggs.

I watched those silver-coated adults slowly creep back into this rapid, I realized that the silver was from an envelope of air that was trapped on the fine hairs that cover the insects' bodies. These were mated females returning to the water to lay their eggs to ensure the next generation: their last act before their death. I watched in amazement as a hundred silver-shrouded female caddisflies crawled back into the river, easy prey for an assortment of predators. They were running a crazy gauntlet, not only in terms of the risk of being eaten but also in terms of the environment. They had just emerged from the watery realm and metamorphosed into air-breathing organisms. And now they were returning without gills.

Caddis are always in creeks and in just about every creek I snorkel. I'm used to them, and I thought I knew their biology. But that day changed all that. I'd never witnessed adult caddis walking back into the water shrouded by a quicksilver layer of air. I never expected it. I'd learned the caddis lifecycle in undergrad and graduate ecology courses. I'd learned that the females lay eggs after they mate, but no one had ever said what that looked like. No one had ever told me what an amazing sight it was to watch adult caddisflies return to the water encased in silver bubbles of air to lay their eggs. No one told me to consider the magnitude of this act. Maybe the professors who taught me didn't know. Maybe they never witnessed the caddis return to water.

If more people knew about the miracles taking place in our creeks and rivers, they might be more concerned about their loss. Not just knowledge of the mechanics but rather what the process actually looks like and how it feels to be a part of it, being a direct witness and to ask questions like, "Why are there silver caddisflies walking down this rock?" If people witnessed this pilgrimage, maybe then people would care more for our most vital resource—water—and maybe then more people would feel alive by experiencing the excitement of discovery.

However, most people don't think of these organisms at all. Some fisherfolk might think of them as fish food and bait to replicate. And how they play a critical link between living and dead plants and fish. But watching these insects reveals them to be much more than a fly pattern, or an ecological function. There is an intelligence we can't comprehend or replicate. They possess beauty in their form that matches their function of converting vegetable biomass to fish.

Leaves twirled in the current like feathers in a breeze. Most of them had dropped off trees about a week prior, in the second week of November, and they populated Deer Creek. I felt like a kid running through blowing cyclones of them as I hung on to a rock in the rapid and leaves whizzed past. Some got plastered to my snorkel and mask.

A little farther upstream, in a more quiet pool, I swam through a snowstorm of sycamore seeds. The frilly tufts that carried them through the air also kept them suspended in the water, and they swirled about like snowflakes. There was a collection of walnuts behind a rock in a small rapid.

This was half of the lifeblood of the stream. The organic inputs from the adjacent forest in the form of leaves, seeds, and twigs provide energy that's converted from plant to animal by a diverse group of insects who shred and ingest the dead leaves. The insects are in turn food for fish. The rest of the stream's energy comes from algae. What I watched was more than just a few leaves twirling in water. I watched an ecological process finely tuned by eons of adaptation. It's part of an interplay of energy between the forest and the stream. In the fall, the net energy flow is downstream with the water. In spring and summer, the stream gives energy back to the forest in the form of hatching insects and migrating fish. Some leaves get stuck to rocks or are captured by sprigs of riverweed as they travel by. Others become waterlogged and gather in eddies on the bottom. I was more than watching a process. I was experiencing it. Another leaf plastered itself to my mask.

There aren't many creek snorkeling trips where I don't witness the intimate relationship between leaves and streams. They end up on the bottom, out of the current, between stones, or pinned by the flow to the upstream sides of rocks. Regardless, leaves are an incredibly important source of energy for our stream ecosystems and constitute a large part of the foundation of the creek food web.

Many aquatic insects eat only leaves that fall into creeks. They even have preferences for different tree species. Leaves with higher nitrogen content are usually eaten first; those with lower nitrogen and higher lignin, an organic polymer that forms cell walls in wood bark and leaves, are consumed later in the season. Do the higher-nitrogen-content leaves taste better to the leaf-shredding community of mayflies, caddisflies, and stoneflies? Or are the higher-nitrogen and lower-lignin leaves consumed first because the high-lignin-content leaves will last longer in the water, and somehow mayflies, stoneflies, and caddisflies know this? Maybe they eat the leaves that will decompose the fastest first so there will be food stores in the stream to last through the winter. Or maybe bacteria and fungi need to process the hard-to-digest lignin before it can be consumed by the creek shredders.

This is just another case of ecological complexity that implies an intelligence at work that we can't comprehend or interpret. Either way, leaves fuel the aquatic insect community, and the aquatic insect community, in turn, fuels the fish, bird, and bat communities that eat the insects, and so on. This is one of the reasons why our creeks need to have forests lining their shores—streams need leaves to fuel their food webs, and forests need creeks to fuel theirs. Trees play other important roles in creek ecology. They provide shade, which keeps creek waters cool. Their roots hold soil in place and reduce the amount of gill-choking sediment entering the water. Nitrogen and phosphorus are nutrients that make plants grow. When excess nitrogen and phosphorous get into the water, they make too much algae grow. Algae doesn't live for long, and when it dies, bacteria use up oxygen as they decompose the dead algae. This results in oxygen-poor water that can't support life, and this process is called eutrophication. Trees filter excess nitrogen and phosphorus from runoff, which prevents eutrophication. One of the simplest things we can do for stream restoration is plant trees.

Even in summer, when the forest canopy is full, and leaves are still firmly attached to their twigs, leaves enter creeks and flow downstream until they become waterlogged or lodged somewhere. In the fall, when the canopy drops, large, flocculent aggregations of yellow, orange, and brown leaves fill the bottoms of the deeper holes and make it look like multicolored decoupage. The life on the bottom of the creek takes advantage of the new cover and food. It's hard for me to snorkel over leaf mats in slower sections of streams without stirring up at least one northern hog sucker, a half dozen tessellated darters, and a bunch of crayfish. So the forest fuels the stream, but we are learning that the stream fuels the forest in return.

Dr. Mary Power, a professor at UC Berkeley, observed that spider webs were much larger farther from the stream compared to the webs close to the stream. She reasoned that the difference in web size was due to food abundance. There are more emerging insects close to the stream, which means those spiders didn't need to invest as much energy in web construction since food was abundant. Spiders in more interior parts of the forest had to build more elaborate webs to capture the same quantity of food. Dr Power tested her theory by trapping insects at varying distances from the stream and estimated that 96 percent of all emerging stream insects become part of the forest ecosystem.

We draw a line between wet and dry, terrestrial and aquatic. But when we look at energy flow, there's no divider. What we do on land affects the water, and water quality affects land-based systems. Terrestrial, aquatic, and human are intimately connected. The boundaries between them are artificial constructions we create.

I witnessed this on the Upper Delaware River one spring. I was waiting for a flotilla of a hundred canoes carrying 200 students to arrive at Worthington State Forest on a beautiful, blue-sky, lazy late May day. This was an annual sojourn trip organized by the Delaware Riverkeeper Network. Worthington was on their third night camping on the river. I provided some afternoon entertainment by taking as many kids snorkeling in the Delaware as wanted to go. While I knew the students wouldn't make shore until three, I always arrived early to enjoy this place. My dad and I used to camp and fish here, and it always brings back memories. While the rickety wooden outhouses have been replaced with slick composting toilets, the river is essentially the same, and I enjoyed remembering those times. I donned my mask, got in, and reveled in clear water. The river here is huge. Fifty yards offshore, a silt island covered in knotweed divides it, and the Delaware extends another hundred yards toward Pennsylvania on the opposite shore. The 50 yards between me and the island are deceiving. It looks placid and calm, but the river is hauling through here, and the bottom drops to at least 20 feet. No wonder drownings are common in this stretch. The river lulls you into a sense of security and then whisks you away. But the bottom on my side gently sloped to deeper water, so I enjoyed pulling myself upstream and drifting back down through wild celery and pondweed beds. It is as close to flying I can get while still on Earth. Smaller smallmouth bass came in close to investigate

Large stonefly nymph.

Newly metamorphosed stonefly adults looking for a mate.

while the larger smallies and huge bigmouth stayed on the cusp of deeper water, curious but cautious. I got chilled in the cool water, so I snorkeled toward land, into the foot-deep shallows, and witnessed stoneflies marching toward the shore.

They were large by benthic macroinvertebrate standards, about an inch and a half, dark brown, almost black, with a flanged thorax that I assume was used to their advantage to keep them plastered to the bottom in swift currents. I got out of the water with them and followed them to the river's edge. Behind me, the large, arching green grasses rustled, but there was no wind. It was as if the grasses were alive and moving. I realized the stonefly nymphs I watched underwater were crawling up these grasses to bust out of the backs of their exoskeletons to become air-breathing winged adults. I knew stoneflies did this. However, the bland word description from my aquatic entomology texts—"stoneflies emerge from the water and molt one last time to become an adult"—were so matter-of-fact and mechanical compared to the marvel I was observing. What a miracle to witness: an animal going from gill-based aquatic to pulmonated-based air-breathing before my eyes.

A slit opened in the back of the exoskeleton of a nymph that had just crawled out of the river. A new animal with wings slowly and methodically emerged. This is the stuff alien space monsters are made of. The new adult stonefly unfurled his or her new wings and dried in the sun. Some of the slightly older adults stood face-to-face on wide arching blades of green riverside grass. I assumed they were male and female getting to know each other, deciding if the other was a suitable mate, the one that was the fittest, the most likely to produce young that were most likely to survive. Reproduction takes a lot of energy, so you want it to count. I wondered what the world was like from their perspective. They only live for a month at most as adults, so I imagined their world was pretty fast-paced.

Eight months later, it was a different world as I slid into the frozen waters of Deer Creek. These wintertime snorkel trips are often just for me to get in the water to experience weightlessness, to have some of the societally imposed, expectation-induced stress get washed away, or at least forgotten while I'm in the moment in the water. They aren't usually about exploring life, but benthic macroinvertebrates often change that motive. I pulled my way upstream against a stiff current as ice chunks pelted my cheeks and clinked off my mask. I enjoyed the feeling of flight as I drifted back downstream with the current and watched caddisfly larvae stick their legs into the water to snag morsels of food. I was just a little too large. The cold took over after a few upstream/downstream laps. I started to shiver, and my hands became difficult to work. I snorkeled toward the shoreside ice sheet and focused on getting out and getting warm, hoping my hands would have just enough strength to unzip me from my drysuit. I looked at the edge of the foot-thick ice as I approached from the current and saw a stonefly adult crawling over the kaleidoscopic-fractured pattern of ice crystals.

I wedged my arm between the ice and bottom since my hands wouldn't work to grip it and let my body trail downstream with the current so that I could watch

An adult stonefly crawls over an ice sheet.

this adult. It was a totally unexpected find. Fly fishers know about winter stonefly hatches, but I didn't, and I was astonished to watch this lowly insect crawl over ice to find a mate.

I hope he was successful. We are experiencing a serious decline in insects, which is a frightening development. Insects are the building blocks of all eco-systems, including aquatic ones. A recent review in *Biological Conservation* concludes that as much as 40 percent of all insects might be endangered in the next few decades. We have already seen significant declines, and aquatic insects are not exempt.

Thirty percent of stonefly species are either endangered or threatened, and 20 percent are already extinct. Eighty percent of caddis are either vulnerable or endangered.

Besides their critical importance to aquatic ecosystems as a link between vegetative and animal biomass, and the ecosystem collapse their disappearance would initiate, they are simply fascinating to watch. Observing their underwater lives could be the subject of an entire book rather than a short chapter.

Other organisms comprise the benthic macroinvertebrate community. Some of the most bizarre life-forms on the planet are included, in fact. A group of us gathered at the base of the Pinchot Dam, in Pinchot State Park, Pennsylvania. We were there to try to catch shad and striped bass that had become stranded in the deeper pool at the bottom of the spillway. July dryness dropped water levels in the lake and, thus, in Beaver Creek that led from the dam to the Conewago River, so the fish were stuck. They couldn't make it up the dam, obviously, and now couldn't head back downstream. I was going to snorkel to document the chase, as well as hopefully the catch and to direct the net-wielding team to where the fish were holding.

It was hot out of the water in my wetsuit, and my large camera housing was clunky and awkward to lug across the boulders that led to the concrete knee wall. I was paranoid about dinging the glass dome on a rock. I propped the camera on the wall, sure it wouldn't fall off, and pulled myself up. I swung my legs over the upstream side, grabbed my camera, and hopped to the bottom 5 feet below. The water instantly churned to murk. This was going to suck, snorkeling in warm, soupy water. But I said I would do this, so I laid down in the 3-foot-deep, greenish-brown filth and snorkeled upstream. I saw the school of shad huddled in a corner of the concrete-lined chute and directed the seine net team to where they were cowering. I snorkeled in the downstream slick of yuck stirred into the water, barely able to see 6 inches in front of me, and almost bumped my mask into a silvery globe of stiff jelly. It looked like an alien brain.

Bryozoan colony.

CHEAHA CREEK

Description: Cheaha Creek was dammed to form Lake Chinnabee. It is now a recreation area within Talladega National Forest. Cheaha Creek upstream of Lake Chinnabee contains good aquatic diversity and interesting geology. Devils Hole is a popular swimming hole at the base of a waterfall about a mile upstream from Chinnabee Lake. While it is an interesting place to see, it is overused, so I recommend snorkeling the easily accessed sections near the lake.

Access: GPS Address: Lake Chinnabee Road, Lineville, Alabama. From Talladega, take 275 north for 4.8 miles to 21 north for 2.5 miles. Turn right on McElderry Road. Lake Chinnabee Road will be on your right in 3.5 miles. Follow Lake Chinnabee Road to the first parking lot on the left. Pay the area use fee, and follow the paved trail to the end. There is easy access to Cheaha Creek from the trail that runs alongside the creek.

Above: Cheaha Creek at Lake Chinnabee Recreation Area, Talladega National Forest.

This was a bryozoan colony. Bryozoans are microscopic animals that live communally, like this 6-inch blob. They are filter feeders, and their presence is supposed to indicate decent water quality, though I think their judgment might be a little off being in this tepid cesspool. The shad outsmarted our net team, and after multiple attempts, we figured we had stressed these fish enough in the name of saving them and decided to leave them be and hope for a rain that would flush them back downstream. The only thing I came away with was a few photos of the alien brain bryozoan colonies. And that was enough. The amazing life in our rivers and streams isn't always large and flashy. Sometimes it's bizarre and cryptic.

Cheaha Creek flows down the mountains in Talladega National Forest into Chinnabee Lake. I was here in February to scout the site for a trip I hoped to run with the Forest Service for kids from the Talladega, Alabama, area. Even in Alabama, rivers get chilly in February. I squeezed into my drysuit and braced for the pain of cold. Cheaha Creek was clear and rocky. It was the perfect venue to run a snorkeling trip in April. I looked for life in its fissures, gaps, and recesses that make the habitat at Cheaha so diverse. There weren't many fish due to the cold. Snails grazed over rocks, and a large crayfish charged me from the shadows, claws erect.

The crests on the ridges on his rostrum, the part of his shell between his eyes, were painted brilliant red and looked like angry eyebrows. His claws were covered in orange spikes, and he came at me with an unmatched intensity. He didn't care that I was a hundred times his size. While bryozoans may resemble assumed alien life-forms, crayfish have served as their models. Besides their large claws, they have smaller pincers on the ends of their eight walking legs they use to bring food to their whirling mouths, so that if I scale this crayfish up a hundred times, or if I shrink to the size of a snail, this pugnacious curiosity becomes a formidable beast. But this one was still just a hundredth of my size and kept coming.

This was a Tennessee bottlebrush crayfish, which was just discovered in 2011. How a large crayfish could go undetected speaks to how we ignore freshwater

Tennessee bottlebrush crayfish.

SUSQUEHANNA AT MCKEE'S HALF FALLS

McKee's Half Falls on the Susquehanna River.

Description: Two rock ledges stretch across the river to form a 1- to 2-foot drop. The bottom is sand, gravel, and cobble below the ledges. It is a very picturesque spot on the Susquehanna. The bank is steep and rocky; however, there are a few trails that lead to the water downstream of the falls. The river is big here, and the water is powerful, so use extreme caution. I do not recommend snorkeling the falls themselves but rather snorkeling downstream.

Access: GPS Address: McKee's Half Falls Rest Area, 8252 South Susquehanna Trail, Port Trevorton, Pennsylvania. This is a rest stop on Route 15. It is on your right, if traveling north.

life, especially non-sport fish freshwater life, and it speaks to their vulnerabilities. If we don't even know they are there, how can we know if what we are doing is having a harmful effect on them? How can we even care if we don't know them on their own terms? And crayfish are some of the most imperiled species on our planet. There are 330 species of crayfish in North America. One-fifth are endangered. One-third of the global species of crayfish are at risk of going extinct. One of the reasons for their decline is the introduction of invasive crayfish species that outcompete the natives.

It was the end of winter. I was on my way up Route 15 to do a presentation about freshwater biodiversity loss at Bucknell University in Lewisburg, Pennsylvania. McKee's Half Falls Rest

Area is a rest stop on Route 15. McKee's Half Falls is a special place for me. My family is from this region, and the falls are prominent in some of our family folklore. The story is that my great-grandfather built eel weirs near here. McKee's really isn't much of a falls. It's a falls by Susquehanna standards, a place where the geology forces the huge volume of the smooth-surfaced Susquehanna to tumble over a 1-foot drop.

I stopped off, squeezed into my drysuit, and got in. The river was up, so I decided to do a drift snorkel, put in at the base of the "falls," float downriver a quarter mile or so, and work to stay close to shore. As soon as the confusion of entrained air bubbles subsided, I watched a crayfish rocket for deeper water. Then I saw another tuck behind a rock as another shot for the deep center of the river. In a quarter mile, I saw twenty crayfish, at least.

They were the invasive rusty crayfish, with huge aquamarine claws and rust-colored patches on the sides of their carapaces. They were strikingly beautiful, but they are so abundant, they must surely have an effect on the ecology of the river, especially on the benthos. Rusty-sided crayfish reduce numbers of bottom-dwelling insects and other invertebrates and displace some fish species, especially bluegill, smallmouth and largemouth bass, and walleye. They deprive native fish of their prey and cover and outcompete native crayfish.

Rusty sides are native to the Ohio River basin and now occur throughout the East and Great Lakes region. They are likely spread as live bait. When fisherfolk have a few pieces of bait left at the end of the day, it is often hurled into the river they are fishing, whether that bait is eel, shiner, or crayfish. Rusty sides are commonly sold as bait. They are large and aggressive, so they easily establish breeding populations in rivers where they are introduced and eliminate native crayfish species.

I enjoyed watching the rusty sides. They are palettes of brilliant aquamarine and red and cream, and while they are hideous concerning how they affect river ecology, they are still striking animals, absent of their negative impact. Five crayfish rocketed in different directions when I moved toward the shore. These human-placed invaders are one of the reasons native crayfish are in trouble. But crayfish aren't alone in being threatened.

There are 900 species of freshwater snail in North America. Ten percent are already extinct. Forty percent are endangered, 25 percent are threatened, and we don't know the status of the remaining 25 percent.

"I'd be a fool not to get in," I said out loud as I stood on a frozen sandbar and watched broken ice sheets float past. The water was clear, and a sign at the canoe launch advised people how they can protect hellbenders—don't turn over rocks, and keep sediments from entering our streams. Not that I expected to see an amphibian out in freezing water, but I have been surprised before. Seeing a hellbender was a long shot, but seep mudalia, a kind of snail only known from the New River drainage, were a more realistic possibility, though I wouldn't know one if I saw it. Part of me hoped the south branch of the New River would have been too muddy to get in. The ice was going to hurt, but I don't get to snorkel the Mississippi drainage very often. I had no excuse. I shivered when a chill wind blew as I geared up.

This place almost wasn't. A dam was proposed that would have flooded this valley and buried this nearly pristine river and all its unique inhabitants under tons of sediments and millions of gallons of water. However, a group of concerned citizens stopped the project and helped to establish the New River State Park in North Carolina. Another reason to get in is to celebrate what was saved.

An ice chunk almost ripped my mask off the instant I pulled into faster-moving water. Ice constantly ground on my mask and hood as it slid past. The bottom was a large expanse of water-smoothed, fractured bedrock. Anchor ice was starting to cling to the bottom and looked like crumpled-up cellophane stuck on orange-encrusted, mica-flecked rock. Olive riverweed grew on top, and casemaker caddisfly larvae hung on just behind the accreting ice. An ice clump occasionally dislodged one, but the insect quickly regained its footing and grasped the bottom. Snails huddled in cracks. I found them! Seep mudalias, endangered in North Carolina. The peaks of their shell spires were eroded so that their normally pointy shells were flattened with the internal Fibonacci spirals exposed in almost fluorescent blue swirls. The rest of their shells were chestnut

Seep mudalias huddle in the lee of a rock for protection from current and ice.

NEW RIVER STATE PARK

Description: The New River is a beautiful waterway, no matter where I access it. It cuts through mountains as it makes its way to meet the Gauley River. The New River at New River State Park is no different. It makes a large oxbow or loop around the US 221 access. Its steep-sided, mountain shore opposite the access is rich in forest. I am grateful to the grassroots group of people who fought against a proposed dam that would have killed this place.

Access: GPS Address: 358 New River State Park Road, Laurel Springs, North Carolina. Follow the park road to the last parking area, which is for a picnic area and canoe launch. The launch is to the left as you face the river and provides easy river access.

Above: New River at New River State Park, North Carolina.

brown, and they clung tight to the rock, for protection from the current and the ice driven by it. I wondered if the eroded shells were normal or a function of water acidification related to climate change. We often hear of ocean acidification, but what about that process in fresh water?

A darter flopped out of the current into the lee provided by one of the fractures and let me take multiple pictures. I wondered if the fish would be this patient in warmer conditions or if its nonchalant attitude was a function of the cold. My mouth was numb so that I couldn't feel the snorkel anymore, and my hands became painful and marginally useful. I stayed in too long and was now paying the uncomfortable price. I crawled through the slushy river, onto the frozen bank thoroughly satisfied at seeing a state-endangered animal, seep mudalias, for the first time and witnessing how they survive winter and avoid getting pummeled by ice.

Snails play an incredibly important role in river ecosystems as grazers. They eat the algae and biofilm that grows on rocks and other substrates in rivers. Without them, the algae would go nuts and clog the river. In turn, snails are food for other organisms, such as fish, birds, otter, and crayfish. They are the link between plant and animal. This became evident while snorkeling the Shenandoah River, near its confluence with the Potomac in Harpers Ferry, West Virginia.

The August waters were warm but still refreshing relative to the oppressive mid-Atlantic, late-summer heat and humidity. The Shenandoah here is near the end of its own identity, close to where it will be subsumed by the Potomac and exist no more, but here, a mile upstream from the confluence, it was still characteristic Shenandoah. I slid into the water on a smoothed bedrock slab that dipped toward the bottom. Instantly, the importance of snails became apparent. The smoothed bedrock slabs dressed in a thin, slick, green algal coat were covered with thousands of little dime-sized knobs, which were crested mudalias. While each individual was light, in aggregate, their mass was huge, and anything with biomass this large had to play a critical role in the river's ecosystem. There were thousands of them grazing, and if I stayed still long enough, I could watch them move. Gold, green, and red metallic jewels glided across the smoothed rock shelves that interrupted the flow of the river. With a little observation, a static collection of drab bumps became a choreographed ballet of color.

Crested mudalias.

I had seen this in a completely different river system, with a completely different ecology, driven by a different hydrology. The flow of the Susquehanna River below Conowingo Dam goes from 8,000 to 80,000 cubic feet per second (cfs) in the matter of an hour based on the number of gates open, which is determined by the demand of energy, which is further dictated by the number of air-conditioning units we turn on. Despite this dramatic swing in depth and flow, a community of Virginia river snail seems to thrive below Conowingo. There are hundreds of thousands of Virginia river snails living here, and one summer, I found densities of more than 300 per square meter of river bottom. I have spent many summer afternoons floating the warm, clear water watching them graze. They are works of beauty, each is its own masterpiece. Their green-and-brown shells are constructed of calcium carbonate that the snail somehow extracts from its environment and knows how to form it into elaborate swirls so that they look sculpted and carved rather than accreted. Their shells are beautiful enough and varied in color from amber to emerald green and chestnut brown. Clean to encrusted in algal growths. The snails themselves look similar to cute bunnies with outstretched noses and ears in the form of antennae, with blue spots that resembled eyes at their bases, though their eyes were really at the ends of the antennae stalks. The coloration on the bodies of the snails was even more striking than that of their shells: intricate, interwoven patterns of gold lines on black, blue on yellow. Their mouths on the ends of their outstretched heads rasped algae from the rocks between diurnal dam-induced scouring floods.

Virginia river snails.

Virginia river snails are still considered abundant, as evidenced by the thousands that covered the cobbled bottom of the lower Susquehanna. Their range extended from Massachusetts to Virginia but is shrinking due to sedimentation and other water pollutants. They are considered extirpated from Massachusetts, critically imperiled in Connecticut, and vulnerable in New York. Just because something is abundant doesn't mean it's not at risk.

The huge spring bowl at Alexander Springs tails out onto a smooth, clean, white sand flat that looks lifeless except for the spotted sunfish that graze across it and the Florida cooters that swim past. I set up a time-lapse camera on the downstream end to capture the comings and goings of fish. What I saw was a video of a hidden world. The sand crawled with snails as they motored across the spring. The entire bottom seemed to come alive and move, they were so abundant. They must be incredibly important in this ecosystem and may be more important than we thought.

Ten years ago, a black algae started to choke Alexander Springs. We assumed it was eutrophication, an increase in nutrients that fuels excess algae growth, but the water chemistry didn't show an increase in these elements. The chemistries did show a slight decrease in dissolved oxygen and a slight increase in chloride or salt. As we punch wells into the aquifer in Florida, we draw water from the top of the aquifer. That leaves water that is just a little lower in oxygen and ever so slightly higher in chloride. Snails that lived in Alexander were just on the cusp of tolerance of low dissolved oxygen and slightly higher chloride. The minuscule shift in these chemicals resulted in the extirpation of three species of snail and the rampant growth of black algae.

Mussels are another group of imperiled freshwater organisms that are incredibly important to river ecosystems. There are 281 species of freshwater mussel in North America. Fifty-five percent are at risk of being eliminated in my lifetime. The Potomac is home to some pretty abundant and amazing mussels. The sun touched the tops of the trees that lined the banks as I put my face into my mask. I wasn't confident that I would see anything, but I was here and waist-deep in the Potomac, so I might as well get all the way in. This was the crucible of the Civil War, and I felt that tension as I submerged.

Algae and rockweed covered rocks and gently waved in the current. The late afternoon sun hit the plants and made the water glow light olive-green. I lounged in the river, floating, completely taken in by the mesmerizing scene. But the relaxing, gentle appearance was misleading, and the current pushed me into a sharp bedrock ridge that split my knee open. I bled into the river as I explored. I hooked my feet on the ledge and let the river push the rest of my body downstream. I undulated in the current with the pale yellow-green elodea and emerald-green, hairy algal tufts. I watched what looked like two minnows wave in the current. But something wasn't quite right. Their movements were too simultaneous and choreographed. As I crept closer to investigate, I saw that they

POTOMAC RIVER AT FIFTEENMILE CREEK

Description: Fifteenmile Creek Campground is at the confluence of Fifteenmile Creek and the Potomac River in Little Orleans, Maryland. The campground sits at mile 140 on the Chesapeake and Ohio Canal towpath, and the area is rich in human and natural history. Little Orleans is a fun, one-store town. Be sure to stop in, and check out Bill's Place. A boat ramp sits below the campground and is easy access for the river. Parking for the ramp is on your left.

Access: GPS Address: Fifteenmile Creek Campground, 11001 High Germany Road, Little Orleans, Maryland. From Hancock, Maryland, take I-68/US 40 west for 12 miles to exit 68. Make a left onto Orleans Road NE, and follow for 6 miles. Make a left onto High Germany Road. The campground will be on your left after driving through a small tunnel under the railroad.

Above: Potomac River at Fifteenmile Creek.

weren't minnows. They were lures made and wiggled by a female lampsilis mussel. They had white, round eyes with black dots for pupils, and the rest of their bodies flowed in the current as she wiggled them. She did a great job mimicking minnows, in structure pattern and movement, and had me fooled for a while.

Freshwater mussels are filter feeders, which means they pull river water in through an incurrent siphon, filter everything out of the water, eat the portion they can eat, and spit out what they can't eat, such as sediment, to the bottom. They expel the cleaned water through their excurrent siphon back into the river.

Females become fertilized when they pull in sperm a male ejected into the water through her incurrent siphon. She produces glochidia, which are essentially larval mussels that need an intermediary host to metamorphose into juvenile mussels. Some mussels are generalists when it comes to their preferred hosts. Other species of mussel depend on a single species of fish as their hosts, so female mussels have developed ingenious ways to lure their fish hosts close to them so that she can infest them with her glochidia and give her offspring the best chance of survival. The glochidia live on their host parasitically for about a month. In that time, they metamorphose into a juvenile mussel and then drop off to the riverbed where, hopefully, they grow into adults.

Some species of mussel have evolved even more elaborate lures than the lampsilis minnows. These include lures that resemble hellgrammites and

Female lampsilis mussel lure.

crayfish. But the mussels I am most familiar with, the ones most common in the rivers I am in all the time, don't put on any showy display to lure host fish to them. They are eastern elliptio, and they are more generalist regarding host-fish needs, though they do seem to have a preference for American eel.

The Delaware had a glassed surface, though it was hauling, evidenced by huge plumes of water deflected off the bottom toward the surface, which caused swirls that quickly moved downstream. The sun was setting, and I would need to wait a few hours until the shad were spawning. I started to hear tail slaps a little before midnight, so I slid into the dark, cold May water. I could only see what came into my light. I wanted to photograph shad spawning, but the shad paced at the periphery of the light in nervous fast circles. I had a hard time holding my place in the river against the current. The dark rock on the bottom and dark night above ate my light. Green water milfoil twirled in the current. Some kind of white flocculent streaked past. It was like cobweb fragments were hurling downstream. Then I realized these were the glochidia of eastern elliptio. While eastern elliptio are not specific in their fish-host requirements, it all of a sudden made sense why eels and elliptio are so closely tied. The sticky glochidia web the elliptios produce get hung in the irregularities of the rocky bottom where they live, the same spaces American eels use. This isn't just a random pairing but rather a uniquely designed and time-honed intentional system, as finely tuned as minnow, hellgrammite, and crayfish lures. It is no wonder that when we disrupt one part of the system, the whole thing begins to topple.

Eels are migratory, so when we obstruct their ability to move between river and ocean, it should be no great surprise that other things are affected. Conowingo Dam is an engineering marvel. It is a hundred-foot-tall wall of concrete that spans the mile-wide Susquehanna 10 miles from its mouth at the upper Chesapeake Bay. It was the largest hydroelectric project in the world at the time of its construction in 1928. As amazing a feat of human engineering as this structure is, it is an ecological disaster and blocks fish from moving from the ocean to the river. Fish lifts have been constructed to help shad and herring up and over the dam, but they are minimally effective and do nothing for other migratory species such as lamprey and eels. The American eel population above Conowingo has been declining, and so has the number of juvenile elliptio mussels. Coincidence? No. This is the result of a fine-tuned system that has been tampered with. The worry is that we are nearing the end of the population of elliptios above Conowingo. These animals can live to be a hundred years old, so as we approach the hundred-year anniversary of the construction of Conowingo, the anniversary of the death of the lower Susquehanna, the old-timers will reach the end of their lives, and the Susquehanna will lose her remaining mussels.

We recently discovered that up to 10,000 baby eels, called elvers, can't make it upriver past Conowingo each day through the summer months, so no wonder there isn't any mussel recruitment above Conowingo. The eels they depend on are dropping in number because their babies can't get back into the river. But there is hope. We are capturing elvers at the base of Conowingo and trucking them upriver, where they are released. One of those release sites is Pine Creek. There hasn't been any elliptio juveniles in Pine Creek until the year after the elver release. This also shows that the finely tuned, time-honed systems are resilient, as long as we give them a chance.

Those old-timers are still there and turn up in the most unexpected places. I slid into the Yellow Breeches for no other purpose than to explore the creek and see what was there. I didn't have an agenda or target species. I just wanted to get to know the creek. A few midsummer thunderstorms traversed the valley, so I expected the breeches to be a bit chocolaty. It wasn't. I glided across a very shallow gravel flat, trying not to scrape the bottom. Blacknose dace with gold sides and well-defined black lines scooted out of my way, and tessellated darters stood their ground for a little with pugnacious upturned snouts before they flicked their tails and sent puffs of bottom into the water as they shot away from me.

I saw a mussel partly dug into the gravel and snorkeled over to it. It looked old. Its shell was battered and scruffy. Layers of shell were worn away to expose concentric green-and-silver lines that resembled a topographic map. What should have been a black shell was exposed white, green, and silver where the shell halves met at the hinge. However, the mussel didn't look like it was awaiting death, but rather it looked vibrant and very much alive. The shell halves were opened a quarter-inch crack so that the frilled indigo incurrent and excurrent siphons could extend into the creek and filter. The mussel's big foot was out, too,

Eastern elliptio mussel.

YELLOW BREECHES

Description: The Yellow Breeches is a world-renowned limestone creek. It starts on South Mountain in Michaux State Forest and flows through farmland and suburbia until it joins the Susquehanna near New Cumberland. The Lower Allen Community Park is a large sports complex with soccer fields and baseball diamonds. The Yellow Breeches flows around its edge, and there are multiple access points.

Access: GPS Address: Lower Allen Community Park, 4064 Lisburn Road, Mechanicsburg, Pennsylvania. Follow the park entrance road to the last parking lot. The Garstad Nature Trail and a canoe launch provide access to the creek.

Yellow Breeches Creek.

and it resembled a large white tongue. This is what we stand to lose but haven't lost yet.

So what if a few snails, crayfish, and mussels go extinct? Most people don't even know they exist. But they know the ecosystem functions they serve. Remember what I mentioned earlier in this book: Species on this planet are like rivets in a plane. They all work to hold the system together. As we lose rivets (species), the plane (our planetary ecosystem) becomes more brittle and likely to crash. Imagine you are boarding a plane. As you step from the jet bridge onto the plane, you notice rivets missing from the door frame. Do you get on with two rivets missing? Ten? How comfortable are you? The same thing applies to species. They are all rivets in our planetary ecosystem, working together to hold it all together. At what point do we say we can't lose any more species, any more rivets, for fear the system will crash? That's why all species matter, even the ones people don't know exist.

But this is all about us—all about what species can do for us. Species deserve to exist because they are. They are part of this amazing creation, whether it was made by a god or the universe. They deserve to exist because they are, regardless of what they do for us, or if they keep our plane flying. Stick your face in the water, and get to know those unknown species—the snails, mussels, and aquatic insects—on their own terms underwater. Settle into the creek to just watch and learn and admire the beauty and intricacy of even the smallest freshwater lifeforms. Your life will be enriched in return, and you will gain a much more thorough understanding of how the world works.